W. F. B. --

An Appreciation

by His Family and Friends

W.F.B. --

AN APPRECIATION
by HIS FAMILY AND FRIENDS

Edited by

PRISCILLA L. BUCKLEY

and

WILLIAM F. BUCKLEY, JR.

Illustrated by

A. DERSO

New York • Privately Printed

1979

Contents

Foreword

THERE'S NO QUESTION that our Father would *not* have liked a book about him to have been written during his lifetime. In fact, he would not have tolerated it. For while he was by no means demure, he *was* self-effacing. He had no interest whatever in himself as a "personality," and would have scoffed at the idea that anyone would want to write about him, or read about him. What interested *him* was what he did, not who or what he was. The reasons why he opposed the recognition of the Obregon government in 1919 were far more important to him than his ensuing dramatic expulsion from Mexico and the painful financial losses that resulted therefrom. In business, it was never the discovery of the oil that excited him, but the chase for it, and even more than that, the techniques and tactics that enabled him to keep his small companies in the field without so much as a by-your-leave to the mastodons that sought to devour him. If his children ended up as captains of their college football teams (they didn't), or editors of the school year book or presidents of the class (they occasionally did), it was all well and good, and he was very proud. But it was far more important to William Buckley that his children be courteous, industrious and God-fearing. And that they know how to laugh at themselves and —cardinal virtue—that their teeth be clean. (Father once estimated that his dentists' bills—he was impelled to make the calculation in surveying the sea of platinum that obscured his children's teeth over a period of ten or fifteen years—cost him more than the formal education of his Father's entire family.) The inner qualities rather than the outer symbols were important to him.

He was a dynamic man, but gentle; and his death was deeply felt by many people. It is for the many who would like something concrete to remember Will Buckley by—the many who knew him, but did not know much about him—that this volume has been written and edited by a few who were close to him. It is not a formal biography; it's not a biography at all, but an appreciation of the man: our tribute to a departed gentleman to whom we were greatly devoted.

His only living brother, Claude Buckley of San Antonio, Texas, who played and fought spiritedly with him as a child, went to the University with him and was later his law partner in Mexico, has written briefly of W.F.B.'s childhood in Duval County, Texas, "a region arid, dotted with mesquite and sparsely settled." Opportunities were few for the large family of an impoverished Irish-Canadian sheriff and sheep rancher, but there Will Buckley developed the moral qualities and intellectual ambition that were to project him into a different life.

The University years are recounted by Judge Walter S. Pope, a former Texas State Casualty Insurance Commissioner, a leading Abilene attorney and a gentleman whom Father always referred to as "my-old-friend-Pope." The University of Texas was as great an experience for Mr. Pope, the farm boy from Santa Anna, as for the older boy from San Diego. They didn't have a penny to squander between them, and the conditions under which they went through college would be unthinkable today. But they thought themselves lucky beyond measure, and were forever grateful for the privilege of education: as were many of the other sunburned, work-toughened young men—Spanish-American veterans among them—who flocked to the University from farm and ranch and cattle town at the turn of the century: many, like Walter Pope, with only a few months of secondary schooling behind them.

If there was ever any one who suffered for his friendship with William F. Buckley, it was Cecilio Velasco of Mexico City. Their intimate association, which lasted until W.F.B.'s death, began in

1909 when Mr. Velasco, as a very young man, joined the Buckley law firm as a bookkeeper. In the ensuing years he was frequently threatened, sometimes jailed, and once kidnapped in the line of duty but, as Father used to tell it, proudly: "No one ever succeeded in scaring Velasco." Mr. Velasco writes about those hectic days in Tampico in the turbulent 1910's.

Dr. Nemesio Garcia Naranjo is a distinguished Mexican journalist, scholar and lawyer, an authority on Cervantes and biographer of Simon Bolivar. A man of wit and sympathy and an old and true friend of Will Buckley's, he tells what it meant to men of his kind in Mexico to find in a foreigner, and particularly in an American, an understanding of Mexico equal to their own.

Of his business associates in the United States, none was closer for a longer time to W.F.B. than George S. Montgomery, Jr. of New York, a senior partner of Coudert Brothers. The business vicissitudes they breasted together would have sundered many a friendship; it only cemented theirs. Mr. Montgomery reports on W.F.B.'s business operations in the post-Mexican period.

The trio known familiarly as "The Sad Young Men" tell what it was like to work for W.F.B. as very junior associates. What made them sad was not only that things often went wrong, but more particularly that when they had warned W.F.B. that the course he had chosen was disastrous—that was when everything went right. John W. Buckley, the eldest son, tells of his Father's madcap affair with oil. Benjamin W. Heath, senior son-in-law and intrepid husband of W.F.B.'s oldest daughter, Aloise, recounts the whirlwind conquest of Tallahassee when the Buckley companies were moving in on Florida. C. Dean Reasoner, of Washington, D.C., a young and very successful lawyer who started working for W.F.B., like John Buckley and Ben Heath, upon his release from the service after World War II, claims that W.F.B.'s first importance to him was as a teacher.

Aloise Buckley Heath recreates the summer evenings in Sharon when "Father was Papa still" and the Homer of the supper table. Priscilla Buckley, the second daughter, contributes a melange of the stories our Father used to tell in later years about his experiences in revolutionary Mexico. (They were almost as good as Raphael Sabatini. Sabatini's heroes were more heroic, but Father's had more fun.) Fergus Reid Buckley, the youngest son, goes back the farthest in time and tells a story about our Father's grandfather who was not only a Protestant, but an Orangeman, and thereby hangs a tale. Douglas Reed, the noted British author (*Disgrace Abounding, Insanity Fair, From Smoke to Smother*), a friend of long standing and, for a time, a business associate of W.F.B.'s, rounds up his entire business career. Van Zandt Wheeler, a Sharon neighbor and free-lance writer, covers the twilight years. He tells of the talks they had, two men born into one kind of America, and living in what seemed to them a different world entirely, two minds that thought alike on almost every subject.

A final contributor is William Buckley himself. Because it was so like him—the analysis, the rhetoric, the principles, the prejudices —we have included in this book about two-thirds of his testimony before the Senate Foreign Relations Committee in 1919. We have also included a sampling of the letters, notes and memoranda through which a very busy man addressed himself constantly to the least problems of his many children.

Finally, there is a short account of his final illness, and a few references to some of the tributes paid him after his death.

P.L.B.

W. F. B. --

An Appreciation

by HIS FAMILY AND FRIENDS

PART ONE

Texas

F. Reid Buckley

Claude H. Buckley

Walter S. Pope

I. *Retold Tale*

By F. REID BUCKLEY

W.F.B.'s youngest son retells a tale, with a digression or two.

WELL, children, the story I am going to tell you is one my Father told me about his grandfather. My Father told me this story three weeks before he died, which we didn't expect, as you now know. You were then, respectively, six and five and three. My Father was seventy-seven. I was twenty-eight.

It may seem like something that happened a long time ago, back in the mists where all things became as shadowy as the dead. Here I am recounting to you a story about a man who was a child more or less your age when Napoleon was master of Europe. Maybe your great-great-grandfather listened to the news of Waterloo, and wondered what it meant (just as I listened to the news about Pearl Harbor, coming back from shooting squirrels on the hilltop copse of Great Elm, and wondered why my Father looked so severe, and my Mother white-faced). It's pretty certain he was a young man when "Old Hickory" marched into Washington and laid siege to the principles of men like Hamilton, as if he were still fighting Indians. He must have been a man in middle-age when the other Jackson, "Stonewall" Jackson, sat a long damp night through over a low campfire with General Robert E. Lee, planning how to lick the Federal Army at Chancellorsville. That was the night Jackson caught pneumonia, you remember. He wasn't killed by his own men. It was the pneumonia setting in after he was weak that

3

killed him: it's the disease following the shots that kills, which is why the Union has been dying ever since the South fell.

I tell you these things that sound like digressions because they were the kind of things that mattered to my Father, although he wasn't given to any kind of imagery. In any case, you think back on it, and the shadowy giants of history were walking battlefields when your Father's grandfather fought *his* battle. So listen to the story my Father told me.

He was an Irish Protestant, and in those days Irish Protestants and Irish Catholics were clawing at each other's throats. The Orange Society of the Protestants had been formed since 1800, and Father's grandfather was a member.

But he married a Catholic girl. This led to problems. The Orangemen used to have an annual celebration in July, and there was always a parade. Part of the parade route cut across the bottom piece of your ancestor's farm. He went to the chiefs of the Orangemen, and he said to them, Now look here, I've married a Catholic girl and I respect her religion just as she respects mine. This year you can't follow the same route.

But they told him that they'd always gone over that lot, and no Catholic, even if she were the wife of a good Orangeman, was going to stop them from going over it this year. He tried to reason with them, but these things weren't to be reasoned over. So he went home.

He went home and waited. The day rolled around. He went out in the morning and stood by the gate the Orangemen would have to cross to get on his land. He waited there until the leader of the parade came up to it. He warned them, *Don't put foot on my land.*

They paid no attention to him, and some of the men in front began climbing across. He took up a plowshare and bashed in the head of the first man to touch down on his land. This was maybe the first time a plowshare had been turned into a sword so quickly.

Well, they threw him into jail. He was there eight days while they waited to see whether the man he hit was going to die or not. He didn't. But after that your ancestor thought it wise to leave Ireland.

That's how we came to be Americans. The family went to

Quebec first, and then to Ontario. The old fellow didn't change his faith, but the children were raised as Catholics. Which gives us some idea about your great-great-grandmother: she must have been pretty enough to arouse her farmer-husband into an act of violence against his co-religionists, or attractive enough to displace, in her passionate husband (if that is what we can judge her husband to have been from the one definite thing we know about him), one passion with another.

A son moved south to Texas. That was my grandfather. We know more about him. His name was John.

John Buckley was a large and a lovable man. His home was in Washington, Texas, which doesn't exist any more, except as a national graveyard, and he was appointed sheriff of Duval County. Like his father—and his son—he was prone to unpopular attitudes: he was a sheep raiser in cattle country, and he never used a gun in his life. He was very strong—and yet he died at 54, when my Father was 23. He had a stroke in Rockport, Texas and was attended by almost all his family when he died. He was taken by special train to San Diego and is buried in Austin. He left five children: and your grandfather had to shift for the family with the help of his older sister.

That's another story. What I want to tell you about here is the making of my Father, and of your Father, and of you. My Father remembered distinctly when his Orangeman grandfather died. My Father was just a boy, about the age of the oldest of you, and as he was coming back home with a load of firewood (mesquite and cottonwood branches, I think we can guess), his Father, John, met him at the doorway and said to him, Come in, Willie. There's something serious your Mother wants to tell you.

My Father put down his wood. If you'd known Grandmother B., Father's Mother, I think you'd guess my Father wiped his hands on his britches and scraped his shoes on the mat of the veranda before walking into the parlor. There was Grandmother B., red-eyed and weeping, the letter that brought the news on a little table in front of her. The little table was round, covered with a velvet red cloth from which tassels hung. Grandmother B. drew my Father to her, and she said, Willie, a grave thing has happened. Your grandfather died last week. She went on: But we have a great consolation. Just before he died, he accepted the last Sacraments.

My Father's Father leaned towards Willie at this point, whispering behind his hand. These words are probably the only words in the history of your family which have come down exactly over the three generations: "He must have been unconscious."

That's all there is to this story. It's just for you children.

II. *My Brother's Early Years*

By Claude H. Buckley

> *"He developed under the loving care and guidance of his sainted Mother known for her devotion and service to God and family. She taught him the fear and love of God and the practice of charity. She taught him to love his country and to revere its flag and all it stood for. The depths of her influence were remarkable."*

WILLIAM FRANK BUCKLEY, the fourth child and third son of a family of six boys and two girls, was born to Mary Ann Langford and John Buckley on July 11, 1881, in what is known as Old Washington, Washington County, Texas. He was named after a paternal uncle. The Town of Washington, some forty years earlier the site of the signing of the Declaration of Independence and later the first Capital of the Republic of Texas, was located on one of the two arms of branches of the navigable stream named years before by the Spanish missionaries "el Rio de los Brazos de Dios," the River of the Arms of God, or, as it is commonly known, the Brazos River. Ever remembering this good and appropriate name, Mary Ann ceaselessly and reverently invoked the Arms of God that they might, as most certainly they did, protect and bless her beloved son throughout his life from helpless infancy to ripe old age.

Will's Father and Mother were of Irish ancestry, their parents having come from counties Cork and Limerick.

The country of the Brazos, known as the "Brazos Bottoms," was humid and malarial. It was here, during a business trip through swampy rural lands, that John Buckley was exposed to rains and cold. As a result he contracted a severe case of bronchitis, which

7

complicated with malaria, developed into chronic asthma. Seeking a more suitable climate for his asthmatic condition and encouraged by a friend who had preceded him, he and his family moved to San Diego, Duval County, Texas, in the Fall of 1882. Here he engaged successively in merchandising, politics, and sheep raising. During the 1890's he served several elective terms as sheriff of the county. He died in 1904, leaving Mary Ann with five children remaining. She was deceased in 1930.

As Will's early life followed the lines of normal boyhood, a brief description of the town of San Diego and its environs will best serve as a backdrop to set his boyhood in relief. San Diego was in the heart of the "Mesquite" Country—commonly known as the "cow country"—of southwest Texas. The region was arid, dotted with mesquite, mesquite grass, and the semidesert shrub, the cenizo, and sparsely settled. The land abounded in cactus and rattlesnakes. The settlement was serviced by the narrow gauge Texas Mexican railway, whose terminal points were Laredo, on the Rio Grande, and, some 153 miles to the East, Corpus Christi, on the Gulf of Mexico.

A typical Spanish and Mexican town, San Diego was built around a plaza some three hundred feet square. On its four sides were to be found a few residences of the earlier and more prosperous inhabitants and the principal business establishments consisting of grocery and drygood stores, the drugstore, the cantina (saloon), and several gambling joints. In the middle of the block to the East and facing the plaza stood the tiny Catholic Church of San Francisco de Paula, whose pastor was to play a vital part in Will's life.

The community was blessed with neither electricity, gas, telephone, running water, nor refrigeration. The water, that served for all purposes, came from a few springs which oozed out of the dry bed of the San Diego Creek. This precious liquid was peddled from house to house, by native "barrileros," in barrel containers mounted on two wheel carts drawn by mules, burros, or oxen. The more prosperous citizens built cisterns to catch the scanty rainfall. Constructed above the, ground and generally uncovered, these deposits served as fertile ground for propagating mosquitoes by the millions during the long summer months.

Of San Diego's population of 2000, some 1800 were of either Mexican or Spanish origin. Among these were Godfearing, highly educated, and refined men and women whose ideals and ways of life were a credit to this isolated community. The rest of the population represented not only many other sections of the United States but also many foreign countries. There were families and individuals from Ireland, from Scotland, Wales, and England, and from Spain, France, and Germany. Others were from Canada, Minnesota, New York, Ohio, Louisiana, and California. The population of the little settlement was unique and cosmopolitan.

While English was, of course, the official language of the state, the county, and the public schools, since about 90% of the inhabitants were Spanish or Mexican, the Spanish language predominated in business and social circles. The town's amusements consisted in the main of dancing, horseracing, cockfighting, and, from time to time, plays, circuses, and medicine shows put on by itinerant performers, mostly of Mexican origin. The festive days of the year were the usual Christmas, New Year, and Easter. But, in addition, with the fervor of a small Mexican town, and reflecting the national characteristics of the inhabitants, there were regularly and enthusiastically celebrated the Cinco de Mayo, anniversary of the defeat of the French at Puebla, Mexico, in 1866 by the Mexican armed forces; and St. John's day, the 24th of June, a day of churchgoing, horseracing, and cockfighting.

The Dieciséis de Septiembre, the anniversary of the independence of Mexico from Spanish rule, was the highlight of the expression of loyalty to ancestors. It was for this particular occasion that the plaza was used. Lined on its four sides by wooden benches and adorned by a central bandstand, it served for a truly elaborate Fiesta. For the entertainment of the townspeople there were imported, from Laredo, a uniformed brass band and, from southwest Texas and points across the Rio Grande in Mexico, gamblers and con men of all kinds. It was indeed a gala affair. It lasted two weeks, just long enough to drain the townsfolk of their meager savings.

It was in this unique environment—a rare interweaving of the frontier and the indigenous—that Will grew from infancy to manhood. He developed under the loving care and guidance of his sainted Mother, known for her devotion and service to God and family. She saw to it that Will was properly and fully instructed in the basic branches of study and that he was instilled with the principles of morality and religion. She taught him the fear and the love of God, His commandments, and the practice of charity towards his fellowmen regardless of race, creed, or position. She taught him to love his country and to revere its flag and all it stood for. The depths of her influence were remarkable and enduring; and love and devotion to his Mother were Will's outstandingly beautiful qualities.

Will attended the small public school, where he applied himself well. He participated with boyish enjoyment actively and whole-heartedly in the frolics, games, and sports of childhood and boyhood. He became a closely knitted part in the community life, and shared its joys and its sorrows. He is remembered most affectionately and not without some pride by those who survive him. He lived through epidemics of smallpox and yellow and typhoid fevers, and the suspense and trials of prolonged drought. He experienced sandstorms in their worst form, whether caused by droves of cattle driven along the trailways to market or to better pasture, or by western winds fanning the parched lands. He knew firsthand of armed risings and rebellions, and of the ruthlessness of the Texas rangers.

Through companionship with his playmates, his fellow students, and the townspeople in general he mastered the Spanish language. He learned to know and love the Mexican people; he became familiar with their way of life; he developed into a champion of their rights and their aspirations. In a word, he acquired an unusual familiarity with the "cow country," the people, and their doings. He was witness to the strange politics of this frontier region.

Will was profoundly influenced by his Mother and by the parish priest, Father John Peter Bard, pastor for some forty years of the church of San Francisco de Paula. He was known throughout and even beyond the "Mesquite Country" as Padre Pedro. A native of the Basque Provinces whose spirit of rugged individualism had nurtured him, he fitted well into the spirit of the particular portion of the New World to which he came as missionary. He was frank, outspoken, of irreproachable character, indomitable will, and inexhaustible energy. He was filled with zeal in pursuit of souls for God. He had travelled extensively throughout the missions of foreign countries and so was possessed of a wide knowledge of many lands and many peoples. He was a scholar and a linguist. Because of his kindness, and solicitude for all the people of his far-flung mission field in the environs of San Diego, because of his selfless interest in the material and spiritual welfare of all fellowmen, he came to be loved and respected by all peoples and all faiths in the Southwest.

It was in this small church and under the instruction of Father Bard that Will was prepared for and received his First Holy Communion. It was here and under the wise guidance of this humble parish priest that he was confirmed by the then Bishop of the diocese, the Most Reverend Peter Verdagüer.

While still a very small boy, Will began to study Latin and to serve Father Bard as altar boy. He continued to do so for fifteen years or more, even during his vacations at home from the University. Father Bard became, so to speak, Will's mentor, confirming and reinforcing the principles which he had received from his Mother. It was from this second Curé d'Ars that Will gained knowledge of the world outside and beyond San Diego. He learned about foreign lands and alien peoples. He became better founded in the elements of the arts and the sciences. His ideals and principles were strengthened and he was filled with ambitions and dreams and hopes.

A third person who had a not inconsiderable effect on Will and his later life was Charles H. Hufford, for some 12 years the principal of the San Diego Public Schools. A native of Nevada and a graduate of the University of Texas, he was a man of great learning and high principles.

On finishing high school in San Diego, Will taught for some two years in the little public school in the rural settlement called Mota de Olmos near Benavides in Duval County. Of the some one hundred pupils that were enrolled in this school only four or five were of Anglo Saxon descent. The others were Spanish and Mexican.

It was from San Diego and its environments, in part wholesome, in part unwholesome; and after having been cabined in the one and the other for some twenty years, that Will, with the blessings of his family and the best wishes of his townsfolk, set out in 1902 for a new and strange world that he might move forward and upward in every possible way, that he might realize to the full his aspirations, his ambitions, and his hopes, that he might accomplish great things. But, first, he must complete and round out his education. With this end in view, he enrolled in the University of Texas at Austin. On the death of his Father, which occurred during Will's second year in college, he realized that he would be able to continue his studies in the academic and law departments of the university only with material assistance from his older sister, Priscilla. At the age of eighteen Priscilla had freely and selflessly given up all that is dear to a young girl and had taken up teaching to help support the family. Now, and for many years later, she dedicated herself to this work, this time, to support and educate her brothers and her sister.

III. *College Days*

By WALTER S. POPE

"When I first met Will, in the fall of 1901, I was a farm-hand, just three months before my 21st birthday, and I had just passed the entrance examinations to the University. In that year, I was the only matriculated student from that vast territory from Temple, Texas, to the Rio Grande. Will's wonderful friendship and personality lifted me from the very depths of inexperience with cultured people, and out of my inferiority complex. Every hour spent with Will was an inspiration to me. We walked everywhere, while others rode the street car. Our strolls through the beautiful Eastwood section were to us a genuine delight. Those moments and hours with Will were like bread cast on the waters. They never returned void, but an hundredfold in friendship and inspiration to me."

WILLIAM F. BUCKLEY, then of San Diego, Duval County, Texas, entered the University of Texas in the fall semester in 1900.

When I began my University work in the fall of 1901 our friendship began at Breckenridge Hall, where we both lived. Lodgings for each of us were less than $5.00 per month. He then had as his roommate his freshman brother, Claude Buckley who was my classmate in Freshman English I, and in time became not only a good friend but a fraternity brother of mine. Board at "B" Hall was $10.00 a month. Our sole diversion after evening meals was to meet in the corridors of the hall or for walks on the campus to visit with

13

each other. We spent no money otherwise than for the $10.00 per year, matriculation fees, each of the first three years in the University, except for our books, stationery and laundry. This was for the good reason that neither of us had any money to spend.

W.F.B. was very neat in person, had a wonderful friendly disposition and personality, a brilliant mind and a marvelous memory. He visited with everyone when time permitted, was an interesting conversationalist and a most polite and wonderful listener. He was so cordial and tactful that he would always bring the best in conversation out of his hearers and would remember in detail their opinions, disposition and personalities. He was a good adviser with the students in their personal problems.

Along about our second year we spent together three or four afternoons a week, as we had no tennis or other equipment and no money for entrance fees to athletic contests in the old gymnasium in the University which was located in the basement under the auditorium in the main building. There we played medicine ball in which we divided the entire group of the gymnasium into two contesting parties, the sole purpose being who could successfully carry the ball over the central line. Will occasionally played handball when there was an opening for him to play.

He was a remarkable student, having mastered the Spanish language in his high school days in Duval County which was in close proximity to the Mexico border. After learning that he could get credit on his degree by majoring in Spanish he immediately enrolled in classes, took examinations which enabled him to get eight credits on his Spanish in and after his sophomore year. He became student assistant to Miss Casis, the outstanding professor of Spanish and Romance languages. He pursued his studies in advanced Spanish Literature with Miss Casis, at her request. He spoke the Spanish language so fluently that he was always in demand for students who wanted to be coached in Spanish and for families and parties who wanted him to accompany them on their trips to Old Mexico. I mention one of these, Mr. R. H. Baker and his family, when Mr. Baker was a high official with the railroads and toured Old Mexico with the family in his private car. In time, and before he finished his University career, Will became the Spanish Translator of the General Land Office of the University of Texas, thus earning a part of his support as he pursued the academic studies in securing his law degree. After finishing six years in the University he remained in Austin for something over a year as an employee of the American Surety Company, with some of whose officials he had made friends. This enabled me to enjoy six continuous years of friendship with Will while he was in Austin.

In the winter and spring of 1904 Buckley and I became members of a small group of friends who made application for a chapter of Delta Tau Delta National College Fraternity. Buckley preceded me in forming this group and extended to me the personal invitation to join. He was at once our leader and outstanding member of the group because of his scholarship, wide acquaintance and leadership, together with his wonderful, outstanding personality. Thus he led us in obtaining our chapter, and acquiring choice men for our membership, including his two young brothers Claude and Edmund, both of whom were splendid young men with very brilliant minds. In after years Will remembered his Delta Tau Delta fraternity and became one of its most liberal financial supporters.

In the fall of 1905 Will became stricken with typhoid fever and while in the hospital in Austin his many student friends rallied and elected him Editor-in-Chief of the University *Cactus*, which was the pride and leading publication of the University student body. Editor-in-Chief of the *Cactus* was the highest office at that time in the gift of the student body. As Editor he and his staff brought out the 1906 *Cactus* which was the most beautiful *Cactus* up to that time in the history of the University. He brought in some new and refreshing ideas on subject matter and made it a work of art so that it was affectionately known as the *Bluebonnet Cactus*.

One of Will's greatest sorrows came while he was in the University in the loss of his devoted father, John Buckley, ex-Sheriff of Duval County, who had been and was to his last hour a very brave, courageous and honorable gentleman, being a highly esteemed citizen, and to his family a most loving husband and father. John Buckley, with his courage and loyalty to friends, enjoyed a warm friendship with some of the leading citizens and officers of that section of the state lying south of San Antonio, Texas. I mention one of these friends, the Honorable Marshall Hicks of San Antonio, Texas, who, while District Attorney in Duval County district, was saved from being assassinated by the courage and loyalty of Sheriff Buckley. He never forgot this friendship, and while Will was in

From the *Bluebonnet* Cactus: *Note W. F. B., Claude H. Buckley, Walter Garnett, Walter S. Pope.*

the University, Hicks, then Senator from the San Antono District, used his influence to secure Will's appointment and thereafter his sister Priscilla's appointment as Spanish Translator of the General Land Office of Texas. Will resigned the office when he began preparing to practice law in Mexico. Miss Priscilla held the office for many years with great success and efficiency, charming and brilliant woman that she was. She is still remembered by many landmen, lawyers and citizens, of South and Southwest Texas where all of the early land titles and papers were recorded in Spanish and had at that time to be translated by the General Land Office Translator. She had a charming personality, it being a pleasure to me for many years to visit her while she was in the Land Office. In that way I kept up with Will and the rest of the family, while he was so busily engaged in the oil business in Mexico and the early days in Venezuela.

Soon after his Father's death, Will moved his Mother and family, consisting of Miss Priscilla who had been engaged to teach school in Austin and Miss Eleanor, a very beautiful and charming sister who entered the University and became a very splendid student, and the aforesaid Edmund Buckley who thereafter began and finished his University academic and law education. Will's Mother was a most charming, gracious and beautiful woman. It was always a pleasure and a privilege for me to visit with her and the family in their Austin home. I enjoyed the friendship with her until she passed away in the fall of 1930. This was a most remarkable family; all of them had brilliant minds, an unusual charm and personality, capable of warm and lasting friendships.

Will was a very devoted and consistent Christian, a loyal member of the Catholic Church in Austin. As to his loyalty to his church I will mention one instance that occurred while he was a student. St. Edwards College, a Catholic University, was and is situated across the river south of Austin. The University of Texas and St. Ed's were great baseball rivals and at this time the ball game was being played in the St. Edwards ball park. When the game was very hot and close a priest called "safe" what appeared to some to be a foul ball. One of the big mouthed Texas students yelled: "That damn priest is lying." With lightning speed Will knocked him down with a fast fist stroke. And that ended that, which turned out to be quite a matter of amusement on the campus as it knew Will's peaceful and inoffensive attitude in almost every instance in which he was concerned.

When we acquired the first University YMCA site which was across the street on the west from the campus, several other churches were interested in building Bible Chairs and churches as close as possible to the University campus in order to look after the spiritual needs of their respective students. I know that Will was very much interested in this movement and anxious that his church avail itself of the same opportunity for service to its members, and as an outcome of this interest, with others, the Newman Hall block of land just south of the University YMCA site was purchased and improved with many of the present buildings thereon.

At the time mentioned, I was student president of the University YMCA and, with the advice of our advisory committee, selected the site for the YMCA on which it still stands. I negotiated for the purchase and paid the sum of $3,600.00 for the dwelling house, fig orchard, and all.

As for the social and recreational life of Will during the summer vacations, I am unable to speak, as I would leave Austin each year on the day after final examinations being about June the 1st for our stock farm some eight miles from Santa Anna, Texas. There I would spend the entire vacation period farming and stock raising with the exception of one summer spent at Austin in the summer school.

When Will moved his Mother and family to Austin, they moved to the residence on the corner of 19th and Lavaca, which site in later years he purchased and built thereon the splendid residence which remained the home of the Buckley family for so many years. His sainted Mother was a semi-invalid during the first years in Austin, and I am sure Will's vacations were devoted to her and the family welfare to the extent that I never knew of him having so much as a date; at least, he never had a regular date with anyone during our school day acquaintance; but with the young women as well as men, he was very popular, and had an easy and sureness-of-himself manner, and was a charming conversationalist, with a spontaneous sense of humor.

I frequently visited their home. I never met a more brilliant family, gracious, companionable, sincerely and devotedly religious and patriotic. Their worth and wealth in his student days was in themselves individually and collectively, and not in worldly goods and possessions, the latter of which, at that time, they did not possess.

Will held, as I remember, every place of responsibility with the fraternity, and with his wide Austin and student body acquantances was a great influence in selecting good men for the fraternity and for the student body officers. He was always interested in University and state politics. Many of us then were mature men. The University enrollment at Austin in the year 1902 reached about 800 students.

Many were young veterans of the Spanish-American War and of scant means, most of which they had earned. To them Buckley was a man's man, and at once a real delight; one who exercised power and influence. Many of these students went out quickly to places of leadership, both in Texas, Oklahoma, and elsewhere. All of them knew Will Buckley.

Our president, David Franklin Houston, became Secretary of Agriculture, and in turn Treasurer of the United States under Woodrow Wilson. Our Austin Board of Regents' member, Watt Gregory, became Attorney General. Albert Burleson, then Congressman from the Austin district, became Postmaster General; and so on. Will's student acquaintances and Austin friends went to places of great responsibility and leadership.

When I first met Will, I was a farm-hand, just three months before my 21st birthday, and I had just passed the entrance examinations to the University. In that year, I was the only matriculated student from that vast terriory from Temple, Texas, to the Rio Grande. Will's wonderful friendship and personality lifted me from the very depths of inexperience with cultured people, and out of my inferiority complex. Every hour spent with Will was an inspiration to me. We walked everywhere, while others rode the street car. Our strolls through the beautiful Eastwood section were to us a genuine delight. Those moments and hours with Will were like bread cast on the waters. They never returned void, but an hundredfold in friendship and inspiration to me.

A Letter from W.F.B. to Walter Pope, eight years later:

The New Willard
May 27, 1914

My dear Pope:

Of the many letters that I received in Vera Cruz, none was appreciated as was yours. I have thought of you so very often, and have started a great many times to write. Writing, however, to me, is a very poor means of communication, and I seldom indulge in it.

I often think of our old friendship, and of what it has meant to me. You were very kind to me at a crucial period in my life when it counted. I have often hoped I might see you in Mexico.

Well, I presume you saw in the papers that I declined the appointment at Vera Cruz. I was only one of the four appointees who did decline, and, consequently, the only one who was not embarrassed a few days later by being decapitated by Washington.

I was in Mexico City when Vera Cruz was taken, and went on down, with the intention of returning to the City with General Funston, to whom I had no doubt I could be helpful. Things were pretty exciting; I hung around Vera Cruz for a couple of weeks waiting for something to happen. Then the Peace Commission came along, and Mr. Rabasa, the President of the Commission, who is my consulting attorney in the City, asked me to come to Washington to deliver to the President a message that the Commissioners could not very well with dignity deliver themselves. I did this, and then went to New York, where I spent last week, and am now back to stay, maybe until the Conference adjourns, or perhaps, a few days.

You must be a very happy man with your sweet wife and your fine boys. I envy you very much. My mother always speaks of you when I come home, and appreciates your always coming to see her.

Pope, I believe I have had as much experience in the last six years (since going to Mexico) as the average man sixty years of age. Mexico is a most interesting country, and business there is so different; everything is done on a large scale, even though the foundation be no more substantial than wind. I have been up against every imaginable kind of game.

I had a terrible time for the first two years. For eight months I worked for a powerful lawyer (a crook) and then quit him, with no money and no friends. He has been a very bitter enemy ever since. For a year, I didn't make a living.

Two years ago I opened a law office in Tampico also and took Claude and Edmund in. Times were getting hard in the interim and I thought I saw a big opening in the oil fields. It was a big step, and another firm, when I told of the opportunity, rushed in and opened their office a few days before mine. I had only about 1,000 (Mex) in cash, and realized that either we or the other people were going to get the big business, and the other firm the small business.

I borrowed money and fitted up a magnificient office costing 7,000 (Mex); I got the District Judge to resign and work for me, and high priced translators, and turned down all small business. The payroll the first month was 2,000. Well, we got the big business, and took in in cash the first year 70,000 Mex. I worked myself down to a nervous wreck and spent all last summer in the North under medical treatment. I then quit the practice and turned the law business over to Claude and Edmund. To me, the practice of law is the most trying thing in the world.

I have some good property in Mexico, worth at least $100,000, American money. From a pecuniary standpoint, I have done all right. All the above, of course, and especially as to my mission to Washington, is confidential.

As ever your friend,

W. F. BUCKLEY

Francisco Madero Sr. Madero Carranza

PART TWO

Mexico

Cecilio Velasco

Nemesio Garcia Naranjo

W. F. B.

Priscilla L. Buckley

Zapata   General Huerta   Pancho Villa   General Obregon

I. *Tampico*

By Cecilio Velasco

"At every meeting that took place in the petroleum club, W.F.B. found himself conducting a heated battle in an attempt to make his fellow Americans understand that they were in Mexico, a free and sovereign nation that demanded and deserved respect. But these gentlemen, who were ignorant of the Castilian tongue, were also ignorant of the English tongue when it was a question of advice that thwarted their ambitions and restricted their profits, and they reached the conclusion that W.F.B. was a poor, ignorant man, sick with a case of Latinism, contracted on the border, a baby in diapers with respect to the material, almost divine power of the unlimited money available to their companies. And at last, W.F.B. was expelled from said association as a pernicious and quarrelsome individual."

I MET HIM in Tampico in 1911, through my friend Mr. William McMahon, who was at that time manager of the Texas Oil Company, and at first sight we felt a kindred spirit. I confided to him that all my life I had been a businessman and that my temporary residence in Tampico, First Oil Port as it was called, was due to my desire to make a change; to find something that, although it might not necessarily offer an unusual future, would at least arouse greater interest in a more varied milieu and sphere of action, in

25

which the nervous system might waste and replenish its energies satisfactorily.

For his part, he confided to me that he was a lawyer, a native of Texas, where he had been graduated and had studied the Castilian language which, indeed, he spoke and wrote perfectly; that also he had been graduated in Mexico City, known as the City of the Palaces, after having completed his studies and having passed the examinations pertaining thereto, and that at the moment he was working in the most important international law office, with head-quarters in the Capital, that is to say, in the populous City of the Palaces. I don't remember now the name of that law firm, but it was a Gringo name of considerable fame and importance. Finally (he told me), the reason for his presence in Tampico was his desire to find his way around and study the place with the idea of running his own office and business as law consultant, provided that he be able to count on the patronage of some of the oil companies already established.

From then on, our relations were friendly and our meetings frequent, and a few months after our first meeting W.F.B. had set himself up in a spacious and magnificent office with a nameplate which read: "Buckley and Buckley, Attorneys at Law. William F. Buckley and Claude H. Buckley." During one of our talks he asked me whether I'd like to work with him, even though this would mean being connected with a profession so far removed from the sphere of my own activities, a proposal which I had to think about a great deal before making up my mind, for I could see no way in which I could be useful in a law office. But I accepted the position he offered me and the first piece of advice he gave me was that in a law office there is no such word as "can't," and that I should never say "No," no matter what proposal might arise in connection with the business and services for which the office had been set up.

It happened that on a certain occasion when his secretary did not turn up for work because of a hangover resulting from some dissipation of the previous night, he asked me whether I could take down in shorthand a contract which he proposed to dictate to me. I had read a little; I knew something about accounts; I could type, compose business letters, and to a certain point, translate. Although it is true that I knew no shorthand, it is equally true that I had considered studying it, and remembering the advice given to me on the first day of my new job, I said to him right away, "Of course."

We got to work; he dictated and dictated, and I wrote and wrote, although naturally very little, if anything at all, of the original dictation. Making use of the few facts which I had succeeded in catching, I drew up my own contract (luckily it was short and not complicated) and when I presented it to him and he read it, realizing that it contained nothing of what he had dictated to me, he said to me, very amiably as was his custom: "Not so bad. Next time you can dictate it to yourself."

W. F. B.—*1908*

The business progressed, the profits rose, but because of I know not what good or evil arts, the expenses absorbed and exceeded the profits. Financial aid to colleagues in the Capital, loans to friends in need, new business projects, etc., etc., kept my cash box empty, and the accounts always with debit balances. To begin with, there was the problem of Buckley's generosity. It was irrepressible.

To give an example, taken from the days shortly after the office in Tampico had been opened: Among other friends, W.F.B. had a friend who was also a lawyer, a one hundred per cent Mexican. This friend came to the office one morning with a very familiar and very urgent need: he had to have five thousand pesos, the good old pesos of long ago.

Mr. Buckley asked the cashier how much was available at that time and the reply was, "Not more than $250.00, including change." In less than a minute Mr. Buckley made up his mind that five thousand pesos would be turned over to his friend that very afternoon.

When his friend left, W.F.B. went straight to a bank where he signed a note payable in fifteen days. That same afternoon his friend left the office comforted by his five thousand pesos and making calculations about the many thousands of pesos that Mr. Buckley must own when with such ease he could relinquish five thousand pesos "which he did not have."

He had, and still has, many friends both in Tampico and Mexico City, some of them Americans and others Mexicans, to whom he never shut the doors of his safe which was sometimes empty of money, but was always filled with optimism with respect to future business. Let those many widows of W.F.B.'s friends, who both in Mexico and the U.S. have lived or continue to live on the contents of that safe, speak for themselves.

W.F.B. soon knew almost everybody in Tampico and had many friends. He possessed great personal charm, he was persuasive, he inspired confidence and all who knew him loved him. He was a man of extraordinary vision and he foresaw a boom in Tampico, with a derivative growth in population, and he constantly talked to me about buying land to be sub-divided. He founded a bank in Tampico under the management of his friend Mr. George L. Rihl, vice-president of the Mexico City Banking Company of Mexico; he acquired undeveloped parcels of land in the suburbs of the City; money came from the United States in appreciable quantities, and he interested his friends in the deal. The undeveloped properties were improved and offered for sale.

Tampico owes to W.F.B. no less than 80 per cent of its development and important works, all developed with foreign capital, which remained in Tampico for the benefit of its residents, for the oil boom was of short duration because of the new petroleum laws, which drove out the oil companies and the businesses which depended on them (very little of the investments made could be recovered). But W.F.B.'s impulse opened the way for many other real estate developers, construction companies, and other works that had a part in the creation of a city, comfortable and happy in spite of its bad climate, whose inhabitants were cosmopolitan and confident, and were good spenders.

His desire was to be an oil man and to run his own company, with the same rights, hopes and probabilities of success as those of the companies that had come in from New York, California, England and Holland; and although his resources were limited, he established the Pantepec Oil Company, a name taken from one of the rivers of the Huasteca Veracruzana in the neighborhood of Tuxpan, where rich oil fields were already being developed. There he began his struggle, undergoing one of the most difficult and exciting phases of his life, but perhaps also the phase that brought him the greatest satisfaction, for he entered the battle with the rank of soldier, and rose on his own merits; and the fight itself was his greatest pleasure.

Through the complaints and pleas for help that came to the law office from his clients he had acquired considerable knowledge of matters pertaining to oil, and he knew all too well the methods employed by some of the old companies in order to acquire lands. He had to stand up to the power of those great enterprises whose moral standards in their dealings were deplorable. They were highly organized, from office and field employees to secret bands of spies, guards, and gunmen in the towns and on the ranches of the Huastecas, and to compete with them it was necessary to bring into play great energy and intelligence, as well as faith; and to that task W.F.B. devoted all his skills.

Much has been said concerning the procedures—extortion, bribery, dispossession and swindling, force-outs and land-grabbings, forged documents, the resurrection of heirs dead for many years, invention of fictitious persons and the use of impostors, crimes and disappearances in desperate circumstances, unbelievable and impossible family connections—used by the oil companies to acquire by purchase or lease coveted lands; for the imagination is filled with bloody episodes in the struggle for oil. I don't know, and it isn't for me to say, but confidentially, all these things, or something of them, very possibly occurred in those fields during those times. But what I have no doubt whatever about is that countless naive and

humble people of the Huastecas were deceived and swindled mer-
cilessly by contracts of lease or sale, ridiculously underpriced and
filled with trick clauses, covering lands of inestimable value which
were deliberately underrated by the agents for the companies as a
weapon in the negotiations, a form of swindle typical of the oil
companies in the early days.

The big leaders of the oil companies in Tampico had a club or
association of oil men, where they met every week or two, according to the demands of the prevailing climate of business. They met
to discuss the rumors that circulated in the Capital concerning
governmental measures aimed at correcting those abuses which
were becoming daily more apparent, and realizing a greater profit
for Mexico itself out of those enormous torrents of black gold flow-
ing from the oil fields of Vera Cruz and Tamaulipas. Among the
outstanding wells of the period were the Juan Casiano well with a
per diem production of 50,000 barrels; the Potrero del Llano well
with some 115,000 barrels a day, and the Dos Bocas well with an
initial production of 250,000 to 260,000 barrels a day, which could
not be controlled, and ran out, with the loss of all the oil it had
produced.

The managers of the leading oil enterprises were in general relatives or proteges of the bosses, most of whom lived in their native
countries. Although cultured and educated to a certain point, they
had a somewhat narrow social outlook; they were ignorant of the
Castilian tongue, just as they were ignorant of the Latin background, character, and customs; they were tactless in their relationships and their official dealings with the government's representatives,
and they scorned the Mexican public. They knew little or nothing
about the industries placed in their hands, but their conduct and
their manners competed with those of any emperor; they knew it
all, but were aware of nothing.

Thus it was that W.F.B. at every meeting that took place in the
Petroleum Club found himself conducting a heated battle in an
attempt to make his fellow Americans understand that they were
in Mexico, a free and sovereign nation that demanded and deserved
respect; that good faith and good deeds were absolutely necessary
in the diplomatic field; that justice, fairness and ethics could not be
dispensed with in their dealings with the landowner; that they
must respect the latter's reasonable rights, granting them appropri-

ate profits and just prices; and that they must treat them with greater generosity and less avarice, if they would avoid lamentable consequences, killing off, all by themselves, the goose that laid the golden egg.

But those gentlemen, who were ignorant of the Castilian tongue, were also ignorant of the English tongue when it was a question of advice that thwarted their ambitions and restricted their profits, and they reached the conclusion that W.F.B. was a poor, ignorant man, sick with a case of Latinism, contracted on the border in the North of Mexico and the South of Texas and that he was a baby in diapers with respect to the material, almost divine power of the unlimited money available to their companies, and of the influence, also infallible throughout the world, of their respective governments. And at last W.F.B. was expelled from said association as a pernicious and quarrelsome individual.

To get some idea of how profitable were investments in the petroleum industry during the First World War, it is enough to say that according to published statistics from 1914 to 1922 the English Aguila Company paid to its shareholders dividends equivalent to nearly 240 per cent interest on their investment.

With the assassination of General Madero and the uprising of General Victoriano Huerta, the warlike atmosphere that reigned throughout the Republic was felt in every aspect of the life of Tampico, manifesting itself particularly in lawsuits by the companies among themselves and with individuals, that had almost the character of a pastime. They were all fighting for something or for nothing, because they all had money to spare to aid the lawyers, who indeed were too few in number to cope with such great confusion. While the Buckley brothers were solving legal problems and fighting in the courts, since I could not fight with judges and tribunals because I had no knowledge of law, I was struggling with governors and mayors (Municipal presidents), fortunately with a fair amount of good luck; only twice was I invited to enter the Tampico jail because the Governor of the State of Tamaulipas did not agree with my lively protests over the failure to fulfill promises made in connection with our urban developments; and once I was abducted, my destination being the middle of the bridge which spans the Rio Grande, which point marks the boundary between Laredo, Texas and Laredo, Mexico; not a comfortable

or comforting destination for me under the circumstances, because
on the one hand I did not have the papers for entry into the United
States, and on the other, they forbade my return to Mexico under
pain of being shot, summarily.

The presence and effective help afforded by Claude Buckley in
Laredo, Texas, helped me out of my difficulty, for he vouched for
me in the United States and I spent fifteen or twenty days in the
hotels of San Antonio and Laredo as a tourist. I owed this abduction
to the Transcontinental Company, a subsidiary of Standard Oil,
because of a lawsuit over rights to certain lands, all of which cor-
roborates what has been said concerning the methods of defense
which the big companies used. I was rescued and returned to
Mexico thanks to opportune orders given by General Calles.

The Revolution was at its height during the years 1912, 1913,
1914 and after, laden with complications because of intrigue and
discord among the groups of revolutionaries, and it involved the
entire nation, including the Huastecas, with many chiefs, generals,
and aspirants to the Presidency of the Republic abandoned by Don
Porfirio Diaz; Villa, Carranza, Obregon, Felix Dias, Victoriano
Huerta, Zapata, and others whose names I don't remember.

How did all those revolutionary forces manage to subsist eco-
nomically in the midst of struggle and the destruction of ranches,
towns and cities? Quite easily. Aside from the loans which they
forced business men and wealthy individuals to make to them, each
general had his own printing press or portable to print his own
currency, with denomination and value according to his whim,
paper money that the people were forced to accept as legal tender
in the regions held by his troops, to a point where money circu-
lating in the North was not recognized in the South, and vice versa.
Some paper money produced in this way reached a point where it
was quoted (a quotation completely without basis) at the rate of a
thousand, two thousand and five thousand pesos to the dollar, until
at last all that money was declared null and void, and was with-
drawn or used to paper rooms of private dwellings.

Life in the oil regions became dangerous. Many bands of rebel
thugs, with or without a flag, sprang up there, some of them victims of the chaos that prevailed, completely at sea with no idea of
which leader they were fighting for, while others were diligent
opportunists devoted to plunder and pillage. Nevertheless, the oil

fields of the Huastecas were the least scourged by the situation and suffered least, thanks to the prudence, level-headedness and justice provided by a self-appointed general who, backed by thousands of his countrymen, took up arms in the year 1914, with no party affiliation, but with a definite aim to maintain order and to keep out of the Huastecas bands of revolutionaries whose sole ideology was easy plunder and pillage of the haciendas.

This general, to whom other groups of revolutionaries gave the sobriquet "The Rebel of the Huastecas," was General Manuel Pelaez, to whom the Mexican nation owes gratitude for loyal and patriotic service, to whom the oil companies owe the order and guarantees which they enjoyed for several years—as long as the control he exercised over the oil regions during the revolutionary period lasted—for he succeeded in establishing discipline and respect, and preventing acts of violence in the oil camps.

Unjustly, tendentious reports published at times by personal enemies of the general have attempted to make him appear as an instrument used by the oil enterprises for their own ambitious ends, but all that has been said on this score, without knowledge of the truth, or with knowledge of the facts but with the purpose of misleading the public, is absolutely incorrect and false. Pelaez was never, in any way or under any circumstances, a tool of the oil enterprises. Quite the contrary; by his opposition to the haughty conduct and inordinate thirst for profit on the part of the oil companies, he compelled them to respect the laws, straightened out their affairs, and guided them along more disciplined paths, without depriving them one bit of their just dues when right was on their side. The first decrees designed to restrict the abuses of the companies in their dealings with the Federal Government and the workers originated with General Pelaez.

Sole bulwark in those days capable of controlling and checking the growing indignation of the despoiled landholders and the workers who felt they were being cheated because of the meager wages they received, and were being injured by the almost inhuman treatment to which they were subjected by cruel foreigners and nationals unconditionally supported by the enterprises, Pelaez served as referee in the disputes. He acted as judge and sentencer— and always left the workers satisfied, for they loved him and respected him; and the companies never refused to heed his decisions. His means of conciliation consisted in obtaining better compensation for the workers and in getting engineers and foremen fired when he had proof that they were tyrannical and despotic with the workers.

The oil companies paid tribute (something like a war tax) to General Pelaez, who, acting independently of the Carranza Government, had need of funds in order to pay his soldiers, who in turn provided the companies with guarantees and peaceful conditions. This tribute was imposed on them by General Pelaez, and the companies, always ready to hand over all they owned to armed bandits whenever they were threatened and in danger, paid their protector reluctantly and against their will, without taking into account that only thanks to him were they able to go on operating their wells. Ungratefully, the companies turned at last to conspiracy against General Pelaez, and in the end succeeded in bringing about the insurrection of his forces in the Huastecas.

All these events and the treacherous, arbitrary and frightful methods practised by the oil companies, which, as I said earlier, precipitated conflicts with labor and conflicts of every kind, are what gave rise first to the nationalization of petroleum, and later to expropriation.

Of all the Americans and Englishmen residing in Tampico, in General Pelaez' opinion W.F.B. was perhaps the only one worthy of his confidence and on whom he could depend safely not to betray him. They maintained very good relations, and it is possible that on some occasions W.F.B. gave Pelaez sound advice concerning the convenient and practical way to conduct himself with the oil companies without neglecting the dignity and patriotism due his Government and his Nation, whom Pelaez never deceived.

The companies took a dim view of the friendly relationship between Mr. Buckley and General Pelaez, and they blamed Buckley for their misfortunes resulting from the increasingly severe intervention in and control of the petroleum industry on the part of the Mexican Government. They declared him their number one enemy, and they maneuvered and conspired with the Government under the presidency of General Obregon until in 1921 they had the satisfaction of seeing Mr. Buckley expelled from Mexico as an undesirable foreigner. At a later date, that same government of General Obregon, realizing the mistake it had made—for it was others who deserved to be deported, not he—invited him to return to Mexico; but W.F.B. declined, at first because it was inopportune, later on because he was already engaged in negotiations for oil in Venezuela. He understood, moreover, that the personal independence, the facilities and guarantees necessary for one to continue working in the oil industry in Mexico were on the verge of disappearing, strangled by the wisdom, intelligence and skill of the managers of the enterprises operating in the Huastecas, stripped now of the security that the "Rebel of the Huastecas" had once offered them.

William Buckley, a man of faith and goodwill, was a great friend to Mexico. He was an outstanding figure in the oil world, in Mexico and in Venezuela. On one occasion, while he was in Tampico in the midst of the scuffle with the other companies, he was offered a job as director of one of the strongest oil companies in the United States, with the fabulous salary of $60,000 a year—but on the condition that he leave Mexico and give up his private activities in the oil business. It was a tempting proposal, he explained to me, which he considered unacceptable, however, because he was certain that they would have turned him into a figurehead, like the majority of managers in Tampico.

W.F.B.'s deportation was deeply regretted in Tampico as well as in Mexico City, for in both places he had countless friends who loved him, particularly among the families of intellectuals and professional people, and the most distinguished members of society.

Those of us who survive him, and there are few of us now, remember him and will continue to remember him with affection, for in many cases his influence on the course of our lives ranged from slight to enormous. His enthusiasm and determination in the enterprises which he undertook were contagious, and completely captured our interest in his affairs. This writer, for example, can say that as regards work he found at W.F.B.'s side the variety of interest and excitement he was seeking to a surpassing degree. In essence, through him, I learned to fight and face life's contingencies, and what began as a simple friendship later turned into everlasting respect and affection.

II. *A Friend of Mexico*

By Nemesio Garcia Naranjo

"William F. Buckley understood and sympathized with the Mexican people, who had been innocent victims of Mr. Wilson's erratic foreign policy. His refusal to serve as Civil Governor of Vera Cruz proved beyond any doubt that he was a friend of my country. His statement before the Senate of the United States reaffirmed his friendship. Could I, as a citizen of Mexico, have anything but admiration and respect and love for him?"

ONE MORNING in the Spring of 1914, I heard the name William F. Buckley for the first time.

In those turbulent days, I was Minister of Public Instruction and Fine Arts in the government of President Huerta of Mexico, and on that particular Spring morning, one of my assistants came into my office to show me a clipping which contained this brief item: one William F. Buckley had indignantly refused to serve as Civil Governor of Vera Cruz, which U. S. troops, under the command of General Funston, had only a few days before taken by violence.

This was indeed extraordinary news, and although Buckley's refusal could do little to change circumstances or shape future events, it did help to restore my confidence in the American people, a confidence I was steadily and surely losing as a consequence of Mr. Woodrow Wilson's policy of what he termed "watchful waiting." My intense dislike for this American president was turning into skepticism for everything north of the Rio Grande. The government of the United States had been arming the rebels under Venustiano Carranza, Pancho Villa and Alvaro Obregon, and the government to which I was attached had more or less been able to hold its own; but to no avail. President Wilson's verdict had been reached many months beforehand: *Huerta* must go; but the pretext for eliminating him had only recently been found, which was the so-called "flag incident" in Tampico where, curiously enough, no flag whatever had been involved.

According to Wilsonian logic, the Tampico incident was warrant for a violent attack on Vera Cruz and a blockade on shipments of arms Huerta was due to receive from Europe. But the American president never owned up to his devious schemes. He was playing the role of the infallible redeemer. His speeches were always apostolic and his vocabulary lofty. And thus while he spoke of "mankind" (one of his favorite words), of "democracy" and "ideals"— "the nature of which I have never been able to ascertain"—he was personally engaged in overthrowing Huerta and putting Carranza in his place, as a venture, pure and simple, in power politics.

Wilson did this intentionally, with premeditation, aided, of course, by the armed forces of the United States which, at that precise moment, were at the service of his personal whims. As a direct result of the bombing of Vera Cruz, many American and Mexican citizens were killed. Many thousands more were to die throughout the tragic eight years his administration lasted, as a consequence of his sinister foreign policy. In my impotent bitterness, I could only ask: How could the descendants of George Washington, Thomas Jefferson and Abraham Lincoln have elected such a puritanical hypocrite to the presidency of the United States? How could they tolerate, to their own moral and material disadvantage, this cruel and unjust aggression against an innocent people?

My personal situation was almost hopeless. Following on the American armed intervention in Vera Cruz, Huerta and his government had, inevitably, to fall. It was a question of days before I would have to pack my bags and leave my country, perhaps never to return. And in my gloom the newspaper clipping cheered me. Here was a citizen of the United States who was not to be bribed by flattering appointments. One American who would never sanction with his presence something he considered morally wrong. Years would pass before I was to have the privilege of meeting Buckley, but his gallant attitude on that occasion was never to be forgotten.

Seven years later I met him. My attention to his vigorous personality had been aroused several months before by the brilliant statement he had rendered in December 1919, before the Subcommittee of the Committee of Foreign Relations of the United States Senate.

The meeting took place in the month of August, 1921. I was in New York City for a short visit, staying at the Hotel Commodore, where General Samuel Garcia Cuellar was also stopping. Garcia Cuellar had been the Chief of Staff of President Porfirio Diaz and, in 1908, while I occupied a room at the Hotel Jardin Mexico City, he and his family had leased the third floor of the same hotel, two years before Diaz was overthrown. We looked upon each other as old neighbors and, in New York, were repeating the circumstances of our long friendship; except that now we were both exiles, and very homesick.

We had gotten into the habit of lunching and dining together, at least three or four times a week, after which we would go to the theatre; and always the chief topic of conversation was our distant Mexico, which we were missing so much.

One day while I was visiting at his apartment, Mr. William F. Buckley telephoned from the lobby to ask the General if he could be received. Garcia Cuellar replied that I was with him at that moment but that I was an intimate friend. Buckley then said that he had been anxious to meet me. He came up immediately and this is how I came to know this extraordinary American whose solid and forceful statement before the Senate Subcommittee had so profoundly impressed me.

What was the purpose of the Subcommittee? Mr. Woodrow Wilson's foreign policy in relation to Mexico had been so incoherent and contradictory, while the criticism of it by such men of renown as Henry Cabot Lodge and Elihu Root had been so incisive, that many members of the Congress had become completely confused. The Senators therefore decided to constitute a Subcommittee of the Committee of Foreign Relations to investigate Mexican affairs. It was before this small group that Mr. Buckley appeared voluntarily to speak of the real situation in my country. I had read in the newspapers a summary of what he testified to and found it so truthful and precise, that I asked my friends in New York who on earth was the informed prompter who had told Buckley what to say.

No one knew; but they all agreed that it was surely necessary, to have spoken so accurately, for the witness to be for all intents and purposes a Mexican. No one else could have sketched so truthfully the tangled jumble of the history of Mexico between 1910 and 1920. I had studied in primary schools in Texas and have felt since then that there are many things about my country that are not intelligible to aliens. Anatole France said in the preface to his biography of Joan of Arc that to understand the past, one must forget the present. Something similar can be said when international comprehension is sought. But how can we ask the French to forget for a moment they are French—in order to understand the Germans? This difficulty is the source of intellectual and moral collisions, especially among neighboring countries. And there will always be scoundrels and fanatics who take advantage of the natural antagonism between contiguous nations to deepen the disparity between peoples who differ in blood, in language, in customs, in religion and in history.

When Buckley entered Garcia Cuellar's apartment, I was awed by his flawless Spanish. The foreign accent was scarcely perceptible and his grammatical constructions were as correct as those of a native professor of Spanish. Indeed, if my English were half as good as the Spanish he spoke and wrote, this tribute to his fond memory would be more readable.

When I asked him where he had mastered our tongue, he replied that he had spent his childhood in San Diego, Texas, a town near the Mexican border where most of the population is of Mexican descent. I inferred that his spiritual development, though so radically different from mine, had many points of contact with it. He had grown up among Mexican children; whereas I a Mexican, had gone to school with American boys and girls.

There were other affinities. His Irish surname indicated a psychology closer to the Latins than to the Anglo-Saxons. His Catholic religion, to which he was deeply devoted, was another important factor of his understanding. In Mexico, Catholicism is the nation's widest and most prominent social phenomenon, so that to understand Mexican affairs, to be a Catholic is almost *sine qua non*. This background enabled him to grasp the problems of Mexico as no other alien I know of had grasped them before. I was later told that no Mexican scholar had prompted Buckley in his statement before

the American Senate. After knowing him it was obvious that he was
as well acquainted with Mexico as he was with his own country.

It is well to remember the events that led to Buckley's refusal to
accept the Civil Governoship of Vera Cruz.

The government of Francisco I. Madero had been overthrown
by a military *coup d'etat*, and General Victoriano Huerta became
President of Mexico on February 19, 1913. Three days later, both
ex-President Madero and Jose Maria Pino Suarez, who had been
his Vice-President, were assassinated in Mexico City, thereby giving Carranza an excuse to rebel, in behalf of a movement that was
to be called the Constitutionalist Revolution.

When Huerta seized the Presidency of Mexico, President William Howard Taft was about to leave the White House and, as is
customary in situations of this sort, left it to his successor, Mr.
Woodrow Wilson, to assume responsibility over whether the government of General Huerta should be recognized or not. It is odd
how history is woven by details that seem insignificant and unim-
portant. Had Mr. Taft chosen to recognize Huerta as President of
Mexico—and this is no criticism of his correct political posture—
much bloodshed evidently would have been avoided, as Mr. Wilson
would have been forced by circumstances to accept what his pre-
decessor had affirmed. If this had occurred, there might never have
been a Constitutionalist Revolution; or if in spite of the recognition,
Carranza had taken up arms against the Huerta government, the
chances would have been one hundred to one that he would have
been defeated.

History is not written of what *could* have happened, but of
events as they actually happened. No one in Mexico has ever been
so popular as was Madero in 1911, just after the downfall of Porfirio Diaz. When he arrived in Mexico City on the seventh of June
of that year, he was welcomed by acclamation. It was he who had
been brave enough to offer armed opposition to the giant who had
ruled the country for more than thirty years, and whose position
seemed eternal and unmovable. And to everybody's amazement,
Madero had won. Repeating the biblical text, David had again tri-
umphed over Goliath who, in the form of Porfirio Diaz, was now
on his way to exile. Decidely, Madero was the people's choice, their
hero and their savior.

Moreover, Madero's romantic dreams of democracy in Mexico were contagious. The people sincerely believed that from then on, effective suffrage would be the rule. They would elect public officials of their choice, and everybody would be free, content, and prosperous.

It requires more courage than talent to incite a mob, and more talent than courage to control it. As the leader of the revolutionary movement, Madero played his role brilliantly and nobody can licitly have doubts as to his personal valor. He had risked his life, his social position and his fortune to achieve his end: the downfall of Porfirio Diaz; and he had succeeded. To the victor belong the spoils, and Madero was elected President in the only true election Mexico has ever known.

It is easier to promise than to fulfill but, unfortunately, Madero did not possess the qualities and skills that make for the successful statesman. His innocent good faith always played against him. His indecisiveness at crucial moments led him from one blunder to another. Hard to believe, but true just the same, the idol of June, 1911, had by February, 1913, entirely lost his popularity and what is more, the respect that is due any Chief of State. To some people he had become a laughing stock; to others, the object of hatred.

There are reports to the effect that Carranza, for sixteen years a senator in the government of Porfirio Diaz and now *maderista* governor of the State of Coahuila, was about to rebel, and that when Madero was murdered, he realized his opportunity, proclaiming that his revolt against Huerta was motivated by a desire to avenge the shameful assassination of his "beloved" chief. The truth of the matter is that Madero and Carranza had already quarreled because the Federal government had cut off Carranza's allowance for the maintenance of State troops. While Carranza's intentions can never be satisfactorily proven, I have nevertheless become convinced that he started his revolution only after Wilson's full approval and support had been assured. Otherwise, the odds would have been too much against him.

When the month of February, 1913, arrived, there had been so many disappointments and resentments, so many awakened but unsatisfied ambitions, that numerous plots and conspiracies ensued. The danger, however, was not to be found in the so-called reactionaries of the old Diaz regime, but rather in the revolutionists who had expected and hoped for more than Madero could give them. It had not been so difficult to start a successful rebellion, as the triumphant and incompetent Madero had proven; but once aroused, the masses were not as easily quieted. The entire country trembled like an expectant mother about to deliver a huge national calamity. Then, on February 9, the military revolt began.

This was the fourth uprising against Madero and the one destined to succeed. General Manuel Mondragon was the first important figure to enter the scene. With armed troops under his command, he proceeded to the Penitentiary and to the Military Prison, respectively, to free Generals Felix Diaz and Bernardo Reyes who had for some time been imprisoned. Together the three continued to the National Palace where a skirmish followed in which Reyes was shot dead. The survivors retreated to the *Ciudadela* where they directed artillery fire against the National Palace. For ten days, the volleys of cannons could be heard all over Mexico City. Madero had appointed Huerta as military commander of the city and the latter conferred with the rebellious generals. They decided it was best for the country to suspend hostilities and to establish a new government. Madero was to be deposed, Huerta to assume the Presidency, and Felix Diaz and Manuel Mondragon were to name the members of the presidential cabinet.

This agreement met with the approval of the representatives of most of the conflicting interests. The Mexican Congress, elected only a few months before, accepted the resignations of President Madero and Vice-President Pino Suarez, by overwhelming vote.

Of the 27 governors of the States of the Mexican Republic, all but two, Jose Maria Maytorena of Sonora and Carranza of Coahuila, recognized Huerta immediately as the new President.

Now no sensible or moral human being can justify murder, and the assassination of ex-President Madero and ex-Vice-President Pino Suarez will always stand out as the most stupid crime committed in Mexico. Although Huerta repeatedly denied that he had given orders to execute these two unfortunate men, he tacitly accepted his government's historic responsibility for the crime.

Woodrow Wilson was inaugurated on March 4th, and a week later gave a statement to the press which was published on March

12, throwing the force of the U. S. government behind "democratic" movements in Latin America.

Carranza was quick to take his cue. Evidently the President of the United States would never coexist with Huerta's violent *coup d'etat*. Therefore, no official recognition would be forthcoming. Could a government in Mexico subsist without recognition from the Colossus of the North? Carranza was willing to gamble, and on the 26th of the same month of March, he and a few followers signed the *Plan de Guadalupe*, initiating the Constitutionalist Revolution which was to be so costly in life and property. With the invaluable help of his friend, Mr. Woodrow Wilson, and of the Army and Navy of the United States, Carranza would emerge victorious, but not for long; because on May 20, 1920, six months after W.F.B. testified before the Senate Committee, he was to die in the village of Tlaxcalantongo, Puebla, murdered by his own men.

We must make a distinction which to me has always been obvious but which was apparently not as clear in President Wilson's mind in the year 1913. It is one thing to deny recognition to the government of another country, another to intervene directly in that country's internal affairs. Any nation, like any individual, has the unquestionable right to choose its friends, and had President Wilson's policy been limited merely to non-recognition of Huerta, the Mexican people might have been able somehow to solve their problems while economizing on the shedding of blood.

But Mr. Wilson was interested only in "mankind" and by that expression, when he referred to Mexico, he meant—Carranza.

While President Wilson had brushed up on the history of Mexico, supposedly because knowledge of the subject would be helpful in dealing with the Mexican problem, all his personal representatives to the various factions engaged at one time or another in the great Mexican civil war, were manifestly ignorant of the country, of the Mexican people's psychology and of the Spanish language. Their ignorance, Mr. Wilson maintained, would, in point of fact, guarantee their impartiality. Believe it or not, this puerile attitude was assumed by a man who formerly had been a professor of Law at Princeton University and was now the President of the United States.

When an English diplomat asked the President to define exactly his policy in regard to Mexico, Wilson is reported to have replied that he was going to teach the South American republics to elect good men to office. "Who were the good men? Wilson thought that Carranza was the best, and that Villa was not as bad as he was said to be."

This is about the most defamatory remark ever inflicted on the poor Mexican people. Less than a year later, in a letter dated June 4, 1914, to Mr. Walter H. Page, American Ambassador to Great Britain, Wilson wrote:

> The thing which seems to me most important now with regard to the Mexican business is that the people over there get a more just and correct view of Villa. Carranza I believe to be an honest but a very narrow and rather a dull person whom it is extremely difficult to deal with but who can be counted upon no doubt to try to do the right thing by those who are now centering their hopes in him for working out a decent solution of the economic problem which underlies the situation in Mexico just as much as the land question underlay the settlement of affairs in Ireland. A landless people will always furnish inflammable material for a revolution.

If the "narrow" and "dull" Carranza was the best man in Mexico, what infamous adjective had President Wilson reserved for the rest of the population?

When Huerta's Minister of Foreign Affairs, Federico Gamboa, replied to Lind's note, he insisted on the sovereignty of Mexico. Refusing to take the bribe, he said simply: "When the dignity of the nation is at stake, I believe that there are not loans enough to induce those charged by the law to maintain it to permit it to be insulted."

Gamboa's answer infuriated Mr. Wilson all the more. Only two or three days before, the President had written to his friend, Mary A. Hulbert:

> Our friend Huerta is a diverting brute! He is always so perfectly in character; so false, so sly, so full of bravado (the bravado of ignorance, chiefly), and yet so courageous, too, and determined — such a mixture of weak and strong, of ridiculous and respectable! One moment you long for his blood, out of mere justice for what he has done, and the next you find yourself entertaining a sneaking admiration for his nerve. He will not let go till he pulls the whole house down with him. He loves only

those who advise him to do what he wants to do. He has cold lead for those who tell him the truth. He is seldom sober and always impossible, and yet what an indomitable fighter for his own hand! Every day the news from Mexico City unsettles the news of the day before. The whole thing is quick-silver. I dare not finish my message to Congress intended for Tuesday till Tuesday's news comes, for fear the things I say in it might turn out to be untrue in fact! Any hour of the day or night I may have to revise my judgment as to what it is best to do. Do you wonder that I have lost flesh a bit?

Mr. Wilson's worries were merely the consequence of his original error of meddling in another country's internal business without knowing anything about it. His stubborness would lead him now to costlier and bloodier blunders. This is how Mr. Buckley related before the Senate Subcommittee the events that followed:

Mr. John Lind[1], the personal representative of Mr. Wilson . . . reported to the President what the President wanted to hear; that is, that the Mexican people were overwhelmingly opposed to Huerta and would very soon drive him out of power. The situation between the two countries became very tense, and the Huerta Government seemed to become stronger instead of weaker; Americans in rebel sections of the country were being mistreated and killed, and there was much general dissatisfaction in the United States with the situation in Mexico. To hurry the triumph of the Carranza revolution, Mr. Wilson raised the embargo of arms and ammunition on the 3rd day of February, 1914, without having first recognized the belligerency of the so-called Constitutionalist revolutionary government—a most extraordinary step. In his message to Congress of August 27, 1913, Mr. Wilson assured that body that Huerta would soon be eliminated by popular action of the Mexican people. On the contrary, the situation continued to lag and Huerta continued in power, much to the annoyance of the American Government. Finally, in March, 1914, the Tampico incident occurred, which gave Mr. Wilson the pretext for which he had long been waiting. A launch carrying marines from one of the American gunboats entered a prohibited zone within the range of firing at Tampico (the town was then being attacked by rebels), and the marines were arrested by a Huerta officer, acting under general orders, taken to military headquarters and there released without having been incarcerated, and, before any demand was made, the Huerta commander expressed his regrets to Admiral Mayo, in command of the American squadron.

. . . The American flag was not [in fact] insulted, and . . . an

[1] About whom more later—see Chapter X (ed.)

apology was made before it was called for. This however, was not sufficient, as the American Government was looking for a pretext for trouble with Huerta, in order to force him from a position where he was causing this Government much embarrassment.

President Wilson was determined to make the most of the Tampico incident so as to assure Carranza's triumph. The American Government therefore demanded that General Ignacio Morelos Zaragoza, who was in command in Tampico, "hoist the American flag in a prominent position on shore and salute it with twenty-one guns. . . ."

Morelos Zaragoza replied that he would have to consult with Huerta, and the latter, after submitting several unaccepted proposals, decided that he was willing to accede to the American Government's demands, if the *Charge d'Affaires* of the United States Embassy, Mr. Nelson O'Shaughnessy, would sign a protocol pledging the United States to salute the Mexican flag in return.

Secretary of State Bryan's telegraphic answer to this request, was that there would be no agreement as to the return salute. "In addition to other reasons," so the telegram said, "signing of protocol would be objectionable because it might be construed as recognition of his government whereas the President has no intention of recognizing Huerta's government."

This message was sent to O'Shaughnessy in the early hours of April 19,1914. When the decision was relayed to Huerta, he determined to stand pat, in spite of the fact that on that day the American government's ultimatum would expire.

The next day, President Wilson was to address Congress to ask for authorization to use United States armed forces in Mexico; but before going to the Capitol, consulted with Senator Lodge, who redacted the following memorandum:

> He [the President] said he wished to read his message and take our opinion upon it. As it was already in print for the press it could not be changed. But he read it. It seemed to me weak and insufficient, although of course well expressed. He then produced the resolution which he wished passed. It was the same as that which afterwards passed the House and authorized hostilities against Huerta by name. This seemed to me most unsatisfactory,

[2] These paragraphs from W.F.B.'s testimony before the Senate Subcommittee on Foreign Relations are repeated in the condensation of that testimony (see Chapter X). They appear twice because they are integral to both chapters.

in reality a declaration of war against an individual. I said that I thought we ought to speak of protection to the lives and property of American citizens as the true international ground. Pres. said that would widen too much and lead to war. I thought it was in any event. He said he wanted immediate action because he wished to intercept a cargo of arms for Huerta due that evening at Vera Cruz on German ship. I suggested that he could not stop the ship without a war blockade. He said that his plan was to take Vera Cruz and seize the cargo after it landed. I pointed out that he would be cutting off arms from Huerta and letting them go to Villa, which would be in the nature of an alliance. He said that was due to circumstances and could not be helped. He then gave to each of us a copy of the resolution which he wished to have passed.

Mr. Wilson had been informed on too many occasions by Mr. Lind and other extremely incompetent advisers, that if the armed forces of the United States landed in Mexico for the purpose of ousting Huerta, they would be welcomed as liberators. He therefore decided to prevent the unloading of arms for Huerta by having Mr. Josephus Daniels, at that time Secretary of the Navy, instruct Admiral Fletcher to take Vera Cruz. Wilson did this on April 21, 1914. The port was bombarded by the American ships; 145 men were killed and 256 were wounded.

This was only the beginning. After Huerta's downfall, the revolutionists were to fight among themselves for several years. To avenge Wilson's recognition of Carranza, Pancho Villa (formerly the American President's pet) assaulted the village of Columbus, New Mexico, where he murdered 17 citizens of the United States. There were to be many more slaughters. The leading men of the revolutions that began in 1913—Zapata, Carranza, Villa and Obregon—were on different dates to die violently, all of them murdered. And all this was nothing as compared with the thousands of innocent people who during those years were to be killed, robbed, starved and raped.

Before the biers of the American bluejackets who had died in Vera Cruz for absolutely no good reason, President Wilson said:

We have gone down to Mexico to serve mankind if we can find out the way. We do not want to fight the Mexicans. We want to serve the Mexicans if we can, because we know how we would like to be free, and how we would like to be served if there were friends ready to serve us. A war of aggression is not a war in which it is a proud thing to die, but a war of service is a thing in which it is a proud thing to die.

Never was a greater untruth spoken. It was uttered precisely by the man mainly responsible for the hell that had broken loose and would continue loose until God alone knew when.

William F. Buckley understood and sympathized with the Mexican people who had been innocent victims of Mr. Wilson's erratic foreign policy. His refusal to serve as Civil Governor of Vera Cruz proved beyond any doubt that he was a friend of my country. His statement before the Senate of the United States reaffirmed his friendship. Could I, as a citizen of· Mexico, have anything but admiration, respect and love for him?

To say that Buckley understood Mexico does not mean that he viewed its problems with impartiality. He was a keen observer, but there was in him—as in nearly every Irishman—more of the fighter than of the mere spectator. He took sides in every conflict probably because he felt that indifference to evil is immoral and cowardly, and that everybody must stand up and fight for what he believes to be right. Thinking of him, I am reminded of Clemenceau who, on being accused of impartiality, replied indignantly: "Traitor, probably; but neutral, never!"

Although in my estimation, he was one of my country's best friends, the Mexican government expelled him in the latter part of 1921. If it is ever proven that he was promoting a revolution [he was—Ed.], I would not in the least be surprised; but at the same time, I am sure he felt passionately that he was right in doing so [he was—Ed.]. On his way north he counter-attacked in a press interview, by saying that President Obregon who had thrown him out of Mexico, was more of an interventionist than he. The revolutionists, among them Obregon, had reaped the benefits of American armed intervention in Vera Cruz, while Buckley had always protested against Wilson's meddling and blundering.

After 1926, when my second exile from Mexico began, we became very good friends. This may be because we had many things in common. We had both been devoted partisans of Porfirio Diaz; I had been a cabinet member during Huerta's regime, and while

W. F. B. designs a house to be built in Coyoacan, Mexico City. But there was one too many revolutions . . .

Buckley was never a *huertista*, he did feel that Huerta was the least of many evils. In my youth, I had been a professor of the History of Mexico, and Buckley knew as much about Mexican history as any professor I have ever known. Now, fate had brought us together, both of us expelled from a country we loved and venerated.

I admired Buckley's vast culture which was never in conflict with his good common sense. His scholarship lacked the academic pedantry that so often accompanies the wisdom of even very learned professors, and makes them dull and tiresome. He read and studied during his 77 years thousands of books, and the erudition derived therefrom was never for the purpose of showing off, but to better his strong spirit and—later in life—competently to advise his numerous descendants.

He believed sincerely in his Catholic faith, and he also believed in the United States of America, of which he was very proud. He rejoiced in his country's wealth and beauty. He gloried in American initiative, in American know-how and in the competitive spirit of the American people.

I envied his business ability and the ease with which he solved the many problems that were presented to him, all of them requiring quick thinking. The main principle of his economic thought was hard work of which at all times he gave an eloquent example. At 75, he was still thinking up new schemes, enterprises and transactions. He believed in a free economy and was convinced that State intervention in this matter produced the opposite of the desired effect. And his convictions were a citadel which he defended with passion.

He was my good friend. May he rest in peace.

Someday, not in the too distant future—because I am now 76 years of age—somewhere, in the light of heaven, I know that our spirits will meet once more. And we will talk of the pioneers that made the United States what they are today, as also of the Spanish missionaries who gave the Mexican people their faith; we will talk of the history of our Continent and of Mexico's beautiful legends; we will surely brag about Buckley's 35—and my 28 grandchildren, and we will both solemnly promise never to speak of Mr. Woodrow Wilson again.

I am looking forward to that pleasant occasion.

INVESTIGATION OF MEXICAN AFFAIRS

HEARING

BEFORE A

SUBCOMMITTEE OF THE
COMMITTEE ON FOREIGN RELATIONS
UNITED STATES SENATE

SIXTY-SIXTH CONGRESS.

FIRST SESSION

PURSUANT TO

S. Res. 106

DIRECTING THE COMMITTEE ON FOREIGN RELATIONS TO
INVESTIGATE THE MATTER OF OUTRAGES ON CITIZENS
OF THE UNITED STATES IN MEXICO

PART 6

Printed for the use of the Committee on Foreign Relations

WASHINGTON
GOVERNMENT PRINTING OFFICE
1919

COMMITTEE ON FOREIGN RELATIONS.

HENRY CABOT LODGE, Massachusetts, *Chairman.*

PORTER J. McCUMBER, North Dakota.
WILLIAM E. BORAH, Idaho.
FRANK B. BRANDEGEE, Connecticut.
ALBERT B. FALL, New Mexico.
PHILANDER C. KNOX, Pennsylvania.
WARREN G. HARDING, Ohio.
HIRAM W. JOHNSON, California.
HARRY S. NEW, Indiana.
GEORGE H. MOSES, New Hampshire.

GILBERT H. HITCHCOCK, Nebraska.
JOHN SHARP WILLIAMS, Mississippi.
CLAUDE A. SWANSON, Virginia.
ATLEE POMERENE, Ohio.
MARCUS A. SMITH, Arizona.
KEY PITTMAN, Nevada.
JOHN K. SHIELDS, Tennessee.

C. F. REDMOND, *Clerk.*

SUBCOMMITTEE ON MEXICAN AFFAIRS.

ALBERT B. FALL, *Chairman.*

FRANK B. BRANDEGEE.   MARCUS A. SMITH.

DAN M. JACKSON, *Clerk.*

II

III. *Witness*

Saturday, December 6, 1919

UNITED STATES SENATE,
SUBCOMMITTEE ON FOREIGN RELATIONS,
Washington, D. C.

Testimony taken at Washington, D. C., December 6, 1919, by Francis J. Kearful, Esq., in pursuance of an order of the Subcommittee of the Committee on Foreign Relations of the Senate.

STATEMENT OF MR. WILLIAM FRANK BUCKLEY

(The witness was duly sworn by Mr. Kearful.)

MR. KEARFUL. You have stated your name. What is your present address?

MR. BUCKLEY. Mexico City.

MR. KEARFUL. Your present address in this country?

MR. BUCKLEY. My present address in this country is Bronxville, N. Y.

MR. KEARFUL. What is your birthplace?

MR. BUCKLEY. San Diego, Tex.

MR. KEARFUL. What is your profession?

MR. BUCKLEY. I used to be an attorney.

MR. KEARFUL. In what business are you now engaged?

MR. BUCKLEY. Real estate and oil leases.

MR. KEARFUL. In Mexico?

MR. BUCKLEY. In Mexico.

MR. KEARFUL. How long have you been acquainted with Mexico?

MR. BUCKLEY. I have lived in Mexico since 1908.

MR. KEARFUL. Are you thoroughly familiar with the Spanish language?

MR. BUCKLEY. Yes.

MR. KEARFUL. Are you able to talk with the natives of Mexico freely upon any subject?

MR. BUCKLEY. Yes.

Mr. Kearful. Have you made a study of Mexican conditions during the time that you were in Mexico and during the last few months in this country?

Mr. Buckley. Yes; I have.

Mr. Kearful. The committee has heretofore had testimony showing in a fragmentary way various incidents which go to make up a picture of Mexican conditions. I understand that you have made such a study of Mexico as to be able to give a more or less complete picture of the situation from the time of the overthrow of the Madero government up to the present time. Such a complete statement would naturally be divisible into various heads. Will you proceed in your own way to make a statement of the conditions covering the entire period mentioned beginning with the overthrow of the Madero government?

Mr. Buckley. To understand the Mexican situation it must be understood in the beginning that the present is more or less the normal condition of Mexico; the era of peace during the Diaz regime from 1876 to 1910 was an abnormal period in the history of that country. All revolutions in Mexico work along conventional lines and the present series of revolutions are in no material sense different from those that beset that country from 1810 to 1876; the abnormal element of the present series of revolutions is the active participation in them by the American Government. During the pre-Diaz period there were hundreds of revolutions and over 50 rulers. All of these revolutions, like the present revolution, promised everything to the people, including universal suffrage, independent judiciary, division of lands, democratic form of government, etc. To the average American the present situation in Mexico is a novel one; to the man who has studied Mexico's history there is not much novelty in it.

There is a distinction between the Madero revolution and the Carranza revolution; the former had for its object the establishment in Mexico of a democratic form of government; the latter had as its object social, and not political, reforms—the principal reforms being the destruction of private property and the expulsion from the country of the Americans. The former revolution was dominated by Mexicans of the old Liberal type and included in its ranks some of the finest men in Mexico. These men were soon disillusioned, quit the revolution, and were succeeded by radicals of an inferior social type who directed the Carranza revolution and now control the Carranza government. The only political reforms that the leaders of the Carranza revolution sought were for the purpose of vesting political power in themselves, and not in the Mexican people. Control of the political machinery would enable them, first, to enrich themselves by graft, and second, to force through their social reforms.

When Madero was President, Carranza was governor of the State of Coahuila. Carranza, as well as other governors, received from the Federal Government an allowance of a large sum of money each month for the support of the State constabulary to put down local revolutions. Limantour had left 63,000,000 pesos in the Mexican treasury, and this was one of the favorite methods used by the groups surrounding Madero to loot the treasury. Of course, troops were not maintained in the several States, or, at least, not more troops than were necessary to cover appearances, and the Governor of the State divided up his monthly allowance with the grafters in Mexico City.

It is stated that because of a disagreement between Carranza and the group surrounding President Madero, Carranza's monthly allowance was cut off and this led to friction between Carranza and Madero and to the formulation of plans by the former to revolt against his chief. It is generally understood that Carranza invited Alberto Garcia Granados, a noted Liberal in Mexico, who formed a part of Madero's cabinet, to join him in his revolt. Garcia Granados had become dissatisfied with Madero, and Carranza thought that he would be friendly to such a suggestion. It is stated that Garcia Granados declined to join in the revolt. After Carranza entered Mexico City Garcia Granados was executed.

Madero was overthrown before Carranza's alleged plans matured. Huerta, the successor of Madero, conducted negotiations with Carranza for some time looking toward recognition of his government by Carranza, but the latter finally broke off negotiations and revolted.

When Madero was killed the agents of Carranza advised him of the bad impression that this outrage had produced in the United States, whereupon Carranza realized his opportunity and proclaimed loudly, especially where Americans could hear, that his purpose in revolting was to avenge the shameful murder of his beloved chief. Carranza's agents in the United States played this up with great effect on the American people.

The Mexican point of view with regard to this assassination has never been understood by the Americans. The Mexican people were not as a rule shocked by the assassination of Madero; you seldom hear reference in Mexico to this crime. As a rule Mexicans who favored Huerta maintained that if Huerta did kill Madero it was good politics; the followers of Madero, while protesting that they were sorry their chief had been killed, admitted that they could understand the attitude of the opposition as constituting good politics.

MR. KEARFUL. What have you to say with reference to the attitude of Mexicans towards Huerta?

MR. BUCKLEY. The mass of the Mexican people have no preferences in politics, for they know nothing about politics. The middle-class and upper-class Mexicans favored Huerta, principally because they were anxious for peace and order and because they had been satiated with the advanced political doctrines announced by Madero and satiated with the shameless graft that surrounded his administration.

Carranza propaganda in the United States, very ably assisted by the American Government, succeeded in instilling into the public mind certain erroneous impressions that have been the basis of American public opinion, where there has been any public opinion, for the last six or seven years.

The Carrancista press explained that there were three classes of people in Mexico—the lower classes, representing what Mr. Wilson has termed "the submerged 80 per cent," the middle class, comprising probably 10 per cent, and the upper class. It is stated that the middle and lower classes were trying to wrest political power from the Cientificos, a so-called party composing the upper classes, that it was alleged had governed Mexico for their own exclusive benefit and the benefit of foreign capital during the Diaz regime.

The peace and order established by the Diaz Government, and maintained for 35 years, enabled the middle class to form. There was no such thing as a middle class in Mexico before the Diaz regime, and the people of the middle class were the strongest advocates of the Diaz regime, for without peace and order it could not subsist.

The "submerged 80 per cent" has no political ambition; does not know how to read or write; lives from hand to mouth, and has no political ideas or preferences; all it wants is to be let alone and be allowed to live in peace and receive those material necessities that are indispensable for the maintenance of life. This class has never received any consideration or protection in Mexico during the regime of Porfirio Diaz.

I do not contend that this is all that the 80 per cent of the population is entitled to, but I do contend, and history shows, that material benefits must come first and that a people does not concern itself with the niceties of government or universal suffrage until after it is provided with bread and clothes.

The educated Mexican, the type that governed Mexico for 35 years, and gave it the only decent government that it ever had—the Mexican whom the American Government has driven out of that country—did not sympathize with Huerta and was not a partisan of Huerta's. To him Huerta was the lesser of several evils; he preferred Huerta to either Carranza or Villa, and subsequent events have demonstrated the wisdom of his choice. The cultivated Mexican, however, would never have chosen Huerta for president of his own free will.

MR. KEARFUL. Will you now proceed to give a statement with reference to the relations of Huerta toward the American Government and the attitude of the American Government toward Huerta?

MR. BUCKLEY. Soon after his election, President Wilson introduced an innovation in the diplomatic policy of the American Government. This Government was represented in Mexico City by an honorable man, who had served his country well—Mr. Henry Lane Wilson—who soon discovered that his Government neither consulted him nor confided in him. Mr. Henry Lane Wilson was the representative of the American Government, but President Wilson preferred to conduct foreign negotiations through his own personal representatives. The State Department was eliminated at once from the field of diplomatic relations with Mexico, and, since the accession of Mr. Wilson to office, has not had anything to do with the carrying out of this policy. Because of his policy of insisting that the rights of Americans in Mexico be respected, and because he showed resentment in not being taken into the confidence of his own Government, Ambassador Wilson was recalled from

Mexico. All manner of scurrilous rumors with regard to this gentleman, among them allegations to the effect that he was responsible for the murder of Madero and had actually connived at this murder, were carefully spread in the United States by Carranza propagandists and by the representatives of the President, among whom Mr. John Lind distinguished himself; rumors which the American Government knew to be untrue and which it could have suppressed by merely denying them. The State Department went so far in conniving at the persecution of this gentleman as to permit an unscrupulous American from Mexico City by the name of Robert H. Murray, the correspondent in that city of the *New York World* and an interested propagandist of the Carranza Government, to secure information from the confidential files of the State Department for the purpose of producing evidence in garbled form against the ex-ambassador.

We will be glad to submit, whenever the committee desires, details with regard to the dismissal of Ambassador Wilson and the conduct of the American Government and its representatives.

Huerta was recognized by most of the first-class powers, but the American Government did nothing. Except for vague statements along general lines that might be regarded as being applicable to Mexico, there was no indication of the President's policy. It will be interesting in this connection, as an indication of the atttude of the high-class Mexican not only towards Huerta but towards the American Government, to state that at this juncture a group of Mexican statesmen in Mexico City, realizing the extreme gravity of the situation and the type of men we had to reckon with in Huerta and President Wilson, discussed the situation with the object of avoiding difficulties. These gentlemen were sufficiently versed in Mexican history, and sufficiently aware of the dependent condition of Mexico with regard to the United States, to appreciate that without the recognition of the American Government Huerta could not remain in power; they felt that the exercise by Mr. Wilson of the great power which the office of President of United States conferred on him to destroy Huerta would be arbitrary and unscrupulous but, nevertheless, they realized what the results would be.

They consequently decided to send an emissary to see Mr. Wilson and ascertain if he was determined not to recognize Huerta's government, and if this were his intention, they instructed their emissary to tell Mr. Wilson that they themselves would soon eliminate Huerta from the Presidency; that they would not permit his vanity to stand in the way of Mexico's welfare. The emissary was instructed to beg of Mr. Wilson that he should not openly oppose Huerta, as this would have the effect of consolidating Mexican public opinion behind him along nationalistic lines; that he permit the Mexican people themselves to eliminate Huerta from the Presidency and thus avoid a disagreeable situation, one which, as a matter of fact, was precipitated by Mr. Wilson's public refusal to recognize Huerta before this emissary could reach Washington, and was aggravated further by his dispatching of Mr. John Lind to Mexico. Mr. Wilson's public announcement, of course, had just the opposite effect in Mexico to what Mr. Wilson thought it would have; it strengthened Mexican sentiment for Huerta and gave him the support of the Mexican people in his personal conflict with President Wilson. Huerta could have been eliminated by the use of some tact.

It was at this juncture that the famous Lind mission was conceived and carried out. John Lind, a Swedish-American from Minnesota, who had never been in Mexico, knew nothing of Mexican affairs or of Mexican character and had no knowledge of the Spanish language, was chosen for a most delicate mission to Mexico City. Could there be anything as different in temperament as a Swede and a Latin-American? Mr. Lind was chosen, so Washington informed the American people, because he knew nothing about Mexico and, consequently, was not prejudiced. Lind proceeded to Mexico City, the details of his trip and mission being given the greatest newspaper publicity, and presented to Huerta, the President of an independent country, the astounding proposition that he eliminate himself from the Government of Mexico by calling a new election in which the Mexican people should *freely exercise their choice* and select another President. The people might not, however, select Huerta, so Lind informed him, not because he might not be the choice of the Mexican people, but because he was not the choice of Mr. Wilson. This proposal was actually given to the press by the American Government. It will not be necessary here to humiliate ourselves by recalling Huerta's answer to Lind. This was the first step of American intervention in Mexico. The President of the

United States told Huerta, and through him the Mexican people, that he would not permit Huerta to be the President of Mexico; it was but a step further to insist that he would permit nobody but a certain person to be President, and Mr. Wilson soon arrived at this step—during the Niagara conference he took the position that he would allow no one to be President of Mexico but Carranza.

There is a very interesting phase in the negotiations between President Wilson and Huerta that has generally been overlooked. Mr. Wilson proclaimed in speeches and interviews that the person of Huerta did not itself matter so much, but that Huerta represented a class—the hated Cientificos[1]—who had oppressed the "submerged 80 per cent" and that Mr. Wilson's interest in the matter, in fact, what he insisted upon, was that a look-in on their government be given to the "submerged 80 per cent" and that they be permitted to establish a government of their own choice; that the rebel leaders, Carranza and Villa, were the genuine popular leaders of this class and that a government must be established by them. As a matter of fact, when to the surprise of the American Government Huerta did not obey its order to retire, this administration, which in its relations with Mexico has never seemed to count in advance on the consequences of the failure of Mexico to comply with its many ultimatums, found itself in a delicate predicament. Mr. Lind was, therefore, authorized to compromise with Huerta, and with the class he represented, by agreeing that if Huerta would call an election in the territory controlled by him, and would not stand as a candidate, the American Government would not only recognize the President elected but would endeavor to see to it that he obtained money; in other words, the President through Mr. Lind said to Huerta: If you will save my pride by leaving office, I will permit you and the class you represent (the Cientificos) to select your successor. Mr. Wilson's protestations of concern for the welfare of the "submerged 80 per cent" seemed to be rather conventional in view of this incident.

The dispatching of the Lind mission was indeed an innovation in diplomacy, both because of its personnel, and the nature of the undertaking. The President seemed highly pleased with the com-

[1] The small group of men who attempted to liberalize the regime of Porfirio Diaz while rejecting reform by revolution. W.F.B. dealt extensively with the Cientificos, whom he greatly admired, in a part of his testimony deleted from this condensation.—Ed.

portment of Mr. Lind, since in his address to Congress on August 27, 1913, he stated that—

> Mr. Lind executed his delicate and difficult mission with singular tact, firmness, and good judgment.

When Huerta refused to accept the dictation of President Wilson, he became stronger than ever with the Mexican people. Mr. Lind, who ever since his trip to Mexico has been an active Carranza propagandist and an ardent opponent of armed intervention, returned to Vera Cruz after his humiliation by Huerta and recommended immediate armed intervention, presumably to avenge Mr. Lind; he advised his American friends in Mexico City to leave the country as intervention was imminent. Mr. Lind remained in Vera Cruz for a number of months where, under the protection afforded him by Huerta's Government, he conspired with the revolutionaries for the overthrow of that government, and actually entered into negotiations with a colonel in the Huerta army to overthrow his chief and let the Zapatista army into Mexico City. He was aided in these negotiations by Mr. H. L. Hall, a discredited American who lived in Mexico and one of the personal representatives of the President. All the details of that arrangement will be given to the committee if it desires.

It may be of interest in passing to refer to an incident indicating the esteem in which Americans in Mexico held Mr. Hall, who, as I have just stated, was one of the many personal representatives of the President. Mr. Hall was kidnapped by the Zapatistas near Cuernavaca, where he had lived for a number of years, and when the Zapatistas sent in a demand for a ransom of thirty pesos, Mr. Hall's neighbors refused to pay it.

MR. KEARFUL. What do you conceive to have been the attitude of the American Government toward Americans in Mexico during this period?

MR. BUCKLEY. The American Government never consulted Americans in Mexico and has always regarded them as unscrupulous adventurers who had left their own country and were in some way or other in league with the Cientificos for the purpose of exploiting the Mexican peon. I cannot explain the reason for this fantastic theory, but this was the theory. Americans in Mexico

City, a colony consisting of between 5,000 and 10,000 persons, realizing that their Government was about to make a decision in its Mexican policy that would be of far reaching importance, and feeling that their Government would be glad to avail itself of the opportunity of listening to the advice of Americans in Mexico, sent a committee of seven Americans to Washington to call on the Secretary of State and the President. Any European government would undoubtedly have been glad of the opportunity to consult its citizens of the type that composed this delegation to Washington and probably every American administration prior to the present one would have sought such advice. After a trip of 2,000 miles this delegation was permitted to see Mr. Bryan for a period of 10 minutes, during which time Mr. Bryan spoke 8 minutes; and was permitted to see Mr. Wilson for 20 minutes, during which their spokesman delivered an address which Mr. Wilson respectfully listened to but with a far-off expression in his eyes. Neither Mr. Wilson nor Mr. Bryan wanted to hear anything from Americans in Mexico or from Americans in this country who knew anything about the Mexican situation, and they ever after formed an effective quarantine against reliable information coming from unprejudiced and honest sources.

There were many incidents where American citizens, who had as their only concern the prestige and honor of their own country, were snubbed and insulted by officials of the American Government. One or two will be sufficient as illustrations. A delegation of citizens of El Paso, headed by Mr. Turney, a prominent lawyer, came all the way to Washington to beseech Mr. Bryan to intercede with the Mexican rebels to provide means whereby the American men, women and children stranded in Chihuahua could be brought to the border. Mr. Bryan did not receive this delegation in his office, but walked out into the waiting room and insulted them, telling them that they were not concerned with American women and children, but were thinking about their own property.

A Congressman from Texas, thinking that because of his knowledge of Mexican character his advice might be valuable, casually remarked to the President at a reception at the White House that he would like to come over some day and talk about the Mexican situation with him, whereupon the President told him very sharply that when he wanted to hear from him about the Mexican situation he would send for him. The President's attitude was so offensive that the Congressman in question never afterwards felt at liberty to call at the White House.

Every honest American who came to Washington from Mexico for the purpose of telling the American Government the truth was insulted, whereas dishonest and discredited Americans who had no regard for the good name of their country and who would stoop to come to Washington and tell the Government what the Government wanted to hear, and what those Americans knew to be untrue, were always received courteously and in a number of cases were rewarded with appointments as personal representatives of the President to Mexico.

In this connection it is worthy of note that during all these troublesome times, when over 100 prominent and cultured Mexican expatriates have resided in New York, there is not a single instance where any of them was called into consultation by the President on matters relating to their country, and concerning which they would certainly be regarded as an authority by unprejudiced people.

MR. KEARFUL. We have heard a great deal about what is known as the Tampico flag incident and the subsequent occupation of Vera Cruz by the American forces, and there have been many conflicting and confusing statements made in regard to those incidents. Are you prepared to give a true story of what occurred at that time?

MR. BUCKLEY. Yes. I was in Tampico up to a few days before the occurrence of the so-called Tampico incident and have many friends and acquaintances there and facilities for acquiring correct information. I was in Vera Cruz the day before that city was occupied by American forces, and returned to Vera Cruz a few days after its capture. I remained at Vera Cruz for several weeks, where I was tendered the position of Administrator of Justice in the American government, established there by Admiral Fletcher, a position which I declined, and had opportunity through association with the American officials in Vera Cruz to ascertain the truth with regard to the landing of the marines and the incidents that led up to the same.

MR. KEARFUL. Will you proceed in your own way to tell the story of the Tampico flag incident and the consequent occupation of Vera Cruz?

MR. BUCKLEY. Mr. Wilson's attempt to eliminate Huerta by using the persuasive powers of Lind, and by employing his favorite method of appealing directly to the people of the country over the heads of its ruler occurred in August 1913. Mr. Lind, who had familiarized himself with the entire Mexican situation by reading the Encyclopedia Britannica, which he afterwards plagiarized in a statement he made on Mexico, and by making a trip from Vera Cruz to Mexico City and back again and then associating with revolutionary spies at Vera Cruz, reported to the President what the President wanted to hear; that is, that the Mexican people were overwhelmingly opposed to Huerta and would very soon drive him out of power. The situation between the two countries became very tense, and the Huerta Government seemed to become stronger instead of weaker; Americans in rebel sections of the country were being mistreated and killed, and there was much general dissatisfaction in the United States with the situation in Mexico. To hurry the triumph of the Carranza revolution, Mr. Wilson raised the embargo on arms and ammunition on the 3rd day of February, 1914, without having first recognized the belligerency of the so-called Constitutionalist revolutionary government—a most extraordinary step. In his message to Congress of August 27, 1913, Mr. Wilson assured that body that Huerta would soon be eliminated by popular action of the Mexican people. On the contrary, the situation continued to lag and Huerta continued in power, much to the annoyance of the American Government. Finally, in March, 1914, the Tampico incident occurred, which gave Mr. Wilson the pretext for which he had long been waiting. A launch carrying marines from one of the American gunboats entered a prohibited zone within the range of the firing at Tampico (the town was then being attacked by rebels), and the marines were arrested by a Huerta officer, acting under general orders, taken to military headquarters and there released without having been incarcerated, and, before any demand was made, the Huerta commander expressed his regrets to Admiral Mayo, in command of the American squadron.

Full details of this matter will be given later but, suffice it to say, first, that the American flag was not insulted, and second, that an apology was made before it was called for. This, however, was not sufficient, as the American Government was looking for a pretext for trouble with Huerta, in order to force him from a position where he was causing this Government much embarrassment.

We might for a moment pause here, in order to judge properly the extreme means that were taken by the American Government in this matter of the so-called insult to the American flag, and consider the sensitiveness of our Government in taking offense here compared with its attitude where the Carranza Government has repeatedly insulted our flag.

For instance, when the American refugees were taken out of Tampico on tankers in June, 1916, at a time when relations with Mexico were strained, a launch from one of the American gunboats carrying armed marines was delegated to escort the two tankers to prevent sniping by the Carranza soldiers, whereupon these soldiers fired on the American launch. When Capt. W. Pitt Scott, the splendid commander of the American gunboat *Marietta*, on his own initiative, called on the commander of the Carranza garrison to disavow the action of his soldiers the commander replied that he would not only not disavow this action, but that the soldiers were acting under his express orders. The American Government ignored this insult to the flag by the Carranza Government.

Not having been able to arouse the spirit of the American Government by this insult, Gen. Emiliano Nafarrate, the commander of the Carranza garrison at Tampico, then proceeded to write a series of insulting notes to Capt. Scott, one nearly every day for a week or so; in these notes he insulted the Captain and the American Government, and expressed his opinion that the Americans were a treacherous race of cowards, that the American Government was playing false with the Mexican Government and was only waiting for an opportunity to conquer Mexico. Such conduct on the part of a Carranza official, one would think, might be construed as an insult to the American Government. I am informed that Capt. Scott reported the first insulting letter to Washington, but that upon receiving no acknowledgment from his Government he filed the rest of the letters away in a scrapbook as they came in.

On June 19, 1916, Carranza soldiers fired upon American naval officers and marines from the gunboat *Annapolis* at Mazatlan on

the west coast of Mexico. I quote from Commander Kavanaugh's
report as quoted in the *New York Herald* of the 23rd of that
month:

> The Government issued manifesto that officers were not to
> land, and guard was placed on dock. I sent ashore Ensign Kessing
> to parley with the Mexicans and ask them to send for the acting
> American consul or for one of the Mexican officials so as to ar-
> range for American citizens coming off to the ship. I sent Pay-
> master Mowat with the party as interpreter, no trouble being
> anticipated, as Mexicans had not molested earlier boats.
>
> I ordered boat officer to keep clear of landing, so that his boat
> could not be rushed, and I forbade him entering the town, the plan
> being that the boat was to lie well clear of the dock, and the
> officers therein to confer with party on shore. By my orders arms
> were carried concealed in the boat, and boat officer had positive
> orders to keep them hidden, and not use them unless fired upon,
> in which case he was to return the fire. The boat was a motor
> sailing launch, with a crew of three men.
>
> Coxswain of the boat reports that after brief parley, Mowat,
> interpreter, informed Kessing that the Mexican said it would be
> all right for them to land. They did so, and were immediately
> seized. Kessing ordered boat to return to ship and report what
> had happened. When Mexicans saw boat start off they motioned
> it to return. Coxswain told them to wait a minute and kept head-
> ing for ship.
>
> When the boat was about 100 feet clear from the dock, Mexican
> custom official, in uniform, fired his revolver at the boat, bullet
> striking near it. Five or six shots were immediately fired at the
> boat by Mexican soldiers.

Needless to say, Carranza was not required to salute the flag. So
far as we know he was not required to make any apology or explanation of any kind.

The New York Herald bureau in Washington had the following
to say about this incident in the same number of the *New York
Herald:*

> That the recent international incident at Mazatlan in which two
> United States naval officers were arrested and an American seaman
> was gravely wounded was almost a duplicate of the incident at
> Tampico which led to the celebrated demand for a salute from
> Huerta was shown in a report received at the Navy Department
> today from Commander A. G. Kavanaugh, commanding the gun-
> boat *Annapolis*. Mr. Daniels, Secretary of the Navy, was ques-

tioned today as to whether a salute from Carranza would be demanded in this case. Mr. Daniels replied with the statement that the situation was so delicate a one that speculation as to action to be taken should be avoided by good Americans. He said, however, that Admiral Cameron McR. Winslow, commander in chief of the Pacific Fleet, had no authority to demand a salute in this case, and also that Rear Admiral Henry T. Mayo had no authority to demand it at Tampico, though President Wilson supported that demand with battleships. Mr. Daniels added that *the Tampico incident was different in that then the purpose was to force Huerta out of Mexico and that was accomplished.*

As a reprisal for the alleged insult to the American flag by the Huerta authorities in Tampico, the American marines were landed in Vera Cruz. It is interesting in this connection to note that, instead of taking the entire city of Vera Cruz, the capture of which could easily have been effected, the American forces took the customhouse and the post office and there waited for several hours while the Huerta garrison in Vera Cruz and the population of Vera Cruz were given an opportunity to arm themselves and attack the Americans. The reason for this was as follows: Lind had reported to the American Government that the people of Vera Cruz would welcome the landing of marines as an act of friendship, since their purpose would be to eliminate Huerta; that it would be merely necessary to capture the customhouse and the post office. Admiral Fletcher, in command of the American battle fleet in Vera Cruz, realized how ridiculous were the representations of Lind, as did also the capable American consul in Vera Cruz, Mr. William A. Canada, and worked out a plan for the occupation of the entire city, which he submitted to the American Government, and which Admiral Fletcher believed could have been effected without the loss of a man. The American Government paid no attention to Admiral Fletcher, but followed Lind's advice and ordered the capture of the customhouse and the post office on the theory that this would meet with the approval of the people of Vera Cruz and it would not be necessary to take the city. The result of this bungling was that over 20 American bluejackets and marines were killed. Mr. Lind, I understand, is still proud of his participation in this affair.

I do not imagine that the families of the boys that were killed in this affair felt compensated for this piece of gross negligence and criminal ignorance by the graciousness of the President in coming to New York and delivering an oration over the biers of the men who were killed, where he took advantage of the occasion to deliver a eulogy on himself. The President stated in part:

> War, gentlemen, is only a sort of dramatic representation, a sort of dramatic symbol of a thousand forms of duty. I never went into battle, I never was under fire, but I fancy that there are some things just as hard to do as to go under fire. I fancy that it is just as hard to do your duty when men are sneering at you as when they are shooting at you. When they shoot at you they can only take your natural life; when they sneer at you they can wound your heart, and men who are brave enough, steadfast enough, steady in their principles enough, to go about their duty with regard to their fellowmen, no matter whether there are hisses or cheers, men who can do what Rudyard Kipling in one of his poems wrote: "Meet with triumph and disaster and treat those two imposters just the same," are men for a nation to be proud of. Morally speaking, disaster and triumph are imposters. The cheers of the moment are not what a man ought to think about, but the verdict of his conscience and the conscience of mankind.

Mr. Wilson was very evidently referring to himself.

Several versions have been given of just why Vera Cruz was taken. In the address just referred to Mr. Wilson stated:

> We have gone down to Mexico to serve mankind if we can find out the way. We do not want to fight the Mexicans. We want to serve the Mexicans if we can because we know how we would like to be free and how we would like to be served if there were friends by ready to serve us.

In his message to Congress, delivered on April 20, 1914, the day before Vera Cruz was taken, Mr. Wilson stated:

> I therefore come to ask your approval that I should use the armed forces of the United States in such ways, and to such an extent, as may be necessary to obtain from Gen. Huerta and his adherents the fullest recognition of the rights and dignity of the United States.

In the resolution that Congress passed on April 22, the day after Vera Cruz was taken, it is stated that:

> The President is justified in the employment of the armed forces

of the United States to enforce his demand for unequivocal amends for certain affronts and indignities committed against the United States.

From this message and the resolution it would appear that Vera Cruz was captured to seek amends for an insult to our flag.

Admiral Badger stated in his message, dated April 21, 1914, to the Mexican commander at Vera Cruz, Gen. Maas:

> The United States naval force seized the customhouse this morning for the purpose of preventing certain munitions of war from being landed in Vera Cruz. The object of this act has been accomplished and the steamer *Ypiranga* is now anchored in the harbor over which the Admiral has control, and the munitions are in his hands.

Here it appears that Vera Cruz was taken for the purpose of depriving Huerta of arms and ammunition.

In Secretary Franklin K. Lane's statement that appeared in the press during the last Presidential campaign he told the truth. The Secretary said that Vera Cruz had been taken to show Huerta that when the American Government told him he had to get out, it meant business. The truth was out at last.

Parenthetically it is very interesting to recall that if the taking of Vera Cruz was to prevent arms and ammunition from reaching Huerta, and in which purpose 20 American lives were sacrified, that the *Ypiranga*, a few days later, went down to the harbor of Coatzacoalcos, a short distance south of Vera Cruz, and there, with 50 or 60 American battleships, gunboats, cruisers, and torpedo boats, in charge of several admirals, patrolling the surrounding waters, landed its arms and ammunition, which a few days later reached Huerta's hands. Carl Heynen, the representative in Mexico of the Hamburg-American Steamship Line which owned the *Ypiranga*, called on the chief of port at Vera Cruz, Capt. Stickney, an unusually obtuse naval officer, and tried to get him to order him, Heynen, or even ask him, not to permit his boat to land the arms and ammunition in question, as Heynen was anxious for an excuse not to obey Huerta's orders, but this brilliant commander practically ordered Heynen out of his office.

MR. KEARFUL. What opportunities have you had to secure personal information with reference to what occurred at the Niagara conference, which was a conference between representatives of the American Government and of Huerta?

MR. BUCKLEY. I was in Vera Cruz in May, 1914, when the three delegates of the Huerta government to the Niagara conference, Lic. Emilio Rabasa, Lic. Luis Elguero, and Lic. Agustin Rodriguez, passed through Vera Cruz on their way to Niagara Falls to attend this conference. These gentlemen asked me to accompany them as counsel, which I did, and we went from Vera Cruz to Habana by steamer, from there to Key West by steamer, and from there to Washington by train. During this time I had the opportunity of ascertaining the ideas and the purpose of the delegates in question. From Washington the Mexican delegation went to New York and a day or so later proceeded to Niagara Falls.

MR. KEARFUL. Were you in close touch with the members of the Mexican delegation from the time of your first connection to the close of the conference?

MR. BUCKLEY. Yes.

MR. KEARFUL. Did you have occasion to confer with American officials on the part of the Mexican delegates at this time?

MR. BUCKLEY. I remained in Washington throughout the conference, except for the last week, and was constantly in touch with the officials of the American Government, principally Mr. William Jennings Bryan, Secretary of State, during this entire time as representative of the Mexican delegation.

MR. KEARFUL. The committee would like to have from you a complete statement in your own way, of the purposes, proceedings, and result of the Niagara conference.

MR. BUCKLEY. A few days after the taking of Vera Cruz the Huerta government received an invitation from Argentina, Brazil, and Chile to participate in a conference with the representatives of the American Government under the auspices of those countries for the purpose of solving the questions that had arisen between the United States and Mexico. A member of Huerta's cabinet, without the knowledge of Huerta, called in secret meeting a group of Mexican statesmen who had taken no part in the Huerta government and informed them that the time had come when they must take an active part in the affairs of their country, regardless of their own preferences, if they would save Mexico from conquest by American troops. It can readily be seen that Mexicans who had not been connected with the Huerta government did not at that time care to become involved with a government that, since the occupation of Vera Cruz by American troops and the backing of the Carranza revolution by the United States, was doomed to last but a few weeks longer. These men foresaw what the consequences of such association might be. Nevertheless these gentlemen agreed with Huerta's minister, and upon the statement by this minister that if they would select a delegation to the conference he would insist that Huerta appoint it, they at once selected probably the three ablest Mexicans in Mexico, Lic. Emilio Rabasa, Lic. Luis Elguero, and Lic. Agustin Rodriguez, all lawyers of note, two of whom, I understand, had never held public office. Huerta appointed these gentlemen.

When the Mexican people saw these three patriotic men leave the country for the purpose of conferring with the American Government, they breathed a sigh of relief, for they felt sure that no mean spirit of partisan advantage would be permitted to stand in the way of an honorable settlement of the difficulties between the United States and Mexico. These delegates represented what was best in Mexico, and the United States could not then or now produce abler men than those comprising the Mexican delegation. No government could have had a better opportunity to learn something about another country than the American Government had in its association with these three gentlemen, and the opportunity of the American Government to reach an understanding with what was best in Mexico was one that few governments would have overlooked.

It was natural to assume, since the object of the taking of Vera Cruz, as set out in the President's message to Congress and in the resolution passed by this body, was for the purpose of compelling Huerta to make amends for his alleged insults to the American flag, that negotiations would be limited to a discussion of this matter. The Mexican delegation came fully prepared to make such amends as the strong American Government might demand, provided they were consistent with the independence of Mexico. They soon suspected that instead the internal affairs of Mexico would be taken up at this conference, and in their impotence to resist this encroachment on the sovereignty of Mexico they reconciled themselves to discuss these matters.

Before arriving in the United States the Mexican delegation learned that the ministers of Argentina, Brazil, and Chile had invited Carranza to send representatives to the conference that was to adjust differences between Mexico and the United States, and had advised Carranza that since his representatives and Huerta's representatives must appear in the same conference, it was only reasonable and just that hostilities should be suspended pending the termination of the same. To this invitation Carranza replied that he would send delegates to treat of the differences between the United States and Mexico—that is, the differences between the United States and Huerta—but that he would not agree to suspend hostilities, and that he would not deal with Huerta. Under the circumstances there was, of course, no object in his sending representatives, and the mediators immediately advised him that since he refused to suspend hostilities they felt compelled to withdraw their invitation to him to participate in the conference.

This invitation to Carranza was in itself sufficient indication that the internal affairs of Mexico were to be discussed and that negotiations were not to be limited to the flag incident, and this impression was confirmed upon the arrival of the Mexican delegates in Washington. The mediators, in a conference they had with the Mexican delegates on the afternoon the latter arrived in Washington, advised these gentlemen that the American Government would insist upon taking up the internal affairs of Mexico and would insist that Huerta be eliminated; that if the Mexican delegation would only agree to this, they would have no trouble with the American Government, everything would be satisfactorily arranged, and the American Government would agree that a government be established in Mexico satisfactory to all parties.

If you will recall the situation in May, 1914, just after Vera Cruz was taken by the American troops, you will remember that the general impression prevailed in the United States that a conflict had arisen between the American Government and Huerta, and there was general insistence that the prestige and pride of the American Government required that Huerta be eliminated from power, even though it be necessary to occupy Mexico for that purpose, and that the press was demanding that Funston's troops be sent on up from Vera Cruz to Mexico City. The predicament of the American Government was most embarrassing, since it had decided to take Vera Cruz on the theory that it would thereby gain the gratitude of the Mexican people, who would immediately overthrow Huerta, but found instead that as a result of criminal ignorance over 20 Americans and hundreds of Mexicans had been killed, and that the Mexican people had rallied around Huerta. The American Government had misjudged the situation; it did not want to go through with its undertaking to eliminate Huerta, since this involved the military occupation of a large part of Mexico; and it did not want to recede in the face of American public opinion, which opinion was not interested in the motives that impelled the American Government to make the decision that Huerta should be eliminated, but whose pride and vanity were aroused when this decision was made, and who insisted that the American Government go through with its project. The American Government eagerly seized at the opportunity for a conference in order to gain time. When the Mexican delegation arrived in the United States the entire press was speculating as to whether Huerta would consent to resign, the general impression being that he would stay in Mexico and die at his post.

This will impress upon you the importance at this time of Huerta's resignation, the intense anxiety that the American Government felt, and its extreme desire to secure this resignation and thus relieve itself of embarrassment. Foreseeing that Huerta's resignation would be required, and that there would be an impasse unless this were forthcoming, the Mexican delegates insisted, as a prerequisite to their acceptance of the mission that Huerta agree to resign, and the latter did so before the delegation left Mexico City. The Mexican delegation realized the importance of coming to an agreement with the United States as soon as possible, but at the same time understood the importance of coming to a definite understanding as to what was to follow this resignation.

The Mexican delegation, at their first informal conference in Washington with the mediators, did not commit themselves to Huerta's elimination, although they heard with satisfaction that if this were accomplished a neutral government satisfactory to all factions would be established in Mexico.

The next day the Mexican delegation went to New York, and spent a day or so there before leaving for Niagara Falls. A prominent Democratic Senator called on one of these gentlemen—they were under the impression that he had come from Washington to see them—and told them that if they would only induce Huerta to resign their troubles would be at an end, and that the American Government would see to it that a neutral government satisfactory to all factions would be established in Mexico.

Although the Mexican delegation had no doubt that what the mediators said was authoritative, as also what the United States Senator said, nevertheless they asked me to remain in Washington and to see the President, either directly or indirectly, the day after they left Washington and inform him officially that Huerta would resign, and that in submitting this offer it was the understanding of the Mexican delegation that a neutral government should be established in Mexico. I called on Dr. D. F. Houston, Secretary of Agriculture, whom I had known for some years, and explained the situation to him and stated the attitude of the Huerta delegation, and informed him of the assurance of the ABC mediators given to the Huerta delegation. Dr. Houston was very much pleased, and stated that, even without the voluntary resignation of Huerta, Mr. Wilson would insist that neither Carranza nor Villa nor any of their active adherents be President of Mexico, under the theory that he had expounded as the basis of his Latin-American policy that he would recognize no man who had risen to office through force, which would eliminate the leaders of the revolution; that, as a matter of fact, these leaders were not seeking power and were unselfish in their efforts to relieve Mexico of a tyrant. This was on Sunday, and Dr. Houston promised to call on the President the next day and advise him of this message from the Mexican delegation. I heard nothing further from Dr. Houston, and advised the Huerta delegation that they could proceed with all confidence.

The Mexican delegation, in order to be sure of their ground, consulted Huerta by telegraph asking him to confirm his offer to resign and advising him that a neutral government would be established. Huerta immediately replied, confirming his authorization to them. The Mexican delegation, in all good faith, officially advised the American delegation and the mediators, at the first full session of the conference, that they were authorized to state that Gen. Huerta had agreed to resign and eliminate himself from the situation.

You can readily see that after Huerta's promise to resign had been published he lost his hold on the Mexican people, as they considered that he had surrendered in his fight with the President of the United States. After this news was published, what prestige Huerta had in Mexico was gone, and there was no way for him to recover it. Thereafter the Mexican delegation was at the mercy of the American Government.

It was natural that since the American Government insisted that the internal affairs of Mexico be settled at this conference, it should also insist, in fact compel, Carranza to participate in the conference. It was expected that the American Government, because of its sponsoring of the revolution, could induce these men through moral pressure, to send a delegation, and all knew that it could compel them to participate by exercising the material pressure at its command. The Mexican delegation, after perfunctorily offering to make amends to the United States in return for the immediate evacuation of Vera Cruz, a request which was refused, asked that an armistice be arranged between the contending parties in Mexico, involving a suspension of hostilities, and that Carranza be asked to send delegates to the conference. The American Government offered to exert its influence to the end that the Carranza revolutionary junta in Washington agree to both of these propositions, and I have no doubt that the Government did use its best offices to accomplish these purposes; but the Carrancistas refused to suspend hostilities.

The Mexican delegation then asked that inasmuch as the Carrancistas would not appear in the conference, they be eliminated from consideration; the American delegation refused to accede to this, and proceeded in the discussions that followed themselves to represent the claims of the Carranza faction. The Mexican delegation then asked that since the American delegation was representing the cause of the Carranza faction, and the latter would receive the benefit of any advantageous arrangements, it agree that the Carranza faction would abide by the results of the conference; this reasonable request was also refused by the American delegation.

Early in the conference the American delegates agreed to waive an indemnity and to waive an apology as a result of the alleged insult to the American flag, which eliminated the international aspect of the conference, and proceedings from then on dealt exclusively with the establishment of a provisional government in Mexico, which was to call elections in order that the Mexican people might be given the opportunity to designate their permanent government. It was agreed that a commission composed of a president, who should be neutral, two Huerta adherents, and two Carranza adherents, should continue the provisional government.

The Mexican delegates to the conference and the mediators were anxious to come to an agreement as soon as possible and conclude their labors. The American delegates delayed matters from one day to another without satisfactory explanation. This was undoubtedly due to the fact that the American delegates soon learned that they had absolutely no authority and were compelled to consult the American Government on each matter as it came up, and to the fact that the American Government could not agree to anything until it had consulted the Carranza revolutionary junta.

It must be remembered that the embargo on the shipment of arms and ammunition to Mexico had been raised some time before, with the result that Carranza and Villa were getting all the arms they needed, but that Huerta was getting none. As a result of the possession of these means of warfare, and as a result of the loss of prestige that came to Huerta after he agreed to resign, the revolution was making great progress. The Mexican delegation had insisted from the very beginning that if the American Government could not induce Carranza to suspend hostilities, it certainly could, to show its good faith, place an embargo on arms and ammunition, pending the conclusion of the conference between the Huerta delegates and Carranza revolutionary junta, represented by the American Government. The American Government, finally, about the 1st of June, agreed to place an embargo on arms and ammunition.

Three or four days after this new embargo was declared, the Ward Line steamer *Antilla* sailed from New York for Tampico with a large supply of arms and ammunition for the Carranza forces. The Mexican delegates immediately wired me, and within a few hours after the boat sailed I called on Mr. Bryan, feeling confident that there had been some mistake.

I reminded Mr. Bryan of the embargo which had been declared

a few days before and asked him how it was that the boat had been permitted to leave the United States, to which Mr. Bryan replied that he understood that the order had not reached New York until an hour or so after the boat left. My recollection now is that the order was issued on Thursday and the boat left on Tuesday. I asked Mr. Bryan how he accounted for this delay, to which Mr. Bryan replied that he really could not account for it. He said that he of course could call in the chief of the proper section of the State Department and ask him, but that this would look as if he were criticizing this chief, and of course he could not do that; or that he might call in the "press boys" and ask them how this had happened, but that it would not look exactly right for him to go outside of his department for information, and that he didn't care to do this. Mr. Bryan, however, seemed to be entirely satisfied to remain in ignorance as to why this order had been delayed four days or so in arriving at New York; the matter did not seem to bother him at all, and it did not seem to occur to him that he of all men ought to know just what had happened.

I then asked Mr. Bryan to have the boat recalled, as it was only a few hours out from New York; Mr. Bryan declined to do this. I asked him then to order the boat to unload the arms and ammunition in Habana, where it touched before reaching Vera Cruz; Mr. Bryan declined to do this. I then asked him to order the captain of the boat not to unload the arms and ammunition in Tampico, but Mr. Bryan declined to do this. In other words, he insisted on breaking faith with the Mexican delegation.

Huerta immediately issued orders to his gunboats not to permit the *Antilla* to enter the port of Tampico, whereupon the American Government announced that the American squadron at Tampico would prevent the Mexican gunboats from interfering with the *Antilla*. The right of the American Government under international law to prevent Huerta from stopping a boat carrying arms and ammunition to the revolutionary faction is, of course, conceded by no one. This determination of the American Government also, of course, constituted another act of intervention in the internal affairs of Mexico. In addition, it is a strain on the honor of the United States.

In connection with the embargo on arms and ammunition, and the promise of the American Government to the Mexican delegation and to the mediators not to permit American arms and ammunition to reach Carranza, I will state that Mr. Lind, personal representative of the President and active Carranza revolutionary agent, was then in Washington, extremely busy as a messenger between the Carranza revolutionary junta and the State Department; he was carrying orders from the revolutionary junta to the department. Mr. Lind stated generally that while no more *Antilla* incidents would occur, the revolutionaries had arranged to get all the arms and ammunition they wanted; that this would be accomplished by having ships take out their papers to Habana and then go to Tampico; and that the American Government had consented to the evasion. I immediately called on Mr. Bryan and asked him if this were true, and he stated that it was. Mr. Bryan stated that these ships would take out papers to Habana, and that the American Government would have no official knowledge that they were going to Tampico; that if, after they got out in the Gulf, they diverted their course the American Government would have nothing to do with it, or as Mr. Bryan insisted, the American Government would have no "official knowledge." Mr. Bryan seemed to draw a very marked distinction between himself as Mr. Bryan and himself as Secretary of State. No further confirmation of the bad faith of the American Government was needed.

Mr. Lind's and Mr. Bryan's words were made good. On June 6 a million cartridges were shipped on the steamship *Sunshine* from Galveston to Tampico. Thereafter the schooners *Sunshine, Grampus*, and *Susan* made six trips from Galveston to Tampico, each time carrying shipments of war materials to the Carranza revolutionaries; all these boats, according to the speech of Representative Rogers, previously referred to, were consigned to Habana, but "by stress of weather they were blown to Tampico."

An incident that occurred in the above conference with Mr. Bryan will indicate the type of mind that the Mexican delegation and the mediators had to deal with. Mr. Bryan stated, leaving aside for a moment the engagement of the American Government, that there was no reason why Carranza should not receive arms and ammunition since Huerta had received them through the *Ypiranga*, the boat which, you will remember, was the occasion of the landing at Vera Cruz according to Admiral Badger, and which unloaded its arms and ammuntion a few days later at Coatzacoalcos, a short distance south of Vera Cruz. I reminded Mr. Bryan that Huerta felt no gratitude to the American Government for getting these munitions, as it was a case of bad management by the American Government. Mr. Bryan then stated that when Admiral Fletcher reported to the Government that these arms were being unloaded at Coatzacoalcos the American Government thought there was a mistake and consequently did nothing until it was too late, as he had received assurance from the German ambassador to the effect that the Hamburg American Line would not deliver this cargo to Huerta; Mr. Bryan then thought a minute, and said that "No; he would not be positive that the German ambassador had given this assurance." He then thought another minute and said that he was quite sure now-that the German ambassador had not given such assurance.

After the American and Mexican delegations had agreed that there would be a neutral government as outlined above, it was arranged with the Mexican delegation that they should name several neutrals who would be considered by the American Government in the selection of one to be President of the new commission. The Mexican delegation and the American delegation discussed this matter for several days, and I discussed it several times with Mr. Bryan. The American Government did not seem to be able to make a choice, and something seemed to be the matter. Finally I had a conference with Mr. Bryan on June 6, in which the situation was defined. I quote from the translation of a letter I wrote to one of the Mexican delegates on June 7:

> I passed the entire day yesterday in conference with Mr. Garrison [Secretary of War] and Mr. Long, Chief of the Department of Latin-American Affairs in the State Department; in the afternoon I saw Mr. Bryan for a moment, and last night I was with this gentleman from 9 until after 11.
>
> The officials of the State Department, including Mr. Bryan, seemed to be very much preoccupied yesterday, but last night Mr. Bryan was again his normal self, due no doubt to his conference with the President.
>
> Mr Bryan, with admirable frankness, advised me of the attitude of the administration, in view of which you may deduce the result of the conference.
>
> The Government [American Government] considers that Huerta cannot remain in power many days longer [Mr. Bryan states]; that everybody knew this when the conferences were initiated, and that since the authority of Huerta was doomed to

disappear, and since Carranza was to enter into authority, the principal object of the conferences was and is now to carry out the inevitable without the shedding of blood and to transfer the Government of Mexico from the hands of Huerta to those of Carranza by peaceful means. That if Carranza were placed under the necessity of conquering the capital he might not be able to contain his people in their desire to commit revenge; that a durable peace could not come as a result of compromise; that he thought the attitude of the Mexican delegation was arbitrary in insisting that Carranza should consent to an armistice, although he personally had tried to persuade him to accept this condition; that the influence of Washington with the rebels was exaggerated, but that even if it did have sufficient influence the government would not exercise it for the reason that what the Mexican delegation asks is that the American Government aid in perpetuating in Mexico, not Huerta but Huerta's regime; that no effort of the Mexican delegation can induce the American Government to break with the Carrancista regime, which this Government considers has the support of the Mexican people and which will form the government which is destined to pacify the country, and with which the American Government must treat; that the government of Huerta had taken every pretext to insult the Government of the United States, and that when the proposition was made to Huerta through Lind that he consent to an armistice he had replied with insults, and that in view of his attitude he could not expect from Washington an attitude hostile to the rebels.

I reminded Mr. Bryan that we had been dealing now for some time on the selection of a neutral for provisional President and that his attitude constituted a decided change, to which he agreed. I then reminded him that the Mexican delegation had participated in the conference and had induced Huerta to agree to resign on the representation and promise of the American Government that it would agree to a neutral as provisional President; at this Mr. Bryan became very much annoyed and stated:

> When you can't keep a promise you can't keep it, and that is all there is to it. I don't want to hear any more about it.

I then asked Mr. Bryan if the American Government would consent to the appointment as provisional President of a constitutionalist who had not taken up arms—that is, a civilian constitutionalist—that if he would consent to this it would help to save the pride of the Mexican delegation and would also show that the American Government was consistent in the doctrine it had laid down that it would not recognize in Latin America any man who arose to power through force. Mr. Bryan thought over this for a long time, and then finally told me frankly that the American Government would agree on nobody for provisional President but Carranza. I finally asked him, then, if the American Government would be consistent in the policy it had announced with regard to Huetra and would agree that since Carranza was to be provisional President he must not be a candidate for permanent President, and that the American Government would not recognize him as such. Mr. Bryan said: "No; Carranza must be provisional President and permanent President." This ended the conference.

Since the American delegation to the Niagara conference had agreed that of the commission of five the President would be a neutral, their position was most embarrassing. A few days after I saw Mr. Bryan and reported the result of the conference to the Mexican delegation, the American delegation weakly proposed that this neutral Provisional President be Gen. Angeles or Gen. Natera, two revolutionary generals. This was so absurd that the Mexican delegates advised the mediators that they would not continue this cynical discussion.

At about that time Villa decided to revolt against Carranza, and Carranza, fearing that he would lose out all around, sent word to the mediators that he would participate in the conference but that he would first have to consult his subordinates, with which maneuver he gained a little time. The mediators, anxious to end this humiliating conference, announced that since all international difficulties had been satisfactorily adjusted, it would be best to adjourn the conference and have the Huerta delegates and the Carranza delegates agree on a neutral government, independent of outside dictation. A few days later, when Carranza had adjusted his difficulties with Villa, he refused to participate in the conference.

In this whole connection it is interesting to speculate on American prestige in Latin America.

MR. KEARFUL. The committee is interested in having a true picture of the Carranza revolution from its inception to the time of his entry into Mexico City. Are you able to draw such a picture?

MR. BUCKLEY. The Carranza revolution, in spite of the encouragement it had received from the American Government, includ-

ing the permission to introduce arms and munitions, had not
progressed as rapidly as its friends had expected. The Mexican
people soon perceived the purposes of the revolution and did not
sympathize with it. At an early stage of the revolution, when
Carranza was in Hermosillo, Sonora, controlling a small portion of
territory, he gave an interview to Mr. Hamilton Fyfe, a correspondent representing a large English newspaper, which shocked
everybody who read it, and which confirmed abroad the impression that the Mexican people had already gained of the purpose
and nature of this new revolution for the redemption of Mexico.
This interview is as follows:

> "Have you any definite plans for land reform and other re-
> forms?" I inquired.
> He thought a moment. Then he replied. "The first necessity is
> the fair and free election of a President. The election which is
> proposed now will be a farce. In the disturbed state of our country
> it is impossible to hold a proper election. Large numbers of voters
> will not know anything about it. We Constitutionalists refuse to
> recognize any President who may be returned at the fraudulent
> election. We shall execute anybody who does recognize him."
> "I beg your pardon," I said. "Would you kindly repeat your
> last statement?"
> I thought I must have misunderstood it.
> "We shall," the general said calmly and as if he were making
> a perfectly natural remark, "execute anyone who recognizes a
> President unconstitutionally elected and directly or indirectly
> guilty of participation in the murder of Madero."

Carranza's revolution never at any time had popular support.
Carranza propagandists in the United States ask, if this is true, why
the Carranza revolution prospered and why Carranza has not been
overthrown. If a government depends for its existence in Mexico
on popular support, these propagandists might answer why it was
Diaz remained in office for 35 years. The truth is that it does not
matter what a great majority of the Mexican people think; the
mass of the people have not the ability to think clearly; and have
not the knowledge on which to base convictions, or the public
spirit to act on them. As a matter of fact, the Carranza revolution
succeeded and the Carranza Government has remained in power,
in the first place, because it has been backed by the American
Government and, in the second place, because it has utilized the

bandits of the country, who had the virility to make subject the entire Mexican population of 15,000,000, with the very valuable support, we must not forget, of the American Government.

The irresponsibility of the mass of the people in Mexico is incomprehensible to the average American. Where a city like Mexico City, with a population comprising 100,000 men, all Catholics, will permit a man like Obregon, and the 3,000 ruffians who comprised his army of occupation, to starve the city and take over 150 priests, march them through the streets of the city to jail, and then load them in box cars and cattle cars and ship them out of the city, without making any resistance outside of a feeble manifestation, such a people have not the public spirit to establish a government based on their own will.

I will not go into details of the Carranza revolution, and shall refer only to certain instances that will explain its nature. Even the peon schoolboy in Mexico knew that Carranza's revolution was a revolution sponsored by the United States and that the American Government had placed Carranza in power. Both because Carranza and his followers are the type of Mexican that make the hatred of the American a religion, and also undoubtedly because of their sensitiveness to the reproach of their own people that they were the puppets of the American Government, the Carrancistas devote a great part of their energy to mistreating the Americans and robbing them of their property.

It had been thought up to the time of the Niagara conference that the American Government was more or less directing the policy and guiding the steps of the revolution. As a matter of fact, a fact easily ascertainable by those who are interested, the Mexican revolutionary junta in Washington was directing the Mexican policy of the American Government. During the course of the Niagara conference Mr. Bryan repeatedly gave me phonographic repetitions of statements that Mr. Cabrera and Mr. Vasconcelos [agents of Carranza] had made to me earlier in the day. Mr. Bryan delayed many of his decisions during the course of the conference so as to ascertain what the revolutionary junta would advise or, rather, direct.

I had a conversation in 1914 with Luis Cabrera, in which Mr. Cabrera very frankly told me that the menace of the American in Mexico must be removed and that the only way to do this was to drive him out of the country and take his property. At a banquet given in Vera Cruz in the latter part of 1915 to Gen. Carranza, which was attended by the consuls of foreign countries, Cabrera dilated on the aims of the revolution and stated that the constitutionalists were going to confiscate American property and take over the American oil wells; and, turning pointedly to Mr. Canada, the American consul, he told him to report this to his President. Cabrera's tone was so offensive that the Cuban consul started to leave the meeting, but was restrained by Mr. Canada, who, being the American consul, had become accustomed to insults from the Carranza authorities.

During the conversation above referred to as having taken place in Washington I told Mr. Cabrera that the American Government would not permit the Carranza government to drive the Americans out of Mexico and confiscate their property, as Mr. Cabrera stated the Mexican Government was going to do, whereupon Mr. Cabrera smiled and told me that he was surprised at the ignorance of the average American on public matters. He explained to me that Mr. Wilson was what he was pleased to term an advanced liberal, a great Democrat, whose concern was for the welfare of the people of the world and was not limited to the narrow bounds of the United States. Mr. Cabrera considered Mr. Wilson to be the same kind of a Democrat as he, Mr. Cabrera, was. He said that Mr. Wilson was opposed to capital in Mexico and everywhere else in the world, no matter to whom the capital belonged, and that in expelling the American from Mexico the Constitutionalists would receive the sympathy of the American Government. The Carranza authorities have proceeded confidently on this theory and have never had the least fear of compulsion from the American Government and have regarded all protests from the American Government as being insincere and merely perfunctory.

It would be tedious to refer to the conduct or words of the officials of the American Government to confirm this opinion of the Constitutionalists, and I will merely refer to an incident that occurred in Tampico in 1916. The Mexican employees of the refinery of the Pierce Oil Corporation had engaged in a strike, promoted by the Carranza authorities, and proceeded to take possession of the refinery. When the American superintendent, Mr. Warren, demanded that the authorities give him possession of his company's property, they paid no attention to him, and when the American Consul made similar demands the authorities did not even reply to his notes. The superintendent of the refinery went to the American consulate, and on finding there the commander of the American gunboats in the harbor, demanded of him that he and the property of his company be given protection, and stated that he was entitled to protection under the rules of international law. The commander in question is a red-blooded American, who undoubtedly did not sympathize with the policy of his Government but who possessed sufficient discernment to understand this policy perfectly. The naval commander informed Mr. Warren that, of course, he was entitled to protection under the rules of international law, but that he, the Captain, represented a government which had repudiated international law; that the American squadron was there not to enforce international law, but to carry out the policy of the American Government, and that under this policy Americans abroad were not entitled to any protection whatever; and regardless of his own opinions in the matter, he had no discretion, since his responsibility was to his Government, and he must, therefore, decline to give Mr. Warren or his property or any other American protection of any kind.

Mr. KEARFUL. From what source do you get the information as to the conversation you have just related?

Mr. BUCKLEY. I was standing in the Consulate when it happened, and I heard part of it and the Captain of the gunboat recounted this conversation to me just after it occurred.

(Whereupon at 12:30 o'clock p.m. a recess was taken until 1:30 o'clock p.m.)

AFTER RECESS

Mr. KEARFUL. You have mentioned Mr. John Lind, a personal representative of President Wilson who was sent to Mexico to eliminate President Huerta. In December, 1914, Mr. Lind published a booklet on page 22 of which he refers to the improved prospects of Mexico under Carranza and says: "The indications are promising. The discipline and restraint shown by the victorious Constitutional armies and their chiefs were most creditable and encouraging." When was it that the victorious Constitutional armies under Mr. Carranza entered Mexico City?

Mr. Buckley. In August, 1914.

Mr. Kearful. I was present in Mexico City in August, 1914, and I know you were. Will you give a description of what occurred there upon the entry into Mexico City of the victorious Constitutional armies of Carranza, with special reference to whether they displayed discipline and restraint, and as to whether what they did was creditable and encouraging.

Mr. Buckley. The Carranza army, upon its entry into Mexico City, did not show the restraint that Mr. Lind speaks about in the booklet you have just quoted. The armies committed all manner of excesses and the officers distributed among themselves the finest dwellings in Mexico City, where they held orgies for several months and which they eventually looted. They sold furniture to pawnshops and libraries to book dealers and wine to the different restaurants in the city. It is notorious that what Mr. Lind states is not true, and his statement is merely the statement of a Carranza propagandist.

Mr. Kearful. Who was in command of the advance forces that entered Mexico City at that time?

Mr. Buckley. Gen. Alvaro Obregon.

Mr. Kearful. What class of people were his forces composed of?

Mr. Buckley. Almost entirely of Yaqui Indians.

Notwithstanding the assurances of Mr. Bryan and Mr. Lind that Villa was absolutely loyal to Carranza, the former did what nearly every revolutionary chief in the history of Mexico has done; he revolted against his civilian superior Carranza. Through the intervention of the American Government, which in its dealings with Mexico has persisted in ignoring the lessons of Mexican history, a convention was arranged between the Villa party and the Carranza party at Aguascalientes. Since this city was then in the territory of Villa, he did just what Carranza would have done if it had been in his territory—surrounded the convention hall with troops and compelled the convention to name as President his own appointee Eulalio Gutierrez, whereupon Carranza repudiated the action of the convention. Of course, the convention was opened, as all Mexican conventions are, with great ceremony, and in this particular case a Mexican flag was desecrated by being kissed by each of the delegates as a pledge to abide by the decision of the convention. Later the flag was stolen by one of the delegates.

The entire Republic of Mexico was then given over to a state of anarchy; Mexico City was taken and retaken time and again within a year by Villistas, Zapatistas, and Carrancistas. Homes in Mexico City were looted and occupied by the different generals, the Carrancistas distinguishing themselves in their barbarous conduct; churches were robbed, prominent Mexicans and foreigners were kidnapped, horses belonging to the diplomatic corps were stolen, several diplomats were driven out of the country, and a general reign of terror continued. The American Government was all the time assuring the American people that conditions in Mexico were rapidly approaching one of peace, and was cooperating with the different revolutionary factions in keeping the truth from the American people. There was little train communication, and it took several weeks for a letter to reach the United States. Representatives of 17 nationalities in Mexico City organized a national committee which unofficially took charge of foreigners and their affairs in Mexico City. This committee made desperate efforts to convey the truth of the situation to the American people and to the outside world, but was unable to cope with the opposition of the American Government.

American newspapers will not print a record of what has happened two or three weeks previously, and it was impossible to keep them advised each day of happenings in Mexico. A rigid censorship was imposed in Mexico City, and any newspaper men who were discovered sending out news unfavorable to the faction in charge was immediately 33d; that is, expelled from the country.[1] Americans for a while sent mail through the American diplomatic pouch, but when the American Government discovered that news of conditions in Mexico was being sent to the American people in this way, it forbade the further use of this diplomatic conduct.

The international committee and the American subcommittee wired full reports of conditions to the American Government, and in vain begged this Government to publish their statements and appeals to the American people. The President replied that he must decline this for fear that the Carranza authorities might make

[1] Articulo 33 of the Mexican Constitution permits the President to expel from Mexico anyone "whose presence he may deem undesirable." W.F.B. was "33d" in 1921.

reprisals on the foreigners sending these reports—rather unusual solicitude for their safety.

Of all the leaders who had charge of Mexico City, Gen. Alvaro Obregon distinguished himself as the worst. It is not out of place to remind the committee that Gen. Obregon is now a candidate for President and is actually posing in the United States as being pro-American. Obregon is regarded as the most bitter anti-American chief in the revolution. During the war, when it seemed that Germany was going to be successful, Obregon wrote a book on his record as a military leader, which was designed to serve as a basis for his appeal for the Presidency, and it was taken from the mails by the American authorities on its way to an American city to be printed. Obregon in this book referred to the disdainful manner in which he had treated Paul Fuller and other representatives of the American Government. He stated that on occasions he refused to meet them, and always told them that Mexico was a free and independent country and would not tolerate any intervention on the part of the American Government; that he approved the attitude of his chief, Carranza, in his endeavors to form a union among Latin American countries to oppose the designs of the Colossus of the North, etc. When Germany was defeated, Obregon modified his book somewhat and eliminated most of the anti-American passages. Obregon is of the opinion, however, that there is no limit to the gullibility of the American people and expects the support of our Government in his aspiration for the Presidency. He and Pablo Gonzalez, the other prominent candidate for the Presidency, are endeavoring now to compel foreign firms in Mexico which have not yet been run out of the country, to contribute the greater part of the funds necessary for their campaign expenses. Of course, when such solicitations are made, funds must be advanced or reprisals will be visited.

Obregon took charge of Mexico City and committed every outrage that his ingenuity could suggest. There were at that time no trains to the north and only at rare intervals a train to Vera Cruz. The plight of 500,000 inhabitants can easily be imagined. Obregon decided to punish Mexico City for reasons that no civilized man could understand. He threw a cordon of troops around the city and would permit the introduction of only a limited amount of food; vegetables he allowed to enter only at certain hours of the day, he cut off train communications with Toluca, and at times with Puebla; his Yaqui Indians killed peaceful citizens in the suburbs of Mexico City, with the same motives that the Germans had in killing innocent people in Belgium—to terrorize the community; the electric lights were turned off after a certain hour each evening, and water was allowed to enter the city only at certain hours during the day; all the controllers were taken off the street cars and shipped to Vera Cruz with the result that the street car system of Mexico City was paralyzed and residents in suburbs had to walk from 3 to 10 miles. These controllers could not be used at Vera Cruz, and the only purpose in taking them was to punish the people of Mexico City.

Obregon had entered Mexico City flying the black flag of anarchy. He made a compact with the I. W. W. whereby the latter were to join in the fight against Villa and be rewarded by owning the Republic. Obregon made speeches and issued proclamations, all of which will be presented later to the committee, calling upon the rabble of Mexico City to loot the city and telling them that if they did he would do nothing to protect property. It was very difficult for him to get the rabble started, so he sent his troops to lead them in looting a prominent church in the very center of the city, the Church of Santa Brigida, and also the adjoining parochial school. After the soldiers had started the looting the rabble went in and took even the tapestry off the walls and also took out the flooring. Some Americans and Mexicans became so indignant at the sight that they seized clubs and dispersed the mob. When Obregon heard of this he dispatched troops to the church, not to punish the mob for looting but to protect it against those who had interfered with the looting. The soldiers pursued the small group of Americans and Mexicans to the American Club, where the latter barricaded the doors and protected themselves against Obregon's soldiers until the Brazilian Minister could arrive at the club and persuade the soldiers to desist. Obregon then delivered the church and parochial school to the I. W. W. to be used as their headquarters.

In casting about for a means of looting the city Obregon imposed a tax of 20,000,000 pesos on business men, for the purpose, so he humorously alleged, of alleviating the condition of the poor. When Mexican business men tried to question him about the distribution of this money and suggested that the same be made under the supervision of a committee appointed by themselves, he had over 100 of these men arrested and placed in the penitentiary. When the foreigners, under the leadership of the Americans, refused to pay this tax Obregon compelled them to close their houses of business, which were kept closed for several days, to the great suffering of the Mexican people.

Foreigners subscribed to a fund to be used by themselves in alleviating the condition of the poor, a condition induced by Obregon and his soldiers, and sent agents to Toluca and other places in the neighborhood of Mexico City to purchase large quantities of corn and wheat, which, however, they were not able to bring to Mexico City for the relief of the starving population in which Obregon had taken such an interest, because the revolutionary chiefs demanded the payment of graft before they would permit the use of trains for the transportation of foodstuffs. The international committee wired to Mr. Bryan, asking him to use his influence with his friends, the military chiefs, to permit the passage of foodstuffs, but to no avail.

MR. KEARFUL. I want to ask you about the international committee. Who composed it?

MR. BUCKLEY. It was composed of the representatives of 17 nationalities residing in Mexico City, most colonies sending one representative, and several colonies, such as the American, English, French, German, and Spanish, having two representatives on this committee.

MR. KEARFUL. The representatives being elected by the respective colonies?

MR. BUCKLEY. Yes.

MR. KEARFUL. I want to ask you further, were you present, and did you personally observe the occurrences that you have just been describing?

MR. BUCKLEY. Yes; I was also a member of the international committee, chosen by the American Colony.

MR. KEARFUL. Please proceed with your statement.

MR. BUCKLEY. As if Obregon was not satisfied to starve the population of Mexico City, he decided to outrage their religious sentiment, and arrested over 150 priests, marched them through Mexico City, and imprisoned them for a day or two. When the populace started to demonstrate against such outrageous treatment, he had his troops fire into them, killing several people and stopping the public manifestation. Obregon then took these unfortunate priests, put them in box cars and cattle cars and shipped them down to Vera Cruz.

While the Mexican people were starving the Carranza officials were looting the country and exporting hides, corn and beans, as well as furniture and everything else of value. That the American Government was cognizant of this, and of the bad impression that the attitude of the Carranza authorities would produce on the outside world, is shown by the note transmitted by the State Department to Mr. Silliman on June 18, 1915, from which I quote the following:

> In your conversation with Gen. Carranza mention that while the *Buford* was unloading 60,000 pounds of corn and beans consigned to the consulate for charitable distribution to relieve famine conditions, and while meat, corn, and other provisions were becoming scarce in Vera Cruz, the Ward Line Steamer *Mexico* loaded roughly 100,000 pounds of beans for export to New York. Such events, presumably with the sanction of the Carranza government, have had wide circulation in the United States as well as similar acts by Federal authorities in the north, and are producing an extremely bad impression as to the motives of leaders who allow such practices, when it is well known that the food supply of Mexico is at the famine point, and that the President of the United States has been in the necessity of appealing to the American people for assistance to satisfy the starving in Mexico.

MR. KEARFUL. Will you proceed now to relate the incidents leading up to the recognition of Carranza by this Government as head of the de facto government of Mexico, including the proceedings of what is known as the Pan-American Conference?

MR. BUCKLEY. Conditions in Mexico had become so intolerable that even the American Government had to take official notice of them. The patience of this Government seemed to be exhausted with the continuation of anarchy in Mexico and with the contemptuous treatment it had received from the revolutionary chiefs it had placed in power.

On the 2nd day of June, 1915, Mr. Wilson issued his famous appeal, in which he called upon the chiefs of the three factions to adjust their differences, with the threat of supporting those who agreed to compromise, or, possibly, of intervening.

Villa and Zapata immediately agreed to arbitrate their differences, but Carranza defied the American Government, whereupon the American Government recognized Carranza.

When Carranza refused to submit his differences to arbitration and insisted that Mexico was a free and sovereign Republic and that he would not permit foreign dictation, Mr. Wilson pursued his customary policy of appealing directly to Carranza's subordinates and sent messages to all of them. These subordinates referred him back to Carranza.

The American Government was apparently greatly incensed at the action of Carranza, and gave every indication that it had finished with him and would withdraw its support, for it ceased its policy of prohibiting the news with regard to Mexico from reaching the American newspapers, and for a period of several months the American press contained long and authoritative accounts of outrages in Mexico, showing the inability of the Carranza government to establish peace, and the incapacity and corruption of the leaders. This was continued until Carranza was recognized, whereupon the American Government immediately shut down on the truth being given out to the newspapers.

The Pan-American conference is interesting now, principally because it indicates the shifty attitude of the American Government with regard to Mexico and the absence of a policy of any kind.

Preparations were being made for the election, and the Democratic National Committee insisted that something be done about Mexico, that it be not permitted to continue in a state of anarchy until the presidential election of 1916. With the idea of placing the responsibility on Latin America, the ministers in Washington of Argentina, Brazil, Chile, Bolivia, Uruguay, and Guatemala, were called into this conference.

The American Government then went through the form, at the first meeting of the conference in New York, of giving to the bright Latin Americans the benefit of the American Government's superior knowledge of conditions in Mexico. As I have stated before, the Latin Americans were, of course, entirely conversant with conditions in Mexico, some of whom had lived there, and for the very obvious reasons that have already been explained, did not sympathize with the attitude of the American Government in supporting bandits in Mexico and thus establishing a precedent for later promoting revolutions in their own countries and overthrowing the very governments which they represented. After a hundred years of experience, all of South and Central America is ruled by the class that ruled in Mexico in the time of Diaz—the so-called "Cientificos." One can imagine the sympathy that these gentlemen had with the attitude of the American Government in overthrowing in Mexico the very type of government that they represented in South and Central America.

At the time the American Government called the Pan-American conference it had the intention of backing Francisco Villa, and shaped its plans accordingly. With the idea of giving to the Latin American diplomats the benefit of the superior knowledge of the American Government of conditions in Mexico, it decided to send to the first session of the Pan-American Conference one of the many personal representatives of the President. The last personal representative of the President to visit Mexico was Duval West, of San Antonio, Tex., who had only recently returned from Mexico, and who had traveled all over the country and had met all the revolutionary leaders, and it was but logical that the American Government should have given to their Latin American associates the benefit of their latest advices and have sent Mr. West to report to those gentlemen. There was, however, a great obstacle to having Mr. West do this, because this gentleman had returned and told the truth about conditions in Mexico and reported that all the factions were composed of bandits. The American Government, therefore, instead of sending West to the conference, selected Mr. Paul Fuller, of New York, who had been to Mexico a year before as a special representative and who had come back, as was usual with most personal representatives, a confirmed adherent of one of the factions—in this case the Villa faction.

Mr. Fuller appeared before this conference and astounded the Latin Americans by explaining to them that Villa was a splendid leader with high ideals; he told them that Villa had a well-disciplined army of thousands of men, although everyone of the Latin American delegates knew that Villa had been driven to the very frontier of the United States and had taken refuge in Juarez. Mr.

Fuller proved that Villa was a leader of high ideals by producing
the Villa revolutionary program, which he himself had translated.
There could, of course, be no more conclusive proof than this!

The Pan-American conference was then adjourned for a few
days for the ostensible purpose of enabling the Latin Americans to
fully digest Mr. Fuller's report; as a matter of fact, the conference
was adjourned for the purpose of giving the American Government
time to complete arrangements to back Villa. Villa had just a few
days before, not fully realizing apparently that the American Government was contemplating recognizing him, gathered together the
merchants in Chihuahua and robbed them. Gen. Scott, Chief of
Staff of the American Army, was rushed to El Paso for a conference
with Villa. I do not know what happened at the conference, although we have Villa's version for a part of it, but the fact remains
that immediately after the conference Villa rushed back to Chihuahua, returned the loot to the merchants and, to show his indignation, had several of his followers executed, presumably for having
robbed the merchants under his orders. This produced a fine impression upon the uninitiated.

The Latin American delegates to the Pan-American conference
were, of course, not among the uninitiated. All these shrewd gentlemen knew just exactly what the American Government was doing and followed all of its steps and the steps of its devious
confidential agents with great interest.

In this connection it is interesting to note that for reasons that it
is difficult to understand the American Government had always
been extremely fond of Villa, and he was decidedly their pet. Gen.
Scott found great pleasure in having his picture taken with Villa;
he seemed to be flattered by the association. When the committee
of Tampico oil men conferred with the President shortly after the
taking of Vera Cruz, the President was gracious enough to tell
them something about conditions in Mexico and assured them that
"Villa is the safest man in Mexico to tie to."

During the progress of the Niagara conference, Mr. Bryan asked
me, upon my suggesting that Villa would undoubtedly revolt
against Carranza, where I had received my information, to which I
replied that I had received it from a perusal of Mexican history,
which shows no instance of a Mexican chief winning a revolution
and handing the fruits over to a civilian. Mr. Bryan smiled with the

assurance of a man who possesses inside information and told me that he knew that Villa was loyal to Carranza because Villa himself had assured him of the fact. This, of course, was final. Mr. Bryan also stated that Villa was an idealist and that reports to the contrary were all manufactured by the Cientificos and Wall Street. He said that, of course, Villa had committed some outrages, but those had occurred early in his career; that the American Government, realizing his possibilities, had sent Gen. Scott to confer with him, who advised him that under the rules of civilized warfare it was not considered proper to kill prisoners, and when he showed Villa a book containing the rules of warfare Villa evinced such an interest in this discovery that he asked Scott for the book. Villa did not know before, apparently, that it was wrong to commit murder; since that moment he had become a changed man. A few years later the American Government apparently discovered that Villa had reverted to his original occupation of being a bandit.

The Latin American diplomats, for reasons that I have already mentioned, were almost without exception opposed to the recognition of Carranza. After finding that it would be impossible to make a satisfactory arrangement with other factions, the American Government decided to recognize Carranza and called the final meeting of the conference.

When the Latin American representatives went to the final meeting they went there knowing that they would be called upon to recognize Carranza and also went there with the feeling which had been derived from reports that had been very assiduously circulated that if they did not recognize Carranza the alternative would be armed intervention by the United States. While the Latin Americans did not want Carranza, they, of course, did not want armed intervention, especially armed intervention coming as a result of a Latin American Conference. When the representatives of the American Government proposed the recognition of Carranza they reluctantly consented.

The Latin American representatives in this case showed the weakness that men of their race usually show in a crisis. There is every reason to believe that the American Government did not intend to intervene at that time. As a matter of fact, by agreeing to the recognition of Carranza the Latin American delegates agreed to a policy that led inevitably to intervention; they agreed, against their own judgment, to recognize as President of Mexico a man who was doomed to failure, and the result of the failure promised to be armed intervention. Whatever the Mexican people may hold against the American Government as being responsible for their plight and their suffering—and there is no doubt that the American Government is largely responsible—the Latin American countries represented in this conference shared the responsibility, and history will convict them of failing at a critical stage in the development of Latin American relations in courage to take the resolution prompted by their best judgment. If the Latin American representatives had declined to recognize Carranza, the American Government would not have dared to do so, especially after having convoked the Latin American conference.

True to the policy of the American Government with regard to Mexico, inspired dispatches from Washington appeared in the press the next morning to the effect that Latin America had achieved a great diplomatic triumph and had forced the United States to recognize Carranza. This false report was, of course, given out for the purpose of laying a predicate for placing the responsibility on Latin America in the event that Carranza should fail.

MR. KEARFUL. You have several times referred to a large number of personal representatives of President Wilson who at various times operated in Mexico. Are you prepared to make a statement in general respecting those representatives and also with respect to the several representatives in particular?

MR. BUCKLEY. Yes. Having discarded the methods usually employed in international matters, the President sent a swarm of personal representatives into Mexico, and the State Department, imitating this policy, also sent a number of special representatives. At times several representatives would be dealing with the same faction, all claiming to represent the real views of the State Department. Often the representatives of Carranza would also be selected to represent the American Government in its dealing with Carranza.

Representatives were sent to each faction—the Villa faction, the Zapata faction, and the Carranza faction—and they became itinerant diplomats, traveling through the country with the chiefs of the various factions. These gentlemen, almost without exception, became ardent admirers and advocates of the cause of the particular faction to which they were accredited and instead of representing the American Government and people they represented the factions in question to the American Government. Their one concern was for the advancement of the particular group in question, and they seemed never to be concerned with the prestige of the American people and the welfare of Americans in Mexico. They never hesitated to advise Americans who appealed to them for help that under the new order of things they were not entitled to any help, that they had no business in Mexico, had been ordered to leave repeatedly, and that their presence in Mexico merely served to hinder the Mexican revolutionaries in carrying out their program for the betterment of the Mexican peon and the establishment of a democratic government.

The majority of these gentlemen became the paid representatives of different factions on their return to the United States, and detailed evidence will be presented to the committee of the financial connections of a number of them with the different factions, if desired. The majority of these special representatives seem to have had strong business inclinations.

The most distinguished of these representatives undoubtedly was Mr. John Lind, who has already been referred to as having been selected because of his ignorance of Mexican affairs. Mr. Lind still gives evidence of being as ignorant of Mexican affairs as he was on the day of his appointment. During the Niagara conference I had a talk with Mr. Lind and found that this gentleman divided Mexico into two classes, the Mexican from the north and the Mexican from the south; just where the dividing fell he did not specify. The Mexican from the north, he said, had been influenced by American ideas and ideals, had become democratic in his instincts and aspirations, was courageous, honest and trustworthy, and American; the Mexican from the south, on the contrary, was still affected by what Mr. Lind was pleased to term European traditions; he was backward, revengeful, monarchical in his tastes, and was altogether bad. This revolution, so Mr. Lind stated, was really a civil war between the north and the south, in which we, the American people, must see to it that the north won out.

Mr. Lind was obsessed with three ideas: A most senstive regard for his own dignity as representative of the President of the United States; the theory just stated that people from the northern part of

Mexico were superior to those from the southern part; and an intense hatred of the Catholic Church. His hatred for Huerta became a personal feeling; it was impossible for him to mention Huerta's name without indulging in profanity. Huerta had outwitted and humiliated him, and Lind could not forget it. He had gone to Mexico on a most ridiculous mission, a demand for the abdication of the President of a supposedly sovereign Republic, a mission which no man with any experience in world affairs would ever have undertaken, and had consequently become the laughingstock of both Mexicans and Americans. Lind seemed to blame Huerta for this situation, instead of blaming himself or his chief. I stated before that in his humiliation he was quite willing that the Army and Navy of the United States be used to avenge him. He has been opposed to armed intervention ever since, when it has been suggested that the Army and the Navy of the United States be used to protect American citizens in Mexico.

Mr. Lind is typical of that provincial American, who, in need of civilization himself, wants to civilize the rest of the world. He believed in forcing American ideas on Mexicans whether they wanted them or not and for some reason, incomprehensible to the American in Mexico, selected Carranza as his instrument.

In private conversation Mr. Lind attributed all the ills of Mexico to the influence of the Catholic Church, and argued that this institution in Mexico must be destroyed. In a conversation with Mr. O'Shaughnessy, on a remark of the latter that he had just received a report to the effect that several Catholic priests had been killed, Mr. Lind stated that this was good news, that the more Catholic priests they killed in Mexico the better it would suit him, and the more pleased the President would be. In Washington, in a conversation that took place during the Pan-American conference, when it was reported that the United States would not recognize Carranza, Mr. Lind exclaimed to the chairman of the International Committee of Mexico City, "My God, poor Mexico will fall back into the clutches of the Catholic Church!"

Mr. Lind has been an active propagandist for the Carrancistas since his return from Mexico. I will be glad to give the committee further details if it desires.

The Rev. John R. Silliman, after years of faithful effort in Mexico, became a missionary and dairyman in Saltillo. He had sold milk to Carranza, the governor of the State, and the relation of dairyman and governor persisted throughout the time that Silliman represented the President before Carranza. Just what qualified Mr. Silliman to represent the President in Mexico has been a mystery to Americans who knew Silliman.

He was always a pathetic figure. His very walk was apologetic. While engaged in social intercourse he seemed to fear that Carranza would appear on the scene and rebuke him. When Americans appealed to him for protection and redress he would explain to them that while he sympathized with them he could not mention such matters to Carranza because Carranza would send an adverse report to the President about him and he might lose his job.

Silliman became so subservient to Carranza that he referred to the Carranza cause as: "our cause" and to the Carrancistas as "we."

A ludicrous situation was brought about in a conversation that Silliman had with Mr. Cornelio Gertz, the German consul in Vera Cruz, which was covered in a dispatch to the *New York Herald* in the fall of 1915, which is in part as follows:

> According to passengers arriving here [Galveston], all Vera Cruz is grinning over the story of a recent interview between Mr. Gertz, the German consul, and John R. Silliman, representative of the American State Department to President Carranza. The story was told by Mr. Gertz himself as a good joke on Mr. Silliman, but there are a good many Americans in Vera Cruz who see more cause for sadness than laughter in Mr. Silliman's alleged partiality to the pronoun "we" under such conditions.
>
> The story, as told by Mr. Gertz, is that he called upon Mr. Silliman the other day and asked whether there was any news and whether there was any change in the situation.
>
> "Oh, things are looking very much brighter," said Mr. Silliman, "conditions are improving rapidly. We have taken Leon, we have defeated Villa, and we will soon occupy the City of Mexico."
>
> Mr. Gertz bounced out of his chair, stared hard at Mr. Silliman in utter amazement, and exclaimed explosively:
>
> "Why, Mr. Silliman, why didn't you tell me that before? I had no idea of such things happening. You should have told me about it so that I could send it to my Government."
>
> Mr. Gertz, of course, thought that in using the pronoun "we" Mr. Silliman was referring to the Americans, instead of which he was referring to the Carrancistas.

The Rev. William Bayard Hale and the Rev. Henry Allen Tupper, two more special representatives of the President, may be referred to briefly. Later, if the committee desires, further information will be furnished. It appears that when the former returned to the States Germany outbid Carranza in securing his services; and, so far as the latter is concerned, it has already been proved in the testimony of Mr. Doheny that he received a check for over $4,000 from the Carranza authorities. We shall present some interesting evidence at a future time, but it will suffice now to say that the Rev. Henry Allen Tupper offered to mention a prominent Mexican favorably in a magizine article for a consideration of P1,000 when exchange was 5 to 1. Dr. Tupper developed great business capacity while in Mexico.

Mr. Paul Fuller was an ardent Villista after his return to the United States.

Mr. Carothers, an American of little prominence in Mexico, was appointed by the President as personal representative to Villa, and has since then been an ardent Villista.

Mr. H. L. Hall was another discredited American living in Mexico and was appointed a special representative to Zapata. He is now and has been for several years a Zapatista propagandist.

Mr. Duval West, of San Antonio, Tex., came back and reported the truth about conditions in Mexico and his services were soon dispensed with by the American Government.

After the Brazilian minister, who had been placed in charge of American affairs on the departure of Mr. O'Shaughnessy, was practically expelled from Mexico by the Carrancistas, the lives of the Americans in Mexico—two or three thousand—and the billion dollars of American property, were left in charge of first one clerk and then another for a period of over a year, at the most crucial time in the relations of the two Governments and when American lives and property were most in need of protection. These clerks were young men, all from 22 to 30 years of age, who were not trained diplomats, had no experience in diplomatic affairs and had not the slightest conception of the meaning of international law. These inexperienced clerks were called upon to measure their wits with brilliant radicals like Luis Cabrera. It is no wonder that the Mexican revolutionaries put through their scheme for the confiscation of American property and the elimination of American citizens from Mexico, when during the course of the constitutional convention lasting for several months, in which these anti-American provisions were being discussed, the interests of the United States were so represented. The American Ambassador, Mr. Fletcher, was held in Washington for over a year at this critical period, and was finally hurried to Mexico with a protest against the passage of the constitution, with the result that the convention hurried up its final vote on the instrument and adopted it within a few days after Mr. Fletcher's arrival.

Mr. KEARFUL. You have heretofore made a statement with reference to Carranza's revolutionary program. What have you to say with reference to the fulfillment of that program?

Mr. BUCKLEY. Everybody knows, of course, that the Carranza Government is a military despotism. It would be a waste of your time to submit the proofs of this. I will merely refer to a few incidents.

In the first place, in the proclamation issued by Carranza ordering elections for Congress and President in 1916, he excluded from the right to vote all citizens who were not revolutionaries.

Section 4 of article 8 of the call provided that those could vote "who were citizens or residents of the respective State at the time of the uprising of Huerta against Madero, provided that they later demonstrated, with positive acts, their adhesion to the constitutionalist cause"—that is, by taking up arms.

State elections have been a farce, and invariably Carranza has placed in power his own choice for governor.

[W.F.B. gave instances of election frauds in eight states] . . .

In many cases opponents have been executed after the writ of amparo, a measure corresponding to our writ of habeas corpus, had been ignored by the military authorities. It will be recalled that I stated that it was reported that during the administration of Madero, Carranza had appealed to a member of Madero's cabinet, Alberto Garcia Granados, to join him in a revolution, which the latter declined to do. As soon as the Carranza forces reached Mexico City troops were rushed out to search and loot Granados's home. Garcia Granados was a high-class Liberal, who had opposed Diaz for many years and who had been repeatedly imprisoned by the latter but who was never involved in any revolts. Granados was tried by a court-martial which absolved him; nevertheless the military commander of Mexico City, Gen. Pablo Gonzales, arbitrarily set aside the verdict of the court-martial and Garcia Granados was executed at once.

In April of this year Gen. Francisco de P. Alvarez was captured by the Carrancistas, tried for treason and condemned to death by the military judge. Alvarez asked for amparo, and the federal judge at Vera Cruz ordered the provisional suspension of execution pending investigation and definite decision by the judge. This would have been sufficient to stay execution under Mexican law, but Alvarez's attorney appealed also to the supreme court at Mexico City, which repeated the orders given by the local judge and communicated the same directly to the council of war, to the local judge, and also to the President of the Republic. Notwithstanding this, Gen. Alvarez was executed. Shortly after an election of supreme court judges was held and the justices, Victoriano Piemental, Manuel Cruz, Santiago Martinez, Agapito Colunga, and Agustin del Valle, who, in the Alvarez case and in many other cases had assumed an independent position, were not reelected. The new court obeys implicitly the orders of Gen. Carranza.

During the first part of October of this year the police found a store of arms and ammunition in Tacuba, a suburb of Mexico City, with the result that an ex-federal general, Leopoldo Diaz Cevallos, was arrested and delivered to Gen. Pablo Gonzalez and taken to a small town near Cuautla in the State of Morelos, where he was executed one night without trial. Within the last few days the judge at Tacuba has decided that Gen. Diaz Cevallos and other supposed accomplices were innocent.

In the address that Carranza's minister of justice, Rogue Estrada, made to the judges of the supreme court of the federal district of Mexico on October 5, 1915, he advised them to carry out the revolutionary program and discard all law. Among other things, he said:

> The revolution, become government, places in your hands its greatest aspiration, justice, and this justice, such as it undoubtedly should become in these times, [consists in] disowning the decisions and annulling the judicial acts of Huerta and the convention. You will say to me the articles [of the Constitution] are to be found in a concentrated form in a book called the law, but I say to you that we are repudiating everything done up to this time,

wherefore there are neither laws nor decrees that dispose that which shall be done.

It is necessary to be filled with a spirit entirely revolutionary in order that the administration of justice may respond to the aspiration of the revolution become government.

I hope from the magistrates composing the Supreme Court of Justice that with good judgment and strict justice they will know how to give their decisions, interpreting clearly the ideals and plans of the revolution become government.

MR. KEARFUL. What in your opinion has been the effect of our Mexican policy on the people of South and Central America?

MR. BUCKLEY. As stated before in this connection, the American Government has diregarded the history of the last 100 years, which shows that up to the present time Latin American countries may only be ruled successfully by their educated classes, and that the mass of the people are not yet prepared to exercise the attributes of democracy. The American Government has insisted on upsetting the natural status in Mexico, and by so doing, with the implication of similar conduct in other Latin American countries, has alarmed those governments. The following are some of the effects of our Mexican policy in Latin American countries:

First. It constitutes evidence of our intention, so they think, of a reversal of our duties and obligations under international law and indicates our intention of interfering in the local affairs of those countries.

Second. The substitution of Pan-Americanism for the Monroe doctrine. It has heretofore been the practice of the American Government to make its decisions alone and unaided with regard to its relations with Latin American countries. Everybody understands, except possibly the Hon. John Barrett, the loquacious director of the Pan-American Union, that there is a community of interest in Latin America opposed to the United States, and that no Latin American diplomat could be relied upon to be impartial in differences arising between the United States and Mexico.

This new departure in policy was forecast in the action of the American Government in entrusting American affairs in Mexico to the Brazilian minister after Mr. O'Shaughnessy was given his passports by the Huerta Government. Although Mr. O'Shaughnessy had left American affairs in charge of the British minister, because of a certain recognized community of interest and ideals between the Americans and the British, the American Government directed that the Brazilian minister take charge of American affairs, thinking, no doubt, that this was an admirable diplomatic stroke. While the Brazilian minister was most solicitous in his regard for the rights of Americans, and all Americans in Mexico remember him with gratitude, nevertheless it was impossible for him to deal with Americans without developing friction, for the very simple reason that there is a fundamental difference in character between the Latin American and the American that can never be reconciled—a difference in their ideas of government which should be recognized and reckoned with in any intelligent policy.

The impression has been produced among the Latin Americans that Latin America, and not the United States, will in the future regulate affairs on this continent. The conduct of our Government has been construed by these countries as a renunciation of the Monroe Doctrine, and a substitution therefor of the Pan-American doctrine in which the Latins will have 20 to 30 votes to 1 for the United States. It has heretofore been maintained that the Monroe Doctrine is a doctrine enunciated by the United States for the protection of the United States, to be enforced by the United States. There is evidence, however, that things have changed. In the President's address to Mexican editors delivered at the White House on June 7, 1918, he made some important statements with regard to our traditional policy which have been taken very seriously by Mexico and to which great importance has been attached by Mexicans and other Latin Americans. While it is true that the statement in the beginning of the address that "My own policy, and the policy of my administration toward Mexico was at every point based upon this principle—that the internal settlement of the affairs of Mexico was none of our business; that we had no right to interfere with or to dictate to Mexico in any particular with regard to her own affairs," is so cynical in its utter disregard of the facts as to cast discredit on what is said in the rest of the address, nevertheless this address is taken seriously by those who desire to profit by it.

After stating that "Some of us, if I may say so privately, look back with regret upon some of the more ancient relations that we have had with Mexico long before our generation; and America, if

I may so express it, would now feel ashamed to take advantage of a neighbor," the President goes on to say:

> Some time ago, as you probably all know, I proposed a sort of Pan-American agreement. I had perceived that one of the difficulties of our relationship with Latin America was this. The famous Monroe Doctrine was adopted without your consent, without the consent of any of the Central or South American States. So [say], "Very well, let us make an arrangement by which we will give bond. Let us have a common guaranty, that all of us will sign, of political independence and territorial integrity. Let us agree that if any one of us, the United States included, violates the political independence or the territorial integrity of any of the others, all the others will jump on her."

That Carranza was quick to perceive the point is evident by what he stated in his message to the Mexican Congress on September 1, of this year:

> As the question of the acceptance of the Monroe Doctrine was taken up at the Paris peace conference, the Government of Mexico found it advisable publicly to declare and officially to inform friendly Governments that Mexico had not and would not recognize that doctrine, because, without the consent of all the peoples of America, it established a criterion and a situation about which they have not been consulted; and therefore that doctrine attacks the sovereignty and independence of Mexico and would establish an enforced tutelage over all nations of America.

It will be noted that in referring to the "consent of all the peoples of America," Carranza uses almost identically the same language as President Wilson.

Third. The encouragement of legislation in Latin America against American investments and the adoption of the so-called "Carranza doctrine." This doctrine, which maintains that a foreigner may not invoke the diplomatic intervention of his own Government, forms the basis of the Carranza foreign policy, and was the basis of his treatment of the foreigner both in executive decrees while he was still a revolutionary chief and in the constitution itself. In the latter instrument it is provided that, before a foreigner may acquire real estate, oil, or mineral rights, he shall specifically renounce the right to appeal to his own Government, and that a mere exercise of this right shall result in the forfeiture of his property to the Mexican Government.

The message to the Mexican Congress just quoted also stated that:

> This Government, for its part, has not made nor will it make any effort to enter this international society (League of Nations) because it is not based, either in its organization or its functioning, upon the complete equality of all nations and all races, the Mexican Government having proclaimed as a prime principle of its international policy that all nations of the globe should have equal rights and obligations, as well as that no individual within the State may invoke privileged position or protection because of his status as a foreigner or for any other reason.

In other words, the Carranza doctrine maintains that Mexico, or any other Latin American country, may confiscate the property of an American without his right to appeal to his Government; that is, may confiscate with impunity. The very enunciation of such a doctrine is inspired by the intention to confiscate.

[Carranza's] Government has broadcast throughout Latin American countries that portion of the constitution imposing restrictions on foreigners and copies of his proposed laws for carrying into effect the confiscation of American oil properties. The result has been that several Latin American countries, notably Colombia, have followed Carranza's advice and example, in view of the impunity with which his program has been carried out, and have adopted similar legislation against Americans.

Fourth. Probably the most costly effect of our relations with Mexico and Latin America is the creation of distrust of the honesty of our Government. The splendid insight into our Mexican policy afforded to Latin Americans in the Niagara and the Pan-American conferences, where the American Government violated its pledged word, deceived its own people, and tried to deceive the Latin American diplomats, would hardly have a very beneficial effect on our Latin American relations.

Mr. Kearful. What have you found to be the effect of our Mexican policy on Carranza himself?

Mr. Buckley. Carranza and his followers distrust and hate the American Government and the American people.

The intervention of the American Government in the internal

affairs of Mexico started with the dispatch of Lind to Mexico, in August, 1913, and has continued to the present time. The American Government has insisted that that unfortunate country be ruled by bandits; it placed the bandits in power by destroying Huerta, and it has maintained them in power ever since. To do this, it has been compelled to tolerate the expulsion of the educated classes from Mexico; the practical starvation of the Mexican people for the last seven years; an attack on religion; the confiscation of foreign property, and the murder of hundreds of foreigners, mostly Americans. To hide the results of its policy from American people, it has not scrupled to use all the powers of a strong government.

Our Mexican policy is disapproved of by the educated classes in Mexico; the common people hate and distrust the United States as a tyrant that has forced the Carrancistas on them; Americans and all other foreigners in Mexico have always opposed this policy; Latin American countries oppose it, and there is nothing to indicate that it is approved by any European government. One would think, then, that surely the Carrancistas must be our friends; as a matter of fact, they are the most bitter enemies of the American Government and people.

It would be without purpose to examine the President's addresses and papers, where he has insisted at one time that the American Government was intervening, and at other times, notably, in the Indianapolis speech, when conditions in Mexico were very bad, that the Government was not intervening.

In the interview published in the *Saturday Evening Post* on May 23, 1914, the President said:

> The settlement of the agrarian question by constitutional means —such as that followed in New Zealand, for example—will be insisted on.

The question arises in one's mind, By what authority can the President insist on the solution of this question? The President goes on to say:

> Every phase of the Mexican situation is based on the condition that those in de facto control of the Government must be relieved of that control before Mexico can realize her manifest destiny.

Later the President states:

> Then came the incident at Tampico. Rear Admiral Mayo, resenting the insult to the flag, issued his demand for an apology, and the President and his Cabinet stepped in behind the Admiral,
> Really it was the psychological moment, if that phrase is not too trite to be used. There was no great disaster like the sinking of the *Maine*, and there was an adequate reason for our action in this culminating insult to a series of insults to our country and our flag.

The psychological moment—that is, the excuse to intervene!

In a communication to Mr. O'Shaughnessy sent by Mr. Bryan on the 13th of November, 1913, after the Lind mission had failed, and when the American Government had ceased quarreling with Huerta, Mr. Bryan instructed Mr. O'Shaughnessy to communicate "the following to Gen. Huerta immediately, as the conditions on which negotiations will be resumed: First, the explicit agreement of Gen. Huerta: (1) That the Congress called for tomorrow shall not assemble; and (2) that Gen. Huerta will absolutely eliminate himself from the situation immediately upon the constitution of an ad interim government acceptable to the United States." What is this if not intervention?

In a report submitted by Mr. O'Shaughnessy to the Department of State in February, 1914, Mr. O'Shaughnessy states that, in a conversation that he had with Huerta, the latter—

> did not criticize the rebels of the north, but said they would never, in the event of their triumph, be able to establish a government in Mexico, and that one of their first acts, if they ever did triumph, would be to turn upon the United States, whom they are now praising.

This was indeed prophetic.

The vacillating policy of the American Government is well exemplified by its policy in placing embargoes on arms and ammunition and then removing them, to the exasperation even of the Carranza Government.

The following data is based on a speech made in the House of Representatives by Congressman Rogers on July 29, 1916:

> In the President's address to Congress held August 27, 1913, he says, "For the rest, I deem it my duty to exercise the authority conferred upon me by the law of March 14, 1912, to see to it that neither side to the struggle now going on in Mexico receives any

assistance from this side of the border. I shall follow the best practice of nations in the matter of neutrality by forbidding the exportation of arms or munitions of war of any kind from the United States to any part of the Republic of Mexico, a policy suggested by several interesting precedents, and certainly dictated by manifest considerations of practical expediency. We cannot in the circumstances be the partisans of either party to the contest that now distracts Mexico, or constitute ourselves the virtual umpire between them."

On February 3, 1914, President Wilson revoked the Taft proclamation of March 14, 1912, in order to enable the rebels to receive munitions of war, and "thereby constituted himself a virtual umpire between the factions."

On April 24, 1914, the President again placed an embargo on the shipment of arms and ammunition to Mexico.

On May 16, 1914, the embargo was raised in so far as to permit shipments by sea. This was for the purpose of shipping arms and ammunition to the rebels, who by that time had possession of the port of Tampico.

On June 4, 1914, Mr. Bryan stated to the newspapers that the mediators had an understanding with the United States that, pending their efforts at Niagara Falls, the United States would permit no arms to be shipped into Mexico either across the border or by water from American ports. We have seen in connection with the Niagara conference how ill the American Government fulfilled this understanding.

On June 2 the steamship *Antilla* left New York for Tampico containing some 3,000,000 cartridges.

On June 6 another million cartridges were shipped on the steamship *Sunshine* from Galveston to Tampico.

On June 10 the United States again imposed an absolute embargo by sea and land.

Thereafter, however, the schooners *Sunshine, Grampus,* and *Susan* made six trips from Galveston to Tampico, each time carrying heavy shipments of war materials. All were consigned to Habana, but "by stress of weather they were blown into Tampico."

On September 10, 1914, the embargo was lifted.

On October 20, 1915, the embargo was again declared, which, however, was not made applicable to Carranza, who was recognized on October 19.

On March 12, 1916, all permits held along the border for exporting explosives into Mexico were cancelled.

Since this time permits for the exportation of arms and ammunition have been given and declined so many times that it makes one dizzy even to go into the matter.

However, it is not necessary to present collateral evidence to substantiate the opinion which the Carrancistas held and hold of the American Government and the American President, for we have their opinion in their own words in the interview published by Gregory Mason in the *Outlook* in 1916.

In answer to the question, "Do you approve of President Wilson's policy in Mexico, and, if not, what do you consider have been its principal mistakes?" Gen. Pablo Gonzales replied: "I do not approve Wilson's policy in general for a reason which is fundamental with me as I believe it is with every honest man, namely, Wilson's policy is not clear; it is not frank; it is not clean. I cannot reconcile the Pershing expedition with the bombastic and oft-repeated declaration of President Wilson of his respect and sympathy for Mexico. I wish that President Wilson would be our friend and give proof of his friendship with deeds, or that he would be our enemy and declare open war on us. But he ought not to exasperate us with his policy of double-dealing, overwhelming us on the one hand with honeyed words and protestations of sympathy, and on the other hand protecting our enemies and obstructing the consolidation of our Government. What I have just said points out the greatest error in Wilson's policy, and, I will repeat, indicates his lack of clearness and frankness."

In answer to the correspondent's question as to what could be expected from the election of Hughes, Gen. Gonzales stated: "I can say that in case the imperialistic reputation of the Republican Party should be confirmed I should prefer frank aggression from Mr. Hughes to the doubtful friendship of Mr. Wilson."

Gen. Alvaro Obregon stated that: "The greatest failing of President Wilson is that his acts so seldom coincide with his words. Wilson makes too many declarations which have no facts behind them; you need not examine his Mexican policy for a substantiation of this; just look at the record of his dealings with Germany."

President Venustiano Carranza, after praising President Wilson for not recognizing Huerta, went on to say:

"But lately, we have had to complain of very serious interference in our affairs by your Government.

"We cannot make such acts of your President accord with his words of sympathy for us. It is this inconsistent policy from your Government which is responsible for the disfavor in which Americans find themselves held in Mexico today. It seems to us that your President has not kept faith with Mexico."

"Can the remarks of Gen. Gonzales in criticism of President Wilson be considered as official?" the First Chief was asked.

"No," was the reply, "Gen. Gonzales's remarks were very interesting, but he spoke only for himself. Nevertheless we would prefer a firm, frank, consistent policy from the United States to such a policy as Wilson's. But, as I have said before, we are grateful to Wilson for understanding that this is a social revolution, and for the sympathy which he expressed in his stand against Huerta. And we believe that your republican Presidents are sometimes inclined to be too overbearing toward weaker nations. On the other hand, their foreign policies usually have the virtue of consistency. What we would like from the next American President, whatever his name may be, is a Mexican policy which will combine sympathy with firmness and consistency."

MR. KEARFUL. Are you prepared to make a statement with reference to the Carranza constitution of 1917? If so, proceed.

MR. BUCKLEY. Yes, sir. The vital elements in the constitution are its effect on real property and its effect on foreigners.

Property in Mexico had the security that it enjoyed in the United States, France, and England; it enjoyed this security in Mexico in practice until 1910 and in theory until 1917.

Since the constitution of 1857 provided for its amendment by an affirmative vote of two-thirds of Congress and a majority of the State legislatures, which could not have been effected without the consent of the people, and since the revolutionary leaders did not have the sympathy of the Mexican people, they decided to write a new constitution without reference to the constitution of 1857.

The constitution of 1857 referred briefly to property in Article 27, as follows:

> Private property shall not be taken without the consent of the owner, except for reasons of public utility, indemnification having been previously made; the law shall determine the authority to make the expropriation and the conditions under which it shall be carried out * * *.

It was necessary that the revolutionary leaders write a constitution which would not only provide for the confiscation of property, but would provide for it in such a way as to make their intention plain, and render the process brief and effective. This was admirably accomplished.

Article 27 of the new constitution of 1917 is a treatise which entirely changed the basis of property in Mexico. It provides at the beginning:

> The property of land and waters comprised within the limits of the national territory corresponds originally to the nation, which has had and now has the right to transmit the same to individuals, thus constituting private property. * * * The nation shall have the right at all times to impose on private property the modifications (modalidades) dictated by public interest, as also to regulate the use of the natural elements susceptible of appropriation in order to make an equitable division of the public resources and provide for their conservation.

The constitution then proceeds to establish three bases on which private property might be destroyed by the executive and legislative authorities:

1. "To this end"—to impose modifications on private property, dictated by public interest—

> the necessary measures shall be enacted (1) for the subdivision of large landed properties; (2) for the development of small properties; (3) for the creation of new centers of agricultural population * * *; (4) for the encouragement of agriculture; (5) for preventing the destruction of natural resources; and (6) to prevent damage to property to the prejudice of society.

2. Although the above provision would be sufficient to destroy the security of private property, another is incorporated which is even more effective, if possible. Article 27 further provides that private property "may not be expropriated except for reasons of public utility and by payment of its price," and then renders ineffective the guaranties implied in the two component elements of this clause—public utility and indemnification. The subsequent provisions with regard to public utility are that "the legislatures of the Federation and of the States, in their respective jurisdictions, shall determine the cases in which the occupation of private property is a public utility, and in accordance with said laws the administrative authorities shall make a corresponding declaration," and that the indemnification shall consist of the value at which the property is rendered for purposes of taxation, plus 10 per cent. The latter is usually between 5 and 15 per cent of the real value of the property. In other words, the State legislature may enact a law providing for expropriation under any pretext or for any reason that it sees fit, and this is final; there can be no possible appeal.

3. As if the two provisions above mentioned were not sufficient, it is further stipulated that the congress of the union and the legislatures of the States are empowered to enact laws for the division of large properties, in which shall be fixed the maximum amount of land that one person or corporation may own and the manner of the expropriation and sale of all land in excess of this area.

Provision is then made authorizing the executive and legislative authorities to carry into effect the above clauses, depriving victims of the protection of the Federal courts under the writ of amparo, and providing for payment of property in 20 annual installments without security other than worthless state bonds.

After providing the reasons that would justify confiscation the constitution then proceeds to declare void and voidable certain classes of existing titles:

1. Towns, settlements and communities may be given adjoining land, and confiscation made by military authorities for this purpose under the revolutionary decree of January 6, 1915, are approved.

2. It declares null and void all "acts, dispositions, resolutions, and operations connected with the subdivision of land and which may have deprived ranches, towns, congregations, tribes, and other corporations still existing of land since the law of June 25, 1856." This provision of the Constitution affects the title of millions of acres of land, and it will be noticed that all such titles are declared null whether acquired in good or bad faith or with or without consideration.

3. The Executive is then empowered to declare void all contracts and concessions since 1876, having for their object the alienation of real property, including oil and mineral rights, by the Federal Government. No trial is provided for; there can be no appeal; the decision of the Executive is final. In other words, property rights are destroyed in Mexico.

On April 30, 1918, the British Government protested to the Mexican Government against the confiscation of the oil properties of British subjects provided for in the Constitution; and in its reply of August 12 of the same year the Government stated the new theory of property in Mexico in the following words:

> If the provisions of the decree are openly made against the laws and in violation of contracts previously made, according to the concept of his British Majesty, such could not rationally

constitute an obstacle to the free development of Mexican property; and this development can demand, as has happened, certain changes of legislation beneficial to the country. This is evident when it is considered that the modern concept of property is that it is a social function bound closely to the prosperity of the State.

This "modern concept of property" as "a social function" has found expression in Carranza's Mexico and Trotsky's Russia.

The confiscation of oil properties is also [made possible] in the constitution of 1917.

The other interesting effect of the new constitution relates to foreigners. The expulsion of the Americans in Mexico has always been known to the initiated as one of the prime objects of the revolution; we say Americans, although the constitution provides the same treatment for all foreigners because the framers of the constitution really had the Americans in mind. Carranza has never deviated from his program in this respect in the slightest degree, and he regards himself as a patriotic Mexican who is stemming the tide of American influence in Mexico which he is convinced will eventually absorb his country.

At the beginning of the revolution foreigners in Mexico enjoyed all of the rights that Mexicans do. Article 33 of the constitution of 1857 stipulated that "foreigners have the right to the guaranties provided in section 1, title 1, of the present constitution" [the right to life and liberty], and article 30 of the "ley de extranjeria" [law regarding foreigners], which was issued under authority of this article and as supplemental thereto, provides that "foreigners enjoy in this Republic civil rights that Mexicans possess."

In consequence, since 1857 the foreigner has enjoyed all the rights in Mexico of a Mexican citizen, with the exception of the right of participating in the political activities of the country, and has been subject to the same obligations as the Mexican, with the exception of those duties derived from political rights, such as military service.

Article 27 of the new constitution provides that the right to acquire the property of the lands and waters of the nation shall be regulated by the following prescriptions:

> Only Mexicans by birth or naturalization and Mexican corporations have the right to acquire the property of lands and

waters and their accessions, or to obtain concessions for the exploitation of mines, waters, or combustible minerals in the Republic of Mexico. The State may concede the same right to foreigners *provided they agree before the Department of Foreign Affairs to be regarded as Mexicans with respect to said property and not to invoke, in consequence, the protection of their Government with regard to the same, under the penalty in the event that they should not comply with such undertaking, of forfeiture to the nation of the property which they may have acquired by virtue thereof.*

The waiver referred to, which is based on the Carranza doctrine, is as follows:

The purchaser shall always be regarded as a Mexican; he shall always subject himself to the laws of Mexico and he shall not enjoy other rights or other privileges than those corresponding to Mexicans. He may not, in consequence, ask or solicit diplomatic intervention in the interpretation of this contract nor the intervention of foreign diplomatic agents in matters relating to the same, the Mexican tribunals being the only ones having jurisdiction to resolve the differences that may arise in this respect.

In order that Americans might not evade this provision and acquire real estate by organizing corporations, the same article, under another section, provides that "Commercial stock companies may not acquire, possess, or administer rural properties." In addition foreigners are absolutely prohibited from acquiring real estate within 62 miles of the border or within 31 miles of the coast.

In addition, article 33 of the new constitution confers on the President of Mexico the "exclusive right to compel any foreigner whose presence he may deem undesirable to abandon national territory immediately, and without the necessity of previous trial." This provision of the constitution adopted by the Government recognized by the United States has enabled Carranza to expel from Mexico not only Americans who reported the truth about conditions in Mexico to the press, or even in confidential communications to their own Government.

In addition to confiscating the church property not already in the hands of the Government, the constitution provides in article 130 that "In order to exercise in Mexico the ministry of any denomination, it is necessary to be a Mexican by birth." In other words, no foreign priest or missionary may legally remain in that country.

This article further provides that "Ministers may not in public reunions or private gatherings * * * make criticism of the fundamental laws of the country, or the authorities, or of the Government in general." The purpose of this article is obvious, and this, with the articles previously quoted forbidding ministers of foreign birth to exercise their office in Mexico, has had a very salutary effect, from Carranza's standpoint, of converting into missionaries for the Carranza government many foreign ministers in that country and of incorporating those ministers in the Carranza propaganda service in return for Carranza's permission to violate the laws of the land by remaining in Mexico. The result has been that a swarm of preachers have been overrunning the United States perjuring their souls by indulging in Carranza propaganda. It never occurred to any of them to admit to the American public that they were not only violating the laws of the benighted Government they defended by being in Mexico at all but that they would have further violated its fundamental law if they had told the truth about that Government.

The Carranza leaders took every precaution in order that there might be no obstacle to putting through the program outlined in the constitution. Although the constitution provided for the life tenure of the judges of the supreme court, it was stipulated that this provision should not go into effect until after 1923, and by this means Carranza has been enabled to count on a subservient supreme court.

Thus has Carranza accomplished three of the great bolshevist objects of the revolution—the abolition of private property, the crippling of the church, and the expulsion of the foreigner. In connection with the charge of the existence of bolshevism in Mexico it is interesting to learn the opinion of Luis Cabrera, minister of finance and the intellectual head and director of the Carranza government. The *Dictamen*, of Vera Cruz, quotes Cabrera in its issue of the 3d of last August, in answer to a question as to whether there was danger that the bolshevist doctrines might spread into Mexico. The article published is as follows:

> Cabrera said that it is not possible for these doctrines to find in Mexico ample field for their development or that they should consitute here the same danger as in Europe and other countries, because conditions here are very different.

He added that he could state that the good part of bolshevism was incorporated in the constitution of 1917, in some of the articles that were given birth by the revolutionary movement * * * ; consequently, concluded Mr. Cabrera, bolshevism is not a novelty in Mexico, nor is there fear, nor is there any reason for fearing, its acceptance here.

There could be no higher authority in this matter than Mr. Cabrera, and no one who knows Mexico is inclined to disagree with him.

MR. KEARFUL. Are you familiar with the vicissitudes of the oil companies in their dealings with the Carranza authorities under the confiscatory clauses of the constitution and confiscatory decrees issued by Carranza?

MR. BUCKLEY. Yes.

MR. KEARFUL. Will you please proceed to state it in detail?

MR. BUCKLEY. Oil property in Mexico has, of course, been confiscated; this is a fact concerning which there can be no argument. The steps that led to confiscation and the attitude of the oil companies are very interesting, because they afford a splendid insight into methods used by the Carranza authorities and the attitude that should be assumed by the Government toward the business interests in Mexico. The question is also extremely interesting, because of the recent publicity given to the oil interests and the attack on them by the Carranza government and its propagandists in the United States, notably L. J. de Bekker, Samuel Guy Inman, Arthur Thomson, and Robert H. Murray, provokers of intervention.

I practiced law in Tampico from 1911 to 1913 and represented nearly every American company in the field at that time as well as several European companies, and because of this connection and subsequent interest in oil leases there I have kept closely in touch with the situation.

There is no question that the oil companies are right in their contention—there is no question that their properties were legitimately acquired, that they have been confiscated, and that they are entitled to the protection of the American Government. On the other hand, there is no question that these companies, through a weak and vacillating policy very similar to that followed by the

American Government in handling the general Mexican situation, have in a large measure brought on the present condition. I am of the opinion that they are as responsible for this particular situation as is the American Government; the oil companies are entitled to protection in their just rights, but like all other citizens they should stand on their rights and render more easy the efforts of their Government to protect them. If the heads of the oil companies in the United States had had a better understanding of the Mexican situation, and if those companies had been represented in Tampico by competent managers, indeed, if there had been one man of real ability among such managers, the oil properties would never have been confiscated.

I would like to say in this connection that the Mexican situation has been made too much of an oil question and has been confused too much with oil. Oil companies have suffered and are entitled to relief, but their suffering has been nothing as compared to that of the American of small means. The latter American has seldom been mentioned in connection with the Mexican situation. Thousands of good Americans went to Mexico on their own initiative, invested all their savings, and were then robbed and driven out of the country. These men have not been heard from; they have not the means to come to Washington or to reach the ear of the American people. They find themselves broken, back in a country in which they have lost their connections, without sufficient funds to enable them to finance propaganda, and what is worse, not even able to count on the sympathy of their own Government which abandoned them and betrayed them in Mexico and has lost no opportunity to malign them to the American people. These are the men who need sympathy and help. We shall present to the committee, if the committee desires, over 100 such men who are now living in different parts of the United States and also witnesses to the killing of 15 Americans, 12 of whom were killed by Carranza soldiers.

In this connection it should be noted that whereas 80 or 90 per cent of the Americans living in Mexico have been driven out of that country, the oil companies and other corporations that were there 10 years ago are still there and doing business; they have suffered, of course, but they have managed to stay on. When an American in Mexico is attacked by the authorities, in the absence of the protection to which he is entitled from his own Government, if he is to stay there he must fight or bribe. The American with $5,000 of property all in Mexico, and no resources in the United States—and this type of American constituted 80 per cent of those in Mexico—could not bribe and it has been hard for him to fight alone; some have fought and are still there. The great majority have lost their small property and were left no course but to abandon the country.

The oil company, able to fight, has not had the courage to do so, and has fallen back on the one alternative—bribery. There is not one of the foreign oil companies doing business in Mexico which has not from one to one hundred Carrancistas on its pay roll. In adopting this contemptible policy, the oil companies have not only contributed to their present plight, but they have failed to seize that leadership in the fight for American rights in Mexico to which they were urged by circumstances, and in so failing they have done incalculable harm to the American of small means and to the American people and American prestige.

For the purpose of inducing foreign capital to develop oil possibilities in Mexico and to spend large sums of money in finding and developing this hidden wealth, a law was passed by the Federal Congress on June 6, 1887, which provided that petroleum mining in all its ramifications, the hydrocarbon products derived therefrom, the capital invested, and the profits, the same as metal mining claims and coal mines, would be exempted from all Federal taxation except the stamp tax, also from State or municipal taxation of any kind whatsoever.

Nothing could be more plain in its meaning and intention than this law. The faith of the Mexican Government was pledged to exempt from taxation the foreign capital that was induced to engage in the hazardous business of developing the oil resources of Mexico, which Mexican capital, because of its timidity, would not develop.

The first encroachment on the rights of the oil companies came in a decree of the State government of Vera Cruz in 1912, during the presidency of Madero, which constituted a half-hearted attempt to begin the imposition of a tax on oil. This decree levied a license tax on companies producing oil, which at the time were limited to the Mexican Petroleum Co. and the Compania Mexicana de Petroleo, "El Aguila"—the Cowdray Co. Although this tax was a license tax, it was termed a "stamp tax" merely for the purpose of evading the law of 1887. The tax was levied on the companies producing oil. At that time the majority of the companies, including the Texas Co., the Gulf Refining Co., the Penn-Mex Fuel Co., the Royal Dutch Co., and many others, while already in the field, had not procured oil, and the Mexican authorities consequently thought that these companies would not join in opposing the decree.

At that time I represented most of the above nonproducing companies. These companies through my intervention agreed to join the Aguila and the Mexican Petroleum Co. in their fight, inasmuch as they regarded their interests as being identical, and I went to Jalapa, the capital of the State of Vera Cruz, as their representative in company with the representatives of the Aguila and Mexican Petroleum, to confer with the governor of the State. Before leaving Tampico I secured an agreement from the representatives of the two producing companies in question to the effect that we would stand on the principle that oil was exempt from taxation and would not compromise the matter on any other basis, for the reason that to compromise would constitute a waiver of the provisions of the law of 1887 and imply a recognition on our part of the right of the Mexican Government to tax oil. The members of the supreme court attended the session and gave as their opinion that the State of Vera Cruz had the right to levy this tax, first, because it was an independent State under the constitution and could not be bound by Federal legislation; and, second, that even if it were so bound the tax was a stamp tax which, under the provisions of the law, could be levied on oil companies. Both of these grounds were untenable because, first, regardless of the form of government, States in Mexico are not now and never have been independent, and besides, mining legislation and oil legislation are within the jurisdiction of the Federal Government; and second, because only the Federal Government levies stamp taxes, and because the law of 1887 in referring to a stamp tax referred merely to the well-known stamp tax existing at that time on bills of lading, receipts, checks, and other commercial instruments.

Notwithstanding the fallacy involved in the defense of this law, and notwithstanding the grave results that would follow the recognition of the right of the Government to tax the oil industry, the representatives of the Aguila and Mexican Petroleum Co., men of small vision who were intent on achieving a temporary victory and receiving the unmerited applause of their principals, compromised with the State authorities and agreed to pay a tax amounting to one-third or one-quarter of the amount specified in the decree; and thus the troubles of the oil companies began.

It is needless to say that a month or so later, without reference to the agreement made by the State with these companies, and in view of the recognition by the companies of the right of the State to tax oil, oil taxes were raised, new taxes were imposed, and taxes have been going up ever since. At the present times taxes on oil imposed by the Mexican Government are confiscatory and amount to from 30 to 45 per cent of the value of the oil at the well.

The oil companies long ago accepted the theory of the American Government to the effect that American property in Mexico is not entitled to protection; their whole attitude has been one of apology. Apparently they have been of the opinion that they did not have the sympathy of the American people, and they have been loath to stand on their rights.

In 1914, during the Niagara conference, I proposed to the companies that they immediately approach the representatives of the Carranza revolution and endeavor to secure an agreement protecting their rights; that if they failed to secure this agreement they approach the American Government openly and try to prevent this Government from recognizing the so-called Carranza Government; and that if they failed in this they measure their forces with those of the Carranza Government, and their own Government, if necessary, and endeavor openly to induce the American bankers not to finance the new Government; that in their first conference with the Carranza authorities they frankly advise these authorities just what their program would be in the event they did not obtain relief. The Carranza revolutionary junta would have understood such reasoning and would have acceded to their request. This program, however, was far too direct and too fundamentally sound to appeal to the oil companies and they turned it down.

Hardly had the Carranza revolutionaries taken Tampico when

they began to issue all manner of military decrees taxing and vex-
ing oil companies. The Federal authorities, the State authorities,
and the municipal authorities all imposed taxes of all kinds. A company was not permitted to drill until after it had secured a permit
and paid the necessary graft; an American could not take a lease or
transfer it without securing a permit from the governor and paying
the necessary graft.

The local commander at Tampico, an ignorant peon by the name
of Emiliano Nafarrate, had the nerve to announce that he would
issue a decree providing, first, that employers should pay their employees, regardless of the contracts that existed between them, in
accordance with a scale of wages fixed by this commander, and
that Carranza paper money, worth at that time about 2 or 3 cents
on the peso, should circulate at an arbitrary value of 10 cents
American money on the peso. In preparation for the promulgation
of this decree, Nafarrate summoned the managers of the oil companies to meet a committee of laborers at his office. The American
consul, Mr. Claude T. Dawson, an intelligent and patriotic American, implored the managers to ignore the summons of Nafarrate
and not to recognize his outrageous claim to the right to arbitrarily
regulate wages and other contractual relations. In spite of the appeal of the representative of their own Government, the weak
managers submissively appeared at the meeting and accepted the
wage scale that Nafarrate handed them.

When Nafarrate, after securing the submission of all of the oil
companies representing assets of hundreds of millions of dollars,
tried to impose this tax on the independent Americans in Tampico
whose property did not exceed in value a few hundred thousand
dollars, men who had gone to Mexico on their own initiative and
for whom no corporation in the United States had purchased a
roundtrip ticket, these men stood on their rights and defied the
military authority, held a meeting, and then formulated a petition
to the President of the United States, which they sent by messenger
to Laredo with instructions to wire it to the President and to the
news bureaus; they also sent a copy of this petition through the
American consul to Gen. Nafarrate. Nothing indicates more
clearly than this petition just what the situation was as that time,
and if you will permit, I will read it in full:

TAMPICO, TAMAULIPAS, May 22, 1916.

Hon. Woodrow Wilson,
   President of the United States of America,
      Washington, D. C.:

The undersigned American citizens, residing in Tampico, in mass meeting assembled respectfully submit the following to your consideration:

That it has become practically impossible for an American to do business of any nature in this section of the country because of restrictions placed by authorities that we believe to be directed primarily against American citizens.

For a year a series of decrees have made their appearance which have been progressive in that they are consistently becoming more anti-American. We believe that the authorities had not the remotest idea when they first began to issue such decrees that they would be able to enforce them, but that when nothing was done by our Government to secure their repeal these edicts have been made more stringent each day, until now our property is threatened with confiscation, and in some cases has been actually confiscated, and our own personal liberty is menaced.

[There follows a list of the oppressive decrees and the failure to secure redress through the courts or by petition to either the Mexican or the United States Government.]

We respectfully state that the military authorities are mistaken in their assertion that the only alternative to submitting to this decree — that is, to confiscation and arbitrary imprisonment — is for the Americans to leave the country. Another alternative is to remain in Mexico and receive from our Government the protection to which we are entitled.

We beg to advise the American Government that we will not obey the decree that seeks to regulate contractual relations where Americans are involved, and that we will not obey the provisions of the decree in which an arbitrary value is fixed on the paper peso. To do so would be equivalent to abandoning our property.

We submit to our Government that we believe that we are in this country not by the grace or favor of the Mexican authorities but because we have the right to be here, and we further submit that we are profoundly convinced that the authorities are anti-American in sentiment and purpose. We firmly believe it is their object to drive Americans out of Mexico.

We conceive it to be our right as American citizens to meet and consider our grievances and communicate with our Government, and we are sending to the American consul a copy of this communication with the request that he transmit the same to the military authorities in this city.

Eighty-four signatures omitted.

This petition is notable because of the fact that it expressed clearly the rights of Americans and expressed a willingness to fight for these rights regardless of the attitude of our Government. It is also notable, because the oil companies without exception refused to adhere to this declaration of Americanism; not a single manager, not a single representative of the hundreds of millions of dollars invested in oil, signed this petition.

Nothing could be more American than this petition; the oil managers would not only not sign it, but they endeavored to prevent the petitioners from using public halls in Tampico to hold their meetings; they were so alarmed at this anachronistic declaration of American rights that some of them went so far as to send word to Gen. Nafarrate that they did not sympathize with the attitude of these turbulent Americans.

When Gen. Nafarrate saw that he had a fight on his hands, that he was up against a group of Americans who understood their rights and did not stand back for their Government to take the initiative, he did what a Carrancista in such circumstances always does, and what the Carranza authorities would have done long ago with respect to the oil industry if this industry had been represented by men with the intelligence to understand their rights and the courage to fight for them—he gave in and exempted the independent Americans in Tampico from the operation of the decree. He did this in the presence of the American consul, but told the consul explicitly that since the oil companies had agreed to his preposterous dictation he would hold them to their agreement.

It is interesting, in connection with the attitude of the oil companies, to note the opinion of Mr. George Agnew Chamberlain, who has just resigned the position of Consul General of the United States in Mexico, expressed in his book *Not All the King's Horses.* Mr. Chamberlain states:

> Take the oil interests; all they had to do was to print the clause of the constitution which stated that petroleum rights were purchasable, and throw in for good measure proof that they did not hold one square foot of ground by gift or concession. If they had stood pat on just that, said it and said it again and not another word, there never would have been an argument.

You will note that [Carranza's] decrees took the legislation of the oil industry back into the Federal Government, but said nothing about the exemption of taxation provided for in the Federal law of 1887, and which was not recognized by the State of Vera Cruz on the ground that oil legislation was a local State matter that could not be controlled by the Federal Government. Now that the Federal Government had taken over oil legislation again, the exception provided for in the law of 1887 was, of course, binding on this Government. However, the oil companies had admitted the right of the Government to tax oil for so many years that even the managers had forgotten that they were entitled to exemption, and I do not recall any instance in which this right was again urged. At about this time Pastor Rouaix, the minister of Fomento, who had charge of oil legislation, visited Tampico for the express purpose, as he stated quite frankly and quite generally in private conversation, of devising a plausible means of confiscating oil properties. The oil managers, true to their policy, lavishly entertained Mr. Rouaix and gave him a banquet the night before he left Tampico.

The Government decided to dredge the Panuco River and arbitrarily, and without any justification whatever, imposed a tax on the oil companies for this purpose which it distributed among the different companies in proportion to the Government's opinion of their ability to pay. The companies all protested vigorously, but did nothing else, and of course paid the tax. An instructive incident occurred in this connection. One of the companies, after its tanker had been loaded and dispatched by the port authorities, and was consequently not any longer legally within the jurisdiction of the Mexican authorities, refused to pay the dredge tax, whereupon the authorities detained the boat. The manager frantically appealed to the American consul, who, being a keen man, saw his opportunity, inasmuch as the boat had been cleared, and conferred with the captain without consulting Washington (this would have been disastrous), to take the tanker forcibly from the Mexican authorities and escort it down to the mouth of the river. When the consul told the manager in question that the gunboat was ready to proceed on this mission, the manager weakened, stated that this was too much responsibility for him to take, and rushed over and paid the tax before the American authorities could possibly give him the protection which he so earnestly solicited.

As stated above, the oil companies have never seemed to be sure of their rights, although there has never been any question of the legitimacy of those rights. Their approaches to the State Department have always been with an air of apology as if they did not have, as American citizens, the same right to appeal to their State Department for the protection that the department was in law bound to give them, as they had to approach a court with a legitimate petition in law.

When the Carranza government, perceiving not only the weakness of our Government but the weakness of the oil companies, attempted to go through with their scheme of confiscation, a scheme which these very authorities did not think two years before they could put into effect, the oil companies selected Messrs. Garfield and Rhodes, men apparently inexperienced in worldly affairs, and certainly extremely ignorant of Mexican conditions and Mexican character, to represent them in their endeavor to persuade the Carranza authorities to set aside the confiscatory provision of the constitution. These gentlemen were selected, not because of their competency in such matters, for they were notoriously and pitifully incompetent, but because Mr. Garfield was a brother of the Fuel Administrator, and the oil companies hoped that they might thus succeed in influencing the Fuel Administrator to report to the Navy Department and the State Department that Tampico oil was indispensable to the prosecution of the European war and thus secure relief.

All through their negotiations the oil companies have been intent on securing the services of a brother or a cousin or a relative of somebody; their policy has been similar to that pursued by the American Government in asking Latin Americans to intercede with the Carranza authorities.

Messrs. Garfield and Rhodes carried out very splendidly the traditional policy of the oil companies and engaged in several months of argument with the Carranza officials, incurred their intellectual contempt, and finally entered into an agreement in which they admitted the principle of nationalization, that is, admitted that all the oil properties belonged to the Government and that the oil companies would in the future operate what had up to that day been their own wells and hold what up to that day had been their own properties, under special license by means of the payment of a rental and royalty to the new owner, the Mexican Government; but they induced the Carranza government to reduce the rental from 4 pesos to 3 pesos per hectare. Satisfied with this brilliant victory, they returned to the States, and what is worse and more humiliating, the highest executive officials of the oil companies in the States, men who had been dealing with Mexico and their properties in Mexico for several years, considered this matter for several weeks and engaged in heated debate among themselves before they decided not to accept and ratify the agreement entered into provisionally by Garfield and Rhodes with the Mexican authorities.

The Mexican authorities proceeded then to put into effect their so-called scheme of nationalization and issued a decree ordering the oil companies to "manifest," that is, to submit a complete statement of their properties, including certified copies of title deeds, leases, inscriptions of registration, geological reports, maps, etc., and fixed a certain period during which this must be done. Instead of meeting this issue boldly and telling the Carranza authorities that they would not make such manifestations, the oil companies sent a swarm of attorneys to Mexico City to argue again with the authorities and beg them from time to time to extend the period during which they must present these manifestations, which in itself indicated an intention to comply with the orders of the Government. In the meantime their attorneys were standing in the halls of the State Department, hat in hand, asking the State Department to take the initiative in a fight in which the oil companies themselves should have taken the initiative, and asking the advice of officials in the State Department, who in their handling of the Mexican situation for the last seven years had proved their incompetency and from whom no American in Mexico who has been able to stand on his own feet wants any advice. Incredible as it may seem, the oil companies without exception proceeded to prepare all this data and must have spent in the aggregate over $100,000 in compiling it, and awaited assurances of the State Department in advance that the State Department would protect them in their rights before deciding not to submit their manifestations, and this decision was not made until the afternoon of the last day of grace, and then, as I have stated, not until after the State Department had taken the initiative and promised to save the oil companies from risk. Could there possibly be an example of greater incompetency and inefficiency than this?

MR. KEARFUL. What, in your opinion, could the oil companies better have done than that which they did?

MR. BUCKLEY. The solution of the troubles of the oil companies, like the handling of the entire Mexican situation, has always been a very simple one; it has been filled with complication by the manner of its handling from this end. If the oil companies, instead of sending numerous delegations to Mexico City to argue with the Carranza authorities, had told the Carranza authorities just what they were going to do, they would have secured relief. If they had frankly told Carranza that they would not permit him to steal their properties; that if he proceeded to do so they would appeal to their Government for relief; and that if their Government did not give them the protection to which they were entitled, they would measure their forces with Carranza and secure their own relief, Carranza would never have gone through with this scheme, and if he had tried to go through with it the oil companies would have won out in the fight.

MR. KEARFUL. How could they have won the fight?

MR. BUCKLEY. The oil companies, after receiving no relief from Carranza, instead of sending a multitude of representatives over to Washington to talk to clerks in the State Department, should have told the State Department just what they had already told Carranza, and if they failed to receive relief here they should have financed a revolution to take over and permanently administer the oil fields, which they could have done for an expenditure of $200,000 a month, whereas they are today paying Carranza over $1,000,000 a month.

MR. KEARFUL. But such proceeding would have been a violation of law, would it not?

MR. BUCKLEY. Yes; of course it would but so would have been the confiscation of their properties by the Carranza Government, and the withholding of protection by the American Government to which these companies were entitled.

During the war, when the representatives of the oil companies were finally given a hearing by the President, who designated Mr. Josephus Daniels to hear their case, and they were asked pointedly just what they wanted and why they wanted it, they did not dare to rest their case on their fundamental right to protection under international law, but weakly stated that they wanted protection in order that oil might be available for the American Navy in the prosecution of the war, and were prompted not by self-interest, but by patriotism. They were promptly, and very properly, told that the American Government was quite willing to assume this risk and that the oil companies could go ahead on the same basis as before.

At a meeting of the oil companies that I attended in New York last December, when it was decided to send a committee to Washington to see Mr. Polk, of the State Department, and ask for the protection which was their right, a discussion was indulged in for three-quarters of an hour in the selection of the committee in their endeavor to send three Americans who might appeal to Mr. Polk; it appeared that Mr. Polk was very temperamental, and liked some people and didn't like others; his ex-law partner was solicitously consulted in the matter of Mr. Polk's likes and dislikes, and finally a committee was selected, not because its personnel was approved by its principals, but because it was calculated that the gentlemen constituting this committee would not ruffle the delicate sensibilities of this official in the State Department.

Mr. KEARFUL. What do you think would be the attitude of the oil companies toward the Mexican problem as a whole, affecting as it does many thousands of other Americans, if they could get the protection they desire and secure a modification of the confiscatory clauses of the constitution of 1917?

Mr. BUCKLEY. In spite of the protestations of the oil companies to the contrary, I believe that they would all, with the exception of one man, quit the fight, which, because of peculiar circumstances, they have been involuntarily waging for the rights of Americans in Mexico.

Mr. KEARFUL. What is your opinion as to the remedy that should be applied to the Mexican problem? Are you in favor of armed intervention by this country?

Mr. BUCKLEY. No; I am not. The present condition of Mexico does not mean that Mexico is not capable of self-government; it simply means that the bandits are not able to govern Mexico satisfactorily. There is a difference between self-government and a democratic form of government; Mexico is capable of the former, although not fitted for the latter. The Government of Mexico for 35 years during the regime of Diaz was beneficial to her people and entirely satisfactory to the rest of the world; during this period Mexico complied with her national and international obligations.

It is true that most Americans from Mexico now advocate armed intervention; they have come to this view as the result of many years of suffering, and because of conditions which promise to last indefinitely, and because of their feeling that for some reason the decent Mexican people will never again be allowed to rule their own country. No American in Mexico wanted intervention ten years ago; any American who has been in Mexico that long would prefer the Government that existed then to armed intervention. Many Americans have reached the point of advocating armed intervention because they have devoted little thought to Mexican history, or are not acquainted with the cultured Mexican and do not understand his point of view and do not understand or have forgotten the capabilities of the high-class Mexican. Our Government has not produced men greater than Limantour, Mariscal, or the Macedos, and there are many such Mexicans today, most of them, unfortunately, in exile. I believe that those Mexicans, with the proper aid, could form a satisfactory government. Armed intervention is, of course, an alternative to the present state of anarchy, but it is not the only alternative, and, in my opinion, is not the best alternative. When the American Government intervened in the local affairs of Mexico it laid the foundation for armed intervention for two reasons: First, because one government cannot control the internal affairs of another people and dictate to them without resorting eventually to the use of armed force—peaceful intervention cannot last indefinitely; and, in the second place, because when the American Government selected men of the type of Villa and Carranza to be the rulers of Mexico it chose men who could not permanently rule that country to the satisfaction of the Mexican people and foreign Governments; it chose a class that was doomed in advance to failure and failure pointed inevitably toward armed intervention. In the history of our relations with Mexico the policy of our present administration will be looked upon as an interventionist policy.

I firmly believe that the solution of the Mexican problem lies either in the positive backing of any one of a number of able Mexicans who would make good presidents of that country, or, in the negative policy of withdrawing recognition from Carranza, and permitting the decent people in that country to form their own government without hindrance on our part. There is no question in my mind but that this latter method would be successful; if, however, we were not sure of its success it would be best to try it before attempting armed intervention. The educated Mexican, the great mass of the Mexican people, have not been given any opportunity in the last seven years. Our powerful Government has made an alliance with men who have oppressed that people and defied all foreign Governments and has been true to this alliance. Now that Carranza has failed, the fear of Americans in Mexico is that our Government will back some other Mexican of the same type; a Government that in the face of all the evidence first backed Villa, then flirted with Zapata, and finally chose Carranza is in danger, is apt, if left to its own devices, to make another unsatisfactory choice.

Mr. Kearful. Why is it that the better class of the Mexican people have not formed an efficient government?

Mr. Buckley. In the first place, because in their majority they have been expelled from that country with the tacit consent of the American Government; because their properties have been confiscated with the tacit consent of the American Government; because a number of them have been killed, also with the tacit consent of the American Government—for we must conclude that where a Government maintains its recognition of another Government that has expelled and outrages its best citizens, this Government consents to that conduct. How could this class of Mexicans, even if they were provided with resources, successfully overthrow the present Government in Mexico when the United States insists that no one in Mexico but Carranza shall have arms and ammunition, and when it holds over them the menace of nonrecognition, without which no Government in Mexico can last?

The effects of armed intervention on the United States and on its future relations with Mexico would, in my opinion, be bad. After the American troops had left Mexico the United States and Americans would be hated by the very people in Mexico who are now clamoring for intervention, and, in their despair, there is no doubt that the majority of people in Mexico want armed intervention. They would forget all the good that the American Government might do and only remember the inevitable wrongs and clashes. It would be a difficult situation for Americans for 10 or 15 years after the American troops left. There is no place where we are disliked more heartily than in Cuba, and intervention in Mexico would have the same result, especially as all Mexicans would realize that we intervened to correct conditions that we had a large part in creating.

The ultimate aim of armed intervention would certainly not be the annexation of any Mexican territory or the formation of a permanent military protectorate over that country. The ultimate end, I assume, would be to turn Mexico's Government over to the Mexicans; and when this is done, whether it be within 1 year or 50 years, that Government will be left in the hands of the very people whom we have driven out of Mexico—the only people who ever gave Mexico a decent government. If it is to be done after armed intervention, it would be better to do it now. It would take a little longer for the Mexican to pacify his own country, but it would be a more secure pacification when it came, and the result would be more permanent.

MR. KEARFUL. We often hear of the necessity to shape American policy in order to meet the sentiment of Latin America, and that a strong policy with respect to Mexico would have a deleterious effect upon our prestige in Latin America. What is your opinion about that?

MR. BUCKLEY. I think we should settle this matter with Mexico without reference to Latin America or to what Latin Americans or anybody else thinks; I think we should settle it in the right way without reference to anybody else. I have always thought that this talk about our Latin American relations that we hear so much about among the officials of the American Government is founded in their provincial ignorance of such matters. Conferences like the Pan-American Conference and the Niagara Conference and our many other conferences do us no good in Latin America—Latin America respects us more when we attend to our own business and do not call Latin Americans in for consultation. Our relations with Mexico are our own business and nobody else's. The use of a firm hand in dealing with Mexico would only strengthen the respect of Latin America for us; I don't mean armed intervention, for, as I stated before, I do not think this is necessary, nor have I in mind just the present situation; but what I mean is that under ordinary circumstances we should insist that every American, no matter how insignificant he may be and even though he be in the most remote part of Mexico, has the right to the protection of his Government and that where he is discriminated against or denied the protection of the law, the American Government would be justified in using its entire Army and Navy to give him protection, and that nothing would have a more salutary effect on our Latin American relations than the use of our Army and Navy where this use is justified. It would instill a wholesome respect in people who would commit the same abuses that have been committed in Mexico if they could do so with impunity. Nothing would have raised our prestige so in Latin America as the dispatching of an army across the border the first time an American was touched and the execution of all those who had injured him. If this had been done seven years ago, in fact, if it had been threatened, Americans would have had no trouble either in Mexico or in the rest of Latin America. As it is, our prestige in Latin America was never so low as it is today.

MR. KEARFUL. Do you desire that your testimony be considered by the committee in executive session, or are you willing that it may be printed as a part of the public hearing?

MR. BUCKLEY. I am perfectly willing that my testimony should be printed and published; I would not give testimony for consideration only in executive session.

(Whereupon the committee adjourned subject to the call of the chairman.)

IV. *The Other Mexico He Talked About*

By Priscilla L. Buckley

> *" 'Señor Buckley,' they said, obviously deeply shocked, 'Monte Michael is going all around town boasting that he will kill you. He is in a bar downstairs now and we will,* con permiso, *kill him.' Would you believe it, they couldn't understand it when I told them I absolutely forbade it, that I didn't want Monte Michael killed? . . ."*

We, as children, never knew much about the foregoing. I doubt if two of us had read his Fall Committee testimony at the time of his death. We were dimly aware he had been counsel for the Mexican Government at the ABC conference at Niagara; that he had refused a proferred commission as acting Governor of Vera Cruz after the marine landings there in 1914, and that he was proud of that refusal. To us, Father's life in Mexico was something altogether different—a mixture of high adventure and misadventure, of wild coincidence, hold-ups and assassinations, of humorous capsules and sweeping generalities, of incidents that had centered around that erect, eagle-nosed gentleman at the head of the table with the thin receding hair, the Wilson-pince-nez, the gentle and courteous manner, and the will of iron.

But it was hard to believe that a man whom we never then or later heard swear (and still doubt that he ever did); who had never (as he told us with increasing emphasis in later years) taken a drink until he was forty, could have figured in those tales of derring-do. But, as he told the stories, of all the identical pairs of blue eyes around the table, the gayest and flashiest were those behind the pince-nez.

None of us remembers Father's Mexican-stories in exactly the same detail. Perhaps he himself changed their emphasis as the years went by; perhaps we in our minds molded them into the form they had to take to fit exactly our wild daydreams about Mexico in revolution. In any case, they were a part of him, a part of us, and a part of Mexico and an America which is gone forever—surviving only, like the ancient legends, in the minds and hearts of those to whom they were passed on.

The marvelous story of La Isleta, Buckley Island, told the first of many times during a walk when we were living at 1 Avenue Ingres, in Paris. Father, with hat high on his high forehead and cane swinging. Mother on one arm. The three oldest of us on the other, and knock-kneed six-year-old Jimmy, in his absorption, walking half backwards, always underfoot, totally impervious to the running commentary, "*Jimmy, get out of the way. . . Mother, tell Jimmy to get out of the way. . . Honestly, if you're not big enough to walk right. . . .*" And through it all a tale traced of delightful skulduggery and counter-skulduggery.

This may not be exactly the way it happened, but this is the way I think Father once said it happened and if it is not so, I for one, don't want to know it. . . . Tampico, as you know, lies on the Panuco River, near the Gulf of Mexico, and is terribly hot. On the river was a sandbar, visible only at low tide. Father thought the sandbar could make a cool breeze-swept residential area, so he persuaded some dredgers already on the job clearing the river channel, to dump their loads of silt on the sandbar. The land which emerged was known as Buckley Island. Well, he developed it, put in streets, and sewers and lights and was ready to sell lots when (". . . that crook, what was the name of that fellow, Aloise, my lawyer. . .") his lawyer, in collusion with the local judge, forged a set of deeds and titles to land which had never existed before. The lawyer forged the deeds, the judge declared them valid and Father, with several hundred thousand dollars sunk in Buckley Island was ordered to get out. . . . "I called in Rox Beaumont (a Texas badman but a good badman because he sometimes worked for Father) and told him to get a dozen of the toughest fellows he knew and go out to La Isleta. They each had a shotgun and I paid them t-w-e-n-t-y-f-i-v-e American dollars a day. Well, the crook was trying to sell lots on the island, but when the customers wanted to see the lots, he couldn't show it to them, not without running into Rox Beaumont. That went on for some time and one day, the judge came to see me. 'Mr. Buckley', he said, 'no one is making money this way. That lawyer of your's is a fool.' So we fixed it up. . . ." Father took the case back to court and the judge declared that the titles and deeds he had previously honored were rank and amateurish forgeries. And Buckley Island was saved.

There was the time the Governor of Tampico found out that his military Chief of Staff was in the pay of the rebels in the hills, and decided to have him assassinated. He, too, called in a Texas badman (Father's designation for any American outlaw in Tampico at that time) and agreed to pay him $5,000 and give him one of his finest horses for the job . . . "So one night this fellow walked right up behind the Chief of Staff and shot him in the neck from a distance of ten feet. But you know, that fellow recovered. He knew, of course, who had paid for his murder and left Tampico just as soon as he could get out. . ." But then—and this is what made it a story worth telling—sometime later, when the Governor told Father about it and Father asked him whether he had paid off the killer, he replied: "Why certainly, Mr. Buckley; when a man shoots another man in the back of the neck at ten paces he has every right to expect that other man to die. . . ." The servant had proved worthy of his hire.

His brushes with petty officialdom. . . . The time he was arrested for driving into Tampico with a faulty headlight and told he would have to leave his car at the police station overnight. "Leave it here? I wouldn't dare. There wouldn't be anything left of it by morning. Everybody knows the police headquarters is the biggest concentration of thieves in Tampico." The police, red-faced and angry, insisted on holding the car. Whereupon Father ostentatiously sent his servant to headquarters to "watch over" the car. The result: a five peso fine for faulty headlights, 25 pesos "por insultas a de dignidad de la policia mexicana. . ." (and how he could roll that out) . . . The time a squatter set out to build a shack on Father's land between his house and the river—and refused to leave. . . . "Just before the shack was completed and the scoundrel moved in,

I called in Ramon (his manservant) and told him, 'Ramon, you see that shack over there on my property? Well, I don't care *what* happens to it. Every stick is yours, provided it is removed before dawn.' Ramon was the world's laziest man but he would work feverishly if he ever had the opportunity to earn a dishonest dollar. . . . Well, sir, I looked out the next morning and there wasn't *a trace* left of that house," he laughed uproariously. "Remember, Aloise, we were having a dinner party that night and the police came in with the squatter to ask what I done with his house. . . . 'I don't know what you're talking about,' I said. 'A house, on my land? I know nothing about a house on my land. *Surely* no one would build a house on my land without my permission. . . .' "

Ramon was the hero of another tale. One night, Ramon heard some noise in a warehouse Father owned at the foot of the hill on which they lived. He loaded his pistol, ran out and, with true Mexican exuberance, shot off his pistol all the way down the hill. By the time he reached the warehouse and caught up with the robber, his gun was empty—and the thief suddenly turned on him. . . . "I'll tell you, you never saw anything quite like it. That scoundrel chased Ramon all the way up the hill, right back into the house. . . . Ramon grabbed a bunch of cartridges and took off after the robber. And do you know, by the time he was at the bottom of the hill again his gun was empty and the other fellow took out after him again. . . ." It went on until one of the two ran out of breath.

. . . and several wild stories about wild train rides. Did both these incidents happen at the same time? Or was Father on two different trains between Mexico City and Tampico that were held up by bandits? In any case, once Father was on a train and had 20,000 Mexican dollars, I think it was. He didn't know where to hide the money. . . . "I put it under the seat and then I thought, maybe the spittoon, but after a while I thought that wouldn't do, so I went into the men's room and I tried to find a hiding place there . . . and about this time, they started to come aboard . . ." (moment of panic among six listening little Buckleys each of whom wondered where he would have put it if only he had been so lucky as to have been in a train that was held up) ". . . so, do you know, I suddenly thought, well there's one place they certainly won't look and I put

that money on the top of my head, under my hat. . . . Would you
believe it, that was the one place they didn't look. . . ."

Another time the bandits blocked the track somewhere in the
mountains between Tampico and Mexico City; but the engineer
refused to give up. Instead, he jammed the train into reverse, and
backed down the mountain roaring and clanking around hairpin
turns at ever accelerating pace. The way Father told it, it sounded
a little like the Perils of Pauline. The bandits got on a flatcar and
took off in pursuit. As they'd round the curves, the outlaws would
shoot at the train and the passengers would fire back until train or
flatcar disappeared around the next curve. Father's train was
brought to a stop when it ran into another train which was starting
up the mountain. . . . The bandits came aboard. "They were furious.
They took the engineer, an American Negro, and they told him
they were going to shoot him. He couldn't understand much Spanish, but he understood that, and I tell you, he went almost white. I
never saw a man so scared." "But Father what did *you* do?" "Well,
some of us tried to protest. I started to get off the train, but a man
came up and stuck his gun in my stomach and told me to get
back. . . . So they took the poor man out and they offered him a
cigarette and do you know they pulled a mock execution . . . gave
the orders and then fired into the air. . . ." No need for him to tell
us it was the next to cruelest thing he had ever witnessed.

On still another train one night, Father heard a group of Mexicans discussing whether it would be all right to ask the *gringo* to
give up his lower birth to the sister of one of them who was exces-
sively pregnant, it never occurring to them that the austere American in the dark business suit and high starched collar could speak
Spanish as well as they. Father hastily offered the woman his berth,
and he and the Mexicans parted the next morning, although still un-
introduced, with protestations of admiration and life-long friendship. . . . "Well, do you know sir, it wasn't three months later that
I went to a reception the new President of Mexico was giving for
the foreign business community. And when I walked in the room
the President hurried over and gave me a great *abrazo*." He was,
of course, the man whose sister Father had aided.

. . . or about his friendly shadows, the three Mexicans who had been ordered by military authorities in Mexico City, during one of Father's altercations with the government, to follow Father wherever he went, under the very well-founded supposition that W.F.B. was in touch with Pelaez, a revolutionary general then in physical control of much of the State of Tamaulipas in which Tampico is situated. Father, always considerate, saw no reason to make life more difficult than necessary for the surveillance team. He seldom entered a cafe without ordering a cup of coffee or a drink for his shadows; he informed them when he was home for good at night; when he expected to leave in the morning and where he would go. On hot and windy days he would invite whichever one was on duty to join him in his car rather than inhale his dust by following in another car on the drives to and from the oil fields. Even so, he was surprised when one evening all three stormed into his room and pulled out from under their coats and panchos an assortment of pistols and guns. . . . "Senor Buckley," they said, obviously deeply shocked, "Monte Michael [a bad Texas badman] is going all around town boasting that he will kill you. He is in a bar downstairs now and we will, *con permiso*, kill him." Would you believe it, they couldn't understand it when I told them I absolutely forbade it, that I didn't want Monte Michael killed . . . in fact, that they simply must give up the whole idea. To them it was so simple. "He says he will kill you. We are your friends. We will kill him." After that, Father said, they guarded him more closely, convinced that there was, after all, something funny about him.

And, as he told it, possibly the funniest story of the lot—though it was a major setback in a lifetime filled with misadventures which kept Father's close associates and colleagues in a state of almost unremitting depression, but which only led to further exuberance on Father's own part—His revolution that failed. Months of hard work had gone into it. General Pelaez' army was ready and waiting. A representative had been sent to Washington to persuade the State Department to remain noncommittal when Pelaez moved out of the Tamaulipas lowlands south towards the mountains and Mexico City. An ammunition train was en route to the Mexican border with the arms Pelaez needed.

"The fellow in charge was an idiot, one of those tall, good-looking Irishmen, always full of himself, and without a brain in his head. . . . I must say, it was no real surprise to me that he lost his way. He guided that wagon train into Mexico, then got lost and led it right back, across the Rio Grande—of course that's the only river within a thousand miles and it happens to mark the boundary but he managed to overlook it and. . . ." (at this point Father could hardly repress his own laughter) ". . . he then got himself arrested on charges of smuggling arms *into* the States. . . . But funniest of all was Garnett. . . ." Dr. Garnett, a close friend of Father's since University days, had been dispatched to Washington to handle the diplomatic developments. ". . . You know when the Revolution collapsed, we all forgot to notify Garnett so he marched into the State Department on schedule, striped trousers and all, and proclaimed himself representative of the Pelaez government. . . . They didn't know what on earth he was talking about. . . . I'll tell you, Garnett was furious. He wouldn't speak to us for months. . . ." and the memory of that abortive interview of long ago would trigger a burst of laughter so infectious that we, who had never seen Dr. Garnett (and privately thought he had been treated rather shabbily) would laugh and laugh, too. And Mother, who didn't *really* like to hear Father talk about fomenting revolution, would giggle as helplessly as the rest.

But more often than not, he was the butt of his own tales. When he established the American Association of Mexico with himself as provisional president and his good friend Paul Greenwood as Secretary-Treasurer, the joke that went around, as he'd tell us was: "provisional president means that Buckley is in charge of provisions. . . ." The "Buckley salad" he used to mention, a recipe an old friend clipped out of a cook book and sent Father (at a time when he and his two brothers were very active in Mexico) and which started . . . "take three hard boiled eggs, sprinkle heavily with pepper. . . ."

But—as we got older—we started asking ourselves, Are all these stories true? We knew by this time Father's version of his engagement to Mother— "We took a carriage drive way out in the country and by the time we got back your Mother's family had the announcement of our engagment printed in every newspaper in New Orleans"—was a Big Joke. And, in the insufferable skepticism of adolescence, we sometimes wondered.

Until the summer of 1936, when Aloise and John were taken to Mexico and had hardly crossed the border before Father commented:

"You know, some years ago, when Edmund (his youngest brother) was still a boy we took a train ride to Mexico City. For some reason, no passenger trains were moving and we had to ride a flatcar. Every now and then, we'd lean over to get out of the way of a corpse hanging from a telephone pole . . . some bandit had been through there and had hung a bunch of soldiers all up and down the line. Edmund finally turned to me and said, 'Gee, Will, isn't this a great country? . . .' "

It had been fifteen years since Father's expulsion and more years than that since he had last lived in Tampico. But the very first night they arrived in Tampico, a man came upstairs to warn them that someone in the lobby with a very old grudge was threatening to "kill Buckley here and now." An incident slightly tarnished, for romance-minded 15-year-old Aloise and 14-year-old John, by Mother's fussy insistence as they went down to dinner that they stand in front of Father. It caused them untold humiliation. . . . And the conversation several days later with a slightly intoxicated American, who when he found out they were the children of W.F.B., simply had to tell them an incident they had never heard before.

It was in 1916, he said, when the Marines had landed at Vera Cruz. The situation was tense, particularly for the Americans stranded in Tampico up the river, with no gunboats standing by to protect them. Most of them gathered together for safety in the hotels and waited. On the balconies, by the windows on the rooftops, lay Mexican sharpshooters waiting, like the Americans in the hotel, for someone to drop the match. The U. S. Government, having precipitated the crisis, had made no arrangements to protect U. S. nationals whom it had left at the mercy of an enraged and trigger-happy Mexican mob. One way or another, the troops had to be brought in.

But how to attract the attention of the nearby German gunboat? "Your Father," the man told Aloise and John, "went out into the middle of the silent square and started hurling obscenities in Spanish such as we never thought to hear from him and didn't know he knew at the Mexicans and he deliberately provoked their fire. . . ."

And an alarmed German naval captain made his way to the plaza with his armed crew, and evacuated the Americans in his gunboat.

When they asked Father about it later that day, he just laughed and changed the subject.

Another six or seven years later, when Father had taken part of the family down to live in Mexico City for six months, he and Priscilla were walking home from a movie one night. As they came out of a side street into a small square, Father stopped and pointed with his cane to the diagonally opposite corner.

"During the revolution . . . the *Zapatistas* had just entered the city. I was coming home from the American Club, along this street when I saw a bunch of troops right over there, where I'm pointing. They had thrown up some kind of barricade and were crouching behind it. Several of the rifles were aimed right at me. I knew that if I went down that way"—he pointed to the left—"they might shoot me. It wasn't beyond them to make a bet on it . . . 'see that fellow there, I can drop him in one shot.' " So Father had walked straight across the square, right at the gun muzzles which had followed his every step. When he got up close, he spoke to the leader: "Señor, have you the time? My watch is broken." Father chatted with them a few minutes. Where were they from? How far had they come today? How was the battle coming? He wished them good luck and lifting his hat, he bade them a courteous "buenas noches."

"You see," he told Priscilla, "no Mexican who had done you a favor would ever shoot you in the back."

The files tell a lot about the climactic experience of this phase in Father's life, his expulsion from Mexico in November, 1921 under "Article 33."

The English language Mexico City newspaper *Excelsior* reported it this way, on November 27, 1921:

> Article 33 of the Mexican Constitution has come into the limelight and on this occasion has been applied to William F. Buckley, president of the American Association of Mexico, with head-quarters in New York. The Association has since its foundation in 1919 been carrying on a propaganda campaign which has been unfavorable to the Mexican Government.
>
> Mr. Buckley, who is well-known in the American Colony and

particularly in oil circles, returned to Mexico about a month ago and spent his time in the Republic in Tampico and in the capital. Article 33 permits the Government to expel from the country any foreigner who is judged as "pernicious" without further trial or charges. The order for the arrest of Mr. Buckley was issued over two months ago, which was one month prior to his return to Mexico. Several days ago it became known that agents of the secret police were looking for Mr. Buckley. He is now in the American Embassy pending the arrangements to be made between George T. Summerlin, United States Charge D'Affaires, and the Foreign Office for his departure from the country.

Alberto J. Pani, Minister of Foreign Relations, is known to have said that the action of the Mexican Government is due to propaganda of the New York Association.

Several members of the American Colony, it is reported, have within the last few days been arrested by the police by mistake, who were looking for Mr. Buckley. Although James C. van Trease denies that he was one of those arrested, it is persistently rumored that Mr. van Trease was detained by the police and later upon establishing his identity was released as were all the others taken into custody by the secret police. . . .

We have a copy of the telegram W.F.B. sent to Albert Fall, Secretary of the Interior, which was much quoted at the time both in the Mexican and U. S. press, part of which reads:

My offense is that since March I have publicly advocated the Mexican policy [Non-recognition of the Obregon government] later adopted by the American Government and that since then I have publicly defended that policy.

[1] *I could have made a profitable arrangement with this Government at any time since last March and could do so today if I were willing to sacrifice my principles and work against the interests of the American people and the Mexican people.*

It is my understanding that the American Government does not admit the right of the Mexican Government to expel an American citizen from the country without trial and without cause — that the American Government will not even by implication approve the expulsion of an American citizen because he has told his government the truth about the Mexican situation. Failure now to impress this policy on the Mexican Government gives sanction to the theory apparently held by the Mexican Government that only unscrupulous and unpatriotic American propagandists may give public expression to their purchased views, and will increase the present deplorable servility of the American Colony in this city.

---

[1] Italicized section omitted from both U. S. and Mexican press reports.

I hope the American Government will, First, insist on copy charges and evidence, Second, advise the Mexican Goverment that it disapproves and will not countenance such procedure and protest emphatically against the same, Third, in case of eventual expulsion insist that a written order of expulsion be delivered to the American Charge. STOP. I address you as you are informed my activities in American Association. Will you kindly see State Department immediately and ask Department give instructions American Charge. STOP I suspect authorities will verbally advise Charge have me leave country quietly. This would leave no record — I will refuse depart under such circumstances. STOP. For your own information I will state that if American Government rules that an American citizen may be expelled from Mexico with impunity and does not insist on written order of expulsion I will leave Embassy and submit to arrest.

We have W.F.B.'s formal statement to the State Department, dated January 20, 1922, part of which says:

I wish to report to my Government on my recent expulsion from Mexico by General Obregon under the authority vested in him by Article 33 of the Constitution, and to invoke the protection and redress to which I may be entitled. . . .

On Wednesday, November 23rd, 1921, while in Mexico City, I learned that the police were looking for me. I so reported to the Honorable George T. Summerlin, American Charge, who called on the Minister of Foreign Affairs that evening to ascertain if the report was true. Mr. Pani confirmed the report that an order had been issued for my arrest; . . . that the purpose was to expel me from Mexico because of my activities in connection with the American Association of Mexico . . . Mr. Summerlin advised Mr. Pani that in his opinion that was political persecution, and took occasion to read to the Minister a memorandum detailing other acts of political persecution, which I had prepared for Mr. Summerlin the day before. . . .

On the following evening the Chief of the Protocol of the Department of Foreign Affairs called on Mr. Summerlin and stated that Mr. Pani had taken up this matter with General Obregon, and that General Obregon had instructed Mr. Pani to advise Mr. Summerlin that he considered it best "for the safety of Mr. Buckley" that he leave Mexican territory; that I would be given protection, would be allowed to leave without a guard, and would be given a few days in which to close my business. Mr. Summerlin communicated this to me that evening. On the following morning I told Mr. Summerlin that the purpose of the Mexican Government was transparent, its object being to have me leave the country quietly on a hint from the Government and thus relieve itself of official responsiblity for this outrage in the event that the American Government should deem the case of sufficient importance for diplomatic intervention. I explained to Mr. Summerlin that if my safety was the only concern of the President, I would remain in Mexico, that I would not voluntarily leave unless Article 33 of the Constitution was formally applied to me and the cause of my expulsion stated; that otherwise I would leave the Embassy and submit to arrest and deportation, and thus place the responsibility where it belonged . . .

That evening (Friday) Mr. Summerlin called on Mr. Pani and advised him that I had refused to leave the country voluntarily. . . . Mr. Pani urged that I depart without further ado. Mr. Summerlin asked for a copy of the charges, to which Mr. Pani replied that "there are no charges"; that the existence of charges was not necessary; that the Mexican Government was under no obligation to communicate with him at all; that the authorities had decided to allow me to leave in this manner out of regard for Mr. Summerlin, whom they held in the highest personal esteem, etc., etc. The position of the Obregon Government with regard to Article 33 was made very clear. Mr. Summerlin replied that the only alternative was for the Mexican Government to expel me forcibly from the country whereupon Mr. Pani formally notified Mr. Summerlin that, under the instructions from the President, the provisions of Article 33 of the Constitution were applied to me because of my activities in connection with the American Association of Mexico.

On Sunday morning, November 27th, Mr. Summerlin communicated in writing to Mr. Pani his version of the above conversation and advised him that I would leave that night for Laredo, if agreeable to the Mexican Government. He also requested a Safe Conduct. The Chief of the Protocol delivered the Safe Conduct the same evening. . . .

All that was in the public record. Father's private files also reveal:

A telegram sent in code from W.F.B. in Mexico City, November 24, 1921 to a friend in New York, Mr. Furman, for delivery to his youngest brother Edmund Buckley:

Following to Edmund from W. F. B. Order issued my arrest. Do not know whether charge activities American Association or complicity revolution. In any case think intention eject me from country.

Am in American Embassy entirely safe and happy. American Charge will ascertain exact charges tomorrow Friday. He will undoubtedly keep State Department advised. You can probably get details there. STOP Am in no danger. Do not come here but suggest Edmund go to Washington and stay there. Please advise Fall (Secretary Interior) Hudson (Paul) Smith (Sidney) and Streeter. STOP Do not advise sister [Priscilla] unless it appears in papers or she hears otherwise. STOP. If charge is activities American Association I will resist on ground American Government does not recognize right Mexican Government expel American citizen for such activities. Also will insist on written order of expulsion. Ask Fall (Secretary Interior) see Secretary of State and insist on these two points in communication to American Charge here. STOP

A telegram to his wife who, with her five-week old baby, was staying with his mother in Austin, Texas the following day, November 25, 1921 in the midst of the negotiations:

> Important business has kept me from going Tampico. Will be several days longer. Love. Will.

But all this was nothing to the way he told it himself, one night in the pine room in Camden, over 36 years later. It was a cold January night and the fatwood fire was blazing away. Mother, Aloise and Priscilla were there. The "girls" (as they still were, and always would be in Father's eyes) had bought a tape recorder that afternoon and had been playing around with it when Father, sitting back in his worn green leather chair, started to tell the story. His voice was a little softer that night and he spoke more slowly. Since his illness, he sometimes had difficulty in finding the exact word he wanted; he rambled a little more. His pince-nez had been replaced by horn-rimmed glasses, but the thicker lenses in them only magnified the mischief and humor in those distinctive azure eyes. He said:

"It was in the Mexico City Bank that I got word the police were looking for me. Two or three fellows, old friends of mine, came in and said: 'They are looking for Buckley and they are going to grab him.' . . . The police went to the American Club and said they wanted Buckley. Van Trease went down and said—'Mr. Buckley isn't here.'—'Is that so,' said the police. 'Come right along.' One grabbed him by one arm, and one by the other. Like van Trease, I had a long nose and was very slim in those days.

"They took van Trease. Van Trease said later: 'I know every dog in Mexico City, but I walked block after block and I never saw a soul I knew that day.'

"They held him in jail for four or five hours.

"There was an article in the newspaper about 'Mr. Bulray,' (they knew perfectly well that wasn't the right name). It said, 'There's an order out for his arrest. He is involved in a revolution in Sonora—that's near Lower California. He will be captured and shot before daybreak."

Was he involved?

"You bet I was. . . . That night Berthier [Emile Berthier, Mother's uncle] took me to the house of Mrs. Bailey. She was married to an Englishman. She began hiding me all over the house and deciding that nothing was good enough. So finally, she opened the window and said 'You stand out on the ledge there." I said, 'Well look here I'd rather be captured than stand out there.'

"The funniest thing happened. All of a sudden about 150 soldiers came up and began marching around the house and shooting their rifles. I thought they were after me. There had been a big shooting scrap in a saloon the night before and they came on account of that. It had nothing to do with me. I lost about eight pounds of weight.

"Next day I called up Berthier. He came and got me and put me in the Bank. I stayed there three or four days. I left in a limousine and went to the American Embassy and stayed there three or four days. There was never any one so sad to see me as Summerlin, the Charge.

"I wanted to know whether the Department of Foreign Affairs had any evidence that I was connected with the revolution. I got a Spanish lawyer, related to de Molinas.

"I said, 'I want you to go to the Foreign Department and find out everything you can.' He came back that evening with all of their files on me. They had ordered me arrested in Vera Cruz three months before. But they had no evidence of my being implicated in the revolution—I was implicated up to my nose—so I wrote an article in the paper the next morning in which I dared them to prove anything. Declared my innocence of this false charge.

"I wrote a letter to the State Department saying that they were going to expel me for my activities with the American Association. I said [to the Mexicans], 'I'll get out of the Embassy and you can

arrest me because I want a clean record.' I don't recognize the right
of the Mexican Government to expel any foreigner without a trial.

"I was very wrong about that. They can expel by executive decree, Article 33, any 'pernicious' foreigner. I said, 'The only thing
I've done is to be president of the American Association which has
given evidence against Obregon to the Fall Committee.' So they
wrote back and said they expelled me because of my evidence to
the Fall Committee. Which was a marvelous thing to [be able to]
show the State Department.

"I went to San Luis Potosi with a friend [S. D. Lester, his secre-
tary]. A guard went the rest of the way. Every time the train stopped the guard would get out on the steps to 'save me from the multitudes.' The papers published reports that multitudes gathered
every time the train stopped, but fortunately these patriotic Mexican guards saved me.

"Not a word of truth in it—I must say, I didn't go out of the
car."

And he smiled, at himself for not having gotten off the train, at
the thought of all the commotion he had caused those many years
ago; he smiled, in retrospect, at the discomfiture of his old friend
van Trease, at the consternation of George Summerlin when he had
walked in the Embassy door, at the whole foolish wonderful affair.

Some one rang for Anderssen, his nurse, who helped him to his
feet, and with a good night kiss all around, he went up to bed. To
his room in the Southern home he loved so well where he could
look out over the camellia and azalea garden he himself had planned; which he had planted, changed, manicured and nurtured for
twenty years until it almost pleased him. To sleep one night more
in an atmosphere of settled elegance and beauty, as removed from
the turbulent Mexican existence he once had lived, as black is from
white. Only such a man as he could have lived happily and fruit-
fully in both those worlds.

Kamschatka, Camden, South Carolina

PART THREE

New York

Douglas Reed

George S. Montgomery, Jr.

C. Dean Reasoner

John W. Buckley

Benjamin W. Heath

I. *Odyssey of an Oil Man*

By DOUGLAS REED

> "*If oil one day should give way, among the require-
> ments of man, to something else that comes out of the
> ground, the big operators when they arrive on the
> scene will find the name of Buckley, or of one of the
> companies he organized on the claim-stakes already
> planted, and Catawba will be pegging claims some-
> where else, outside the range of that moment's interest.
> That will happen if W.F.B.'s philosophy is continued.*"

WILLIAM FRANK BUCKLEY was a latterday pioneer who never
believed that frontiers will ever cease to move for free men; he
always saw new oilfields beyond the next horizon and moved on,
ahead of the crowd.

He was often thought wrong by those he left behind and they
frequently found he was right when they caught up with him.
When the process became like financial tightrope walking, which
was not seldom, they accounted him a man who had once had a
lucky strike and was pressing his luck too hard. Sometimes the old-
timers reckoned he was washed up; later, when they studied the
stock quotations of another new Buckley company, they had to
reckon again. As I write this (1956)[1] the net worth of the companies
under Buckley's guidance is around $110,000,000, having risen to
that from $25,000,000 in the ten post-war years, and the Buckley
group is ensconced in the oil situations of Venezuela, Canada,
Florida, the Philippines, Israel, Australia, and Guatemala.

[1] The article was revised after W.F.B.'s death.—Ed.

This was system, not just episodic speculation. At the root was a tenacious philosophy of independence. W.F.B. was often called (by himself and by others) a gambler, but the strong conviction was basic. He was primarily resolved to prove and practise his philosophy, which he wore like a panache, and then to make money.

This innate passion for independence of thought and action was the product of his pioneer stock and native clime. Will Buckley cannot be pictured, at twenty, working for someone else; at three score and ten he was still, above all, an independent oilman in a world of oil Titans, whom he held in no awe.

He upheld this banner through fifty years against the general trend of government (home and foreign), dictators on confiscation bent, punitive taxation, discriminatory laws, and the timid giants (as he saw them) of the industry. As he went along, his accumulating experience taught him how to turn his philosophy to practical profit despite the Ogs, Gogs and Magogs of oildom, officialdom and bumbledom.

To most young Texans fifty years ago the word "oil" was as glamorous as "space" is to youth today. Texas was not large enough for all its would-be oilmen and this young man went South to Mexico, where room and a looming oil boom beckoned. W.F.B., who grew up just north of the border, left the University of Texas with a legal degree and founded in Mexico City, with his brother Claude, what quickly became a leading foreign law firm.

That was his doorway to oil, for the major companies needed abundant legal help in those days of predatory politicos and revolutionary generals. Buckley & Buckley soon represented several big companies and in 1911 opened a branch office in Tampico, the center of the oil industry and of the series of revolutionary wars which ultimately brought about the confiscation of the oilfields.

Buckley played an active (and still untold) part in those years of commotion. He impartially incurred enmity and respect among the various parties to them, who impartially recognized his international stature at the age of thirty. When Argentina, Brazil and Chile offered to mediate between the United States and Mexico after the American occupation of Vera Cruz in 1914, the Mexican Government appointed Buckley counsel to its delegation at the ensuing "A.B.C." Conference at Niagara Falls; afterwards W.F.B. became William Jennings Bryan's closest adviser on Mexican affairs as long as Bryan remained Woodrow Wilson's Secretary of State.

The trend of high policy, even then, was towards compromise or oil might have lost Buckley to statesmanship, for he was hewn from the timber of Pitt and Burke, Hamilton and Calhoun. He inflexibly opposed confiscation in any guise, wolverine or woolly, and has never concealed his poor opinion of the policies, both of the Woodrow Wilson government and of the big oil companies, which he thought timorous and flabby. Under Secretary of State Buckley (if imagination be allowed the flight) there would have been no truck with or knuckling down to discriminatory or confiscatory laws or taxes anywhere. Hence W.F.B.'s future lay in oil.

When the revolutions ended W.F.B. had given up the practice of law (he was not the man long to represent any but William Buckley) and gone into the oil business for himself, founding the Pantepec Oil Company of Mexico, the stem from which today's far-flung group of Buckley companies indirectly derives. He chose a difficult time to set out as an independent operator, for the opposing generals in the successive revolutions shared one aim: they wanted the oilfields.

During those wild years he contrived to have some profitable fun, in a spirit of unsubduable independence. The oil companies once dredged the Panuco River upstream to Tampico. There was a muddy island in the Panuco River bordering the City of Tampico with a narrow channel between the river and the city. Buckley connected the island with Tampico, building a wide and firm passage, contracted for part of the silt being dredged from the river to raise the island some two yards higher, developed it and sold it as real estate.

Then a real estate development built in Tampico by Buckley was invaded by squatters. Buckley convinced the authorities that the neighborhood sportsmen sorely needed a rifle range on his property for practising their marksmanship and the squatters retired, persuaded of the basic human right which they had challenged.

W.F.B.'s early experience as a negotiator (none has ever denied that he was a formidable one) thus was gained in a tough school, not limited to oil. His annals record a belated realty venture after World War I, when he arranged to finance the purchase of the

Galapagos Islands, an equatorial group of little interest to any after Darwin, from their owner government, for resale to the United States as a navel base. The deal, which carried a profit of millions, was all set when it was sunk by the postwar wave of anti-militarism, then at its crest.

Buckley's talents as a real estate man were obviously of rare order, but these ventures were essentially sidesteps for his destiny had obviously decided that he should become an oilman, though not in Mexico. He backed the wrong general in the closing revolutionary phase and, after leading American opposition in Mexico to the recognition of General Alvaro Obregon, was expelled as a "pernicious foreigner" in 1921 when Obregon received Washington's recognizing nod.

He had another last laugh in 1924 when President Calles invited him to return (after W.F.B. had told the *New York Times* he agreed with Calles' published opinion that the oil companies had pursued a hypocritical policy, professing friendship to the Mexican Government in Mexico City and advocating armed intervention in Washington).

Buckley acknowledged the courtesy by returning to Mexico but his experience had taught him that it was not the place for an independent oilman and for some years his scouts had been quietly surveying the ground in Venezuela. He transferred to that country in 1924, and Pantepec became the Pantepec Oil Company of Venezuela.

This move, which committed him finally to oil, was the second stage in the Buckley odyssey, which some orthodox operators at all its stages regarded as the Buckley oddity, unaccountably favored by fortune. The glamorous aura of a man of mystery accompanied him from Mexico into Venezuela and the stern eye of that day's dictator, General Juan Vicente Gomez, at once fell on him. Gomez consulted his Secret Police Chief about the lone ranger from Texas and lonely stranger from Tampico and received the advice (this is authentic), "Buckley is too big a man to trifle with; either throw him out of the country or make a deal with him."

In the ensuing negotiations Gomez tried to make the deal a hard one. His responsible Minister consented to grant concessions against an agreed payment and then was directed by Gomez to demand a much higher sum. W.F.B. told the Minister, as between hidalgos, that he insisted on the terms agreed and expected the Government, as he would expect a private person, to honor its given word. His knowledge of the language and character was effective; Gomez yielded and thenceforth treated W.F.B. as *muy simpatico*.

To the now-it-can-be-told chapter of that period belongs the story of another Minister who showed himself actively anti-Buckley. An article depicting Gomez as an ignorant man and the anti-Buckley Minister as the true brain of his Cabinet appeared in a New York Spanish-language newspaper. Friends of Gomez told him that the writer behind the pseudonym could only be Señor X, the anti-Buckley Minister, who then was dismissed and exiled. In fact the author, though eloquent in Spanish, was not that Minister.

W.F.B.'s Venezuelan venture grew naturally out of his Mexican experience, as his original move into Mexico had grown out of his youthful environment in Texas. He had learned in Mexico what it took to be an independent oilman. You needed, first and foremost, to be an early comer in an area of new interest; after that, the requisites were geologically promising concessions, good titles to them, dependable oil laws, and political stability. In the oil business, he already knew, these loved ones seldom are to be found at one place and time all together.

He had valuable intangible assets: full command of the language, deep understanding of the Latin American character and methods, and a specialist's knowledge, gained in Mexico, of concession practice, oil laws and title (in oil exploration title is of paramount importance).

Beyond that, he had vision. Today, Venezuela is so rich (chiefly through oil) that its diplomats' entertainments in the world's capitals are renowned for their splendor and their gushers of champagne. Thirty years ago, when interest in Venezuelan oil was only beginning, very few foresaw this rising future.

W.F.B. either calculated rightly or was lucky. At the time he seemed to be wrong or unlucky, for twice seven lean years followed, during which he became known (he recalls) as "Dry Hole Bill," and much money went down the drill-stems. He held concessions of more than 3,000,000 acres, strategically distributed over the most promising geological areas, but his invisible assets were not supported by much visible cash and the overheads and undergrounds of the oil business are heavy.

In oil exploration, a new company may go to the public for money once, or possibly twice, on a wave of enthusiasm for a new area, but thereafter John Doakes, as a source of finance, also becomes a dry hole and the independent usually has to fade out or sell out. This was particularly the case during the thirties, and Buckley's achievement in keeping Pantepec together and raising funds for rentals and exploration during fourteen years still commands the surprised admiration of old-timers.

It was done through a series of deals in which great tenacity and resourcefulness were shown, especially in negotiations with the major companies. Giants by nature move slowly and W.F.B. sometimes found ways to prod them into action which, he held, they ought in their own interest to take. Some dragging parleys between him and Company A once reached sudden agreement when W.F.B. received a private cable from a friend urging him not to close because Company B was eager to deal. Its contents evidently became known to Company A and W.F.B. later gravely commented on the alertness of that company's intelligence service.

A serene self-confidence that nothing ruffled was either native to him or was acquired in the years of matching wits with protagonists of a stature ranging from bandits and squatters to attorneys, revolutionary generalissimos, great oil companies, cold-eyed bankers and governments. Without the gift of imperturbability (he was never known to lose a night's sleep through the oil business) he might not have weathered those years. The most immoderate language ever heard from him came on a recent occasion when, contrary to his expectations, a New York arbitrator awarded against Pantepec in a dispute involving over $3,000,000; "I have never been so put out," he said severely.

The unclouded surface of this sangfroid reflected no change in moments of triumph or of disaster. On the eve of the 1929 depression he obtained $2,500,000 to carry on work on Pantepec's concessions from a French financier, Marcovici. The crash followed and Marcovici's wife appealed to W.F.B. to turn the money back, whereon he destroyed the check. At that moment Pantepec was almost out of funds and his own resources consisted principally of Pantepec stock.

When the big payoff came at last, about twenty-five years after Buckley's first Mexican venture into oil, luck was undeniably with him, for no calculation could have ensured that it would come in the nick of time. But for that lucky strike the restrictions of war-time would have left his Venezuelan concessions in suspense for many years, if he could have held on to them for so long. He made his first major deal with Standard just in time for a big oilfield to be found on Pantepec's Venezuelan concessions on the eve of World War II.

Under this farm-out agreement, Standard's Venezuelan sub-sidiary, Creole Petroleum, began to explore and develop part of the Pantepec properties and the first discovery was followed by a second a little later.

Buckley has often been called the inventor of the farm-out sys-tem, which today is widely used in the oil business. If his sole origination of it cannot be established, he was certainly one of the originators and most successful practitioners.

The farm-out is in effect a sub-lease; the sub-lessee accounts the prospects good enough to take over the cost of exploring, drilling and developing and to pay the lessee an agreed share of the profits from oil or gas produced. It also somewhat resembles share-cropping in reverse, the wealthier partner deeming it worth his while to do the work and share the yield, in cash or kind. This was the basis of all Buckley's subsequent ventures. The concept is simple; its execution, like figure-skating, is also simple if you can do it.

All depends on the foresight of the pioneer, who has to implant himself at an early age in an area which later becomes attractive to the great operators. He has to sally forth into unknown territory, make sure that he gets the right land, and then convince the in-dustry of its underlying values. To that end he has to find the money for the initial expedition, for the rental of concessions, for the geological survey, and for enough drilling to keep the permits alive until the evidence is produced, if it is there.

The Creole-Pantepec discoveries at length justified the method. Production went on through the war, from which Pantepec thus emerged with a half-share in two producing oilfields, and then the big new deals began at once, for interest in Venezuela was mush-rooming. The Atlantic Refining Company took a half-interest in Pantepec's remaining concessions and soon found two more fields; the C.F.P. (Compagnie Française des Petroles) agreed to purchase

Pantepec's remaining concessions and soon found two more fields; on the drilling of a stipulated number of wells, for an option to purchase a half-interest in Pantepec-Creole's shared properties.

The portents were good. Peace had broken out, oil was coming up, money was coming in. After thirty years Buckley was able to give full rein to his ideas at last, and he went all out. At that point his basic philosophy put out two new guiding principles, which grew as naturally from his lengthening experience as the original method of pioneer claim-staking in a new area from his initial essay in Mexico.

The first was that the policy of all-eggs-in-one-basket was unsound in the case of a naturally depleting resource and in a time of ever-changing oil and tax laws and labor costs, which could quickly convert a good situation into a precarious one. Sound strategy lay in diversification and expansion (some resemblance might be traced between this idea and Bismarck's policy of reinsurance in the field of foreign relations).

The second new principle was that, in an age of punitive taxation of income, the stockholder's interest, whether he realized it or not, lay in capital appreciation rather than in dividends. W.F.B., as was to be expected, believed he knew what was best for stockholders; to him it seemed obvious that the stockholder should prefer a capital-gain run for his money to sitting waiting for dividends, ever more heavily taxed, from the same source, ever depleting.

He set out at once to put his philosophy, as thus developed, into practice and at his first diversive venture ran at once into strong stockholder resistance. At that time Florida was a center of great interest and Buckley, early on the scene, had obtained for Pantepec a large spread of offshore leases there, thus ensuring that the major companies would find him strongly entrenched when, if history repeated itself, they decided to get busy in Florida. At the same time he was quietly sizing up the field in Canada.

A large group of Pantepec stockholders opposed this foray into Florida. They wanted to realize on Pantepec profits through dividends and objected to the use of its funds for new ventures. That seemed fair enough at the time (though events soon proved them wrong).

W.F.B. won handily the violent proxy fight that followed, and in victory then applied the judgment of Solomon. He split Pantepec in two companies: Pantepec, which kept its half-interest in the two producing fields and was committed to dividend-paying; and Pancoastal, which acquired the remaining Pantepec properties and the Florida leases and was dedicated to expansion. Pancoastal was safeguarded against future stockholder opposition in its ventures by being placed under a voting trust for ten years (it was lucky from the start, Atlantic discovering the two new fields on the Venezuelan properties received by it from Pantepec).

After this bifurcation Pantepec's experience soon showed that Buckley had correctly judged the future. The backwash of World War II (as of World War I) threw up various revolutionary movements and regimes, among them that of Romulo Betancourt in Venezuela, and in Buckley's experience the Mexican period began to repeat itself. Betancourt arbitrarily enacted a retroactive 50 per cent tax-on-profits law, on top of the 16 2/3ds royalty which the foreign oil companies had contracted to pay on their concessions, and equally arbitrarily increased oil workers' wages by 50 per cent.

These were heavy blows to a company dedicated to dividend-paying. After thirty years W.F.B. again found himself between a revolutionary regime, on the one hand, and, on the other, a home government and big oil companies which both had acquired the habit of capitulation. As on the earlier occasion in Mexico, he urged Washington and the major companies, respectively, to deny recognition to Betancourt and to refuse to deal with him under duress. Once again, both gave way and Buckley was left alone.

A leaf from W.F.B.'s notebooks records that on this occasion the State Department met his recommendation with the opinion of one of its leading South American experts, who advised that Betancourt could be trusted to respect the position of the oil companies and, if he were overthrown, would be succeeded by Communists, which would be disastrous. This expert, a Mr. Lawrence Duggan, was later named as a Communist agent by Elizabeth Bentley and Whittaker Chambers and met his death in a mysterious episode of defenestration.

In Venezuela W.F.B., left on the burning deck, urbanely took the issue to court on constitutional grounds. Betancourt was no

Gomez and was not amused. Moreover, when he was overthrown, the 50-50 tax lived after him.

Pantepec soon ran into the sea of troubles which Buckley, through long experience, had foreseen. It could not expand in Venezuela because no new concessions were granted after 1943 (this policy was only revised in 1955). Under the new tax-and-wages incubus dividends had to be passed and tax arrears mounted. A farm-out agreement with Clint Murchison, for the drilling of wells against a half-interest in the deeper zone of one property, promised relief; but it had to be cancelled when the Government after one unproductive well, forbade further deep drilling as wasteful of gas. Then Compagnie Francaise, charging default on the drilling obligation, began suit to recover its option money. Thereafter, the force of events soon impelled Pantepec to emerge from its isolation and join Pancoastal in diversification ventures.

While Pantepec's eggs-in-one-basket policy was addling, Buckley was serenely moving, through Pancoastal, into Canada, which became a new center of interest after 1947. At an early stage he acquired extensive permits, carefully chosen to give a commanding position in negotiation when competition became keen, in Alberta, Saskatchewan and British Columbia.

At about this time it became apparent that Buckley could best serve the interests of both companies, and of the new ones in prospect by forming in the United States a single organization which could provide each of them with the benefit both of his own experience and vision and of the services of the staff he had trained in his business philosophy. Thus was the Catawba Corporation founded.

Through Catawba, Buckley brought to the companies spun off from Pantepec and then Pancoastal a diversity and quality of talent, and an experience in intercontinental oil which was unique among independents, and which none of the newer companies could have afforded alone.

Under the guidance of Buckley and of Catawba's staff, diversification went on apace and on at least one occasion too fast. First, Pancoastal added to its Canadian and Florida properties a half-share, acquired through a Canadian subsidiary, in concessions of 1,600,000 acres held by the Manabi Exploration Company in Ecuador; another strategic position was secured against the day of rising interest.

In Canada itself the new venture promised to more than offset the difficult situation in Venezuela. A heavy oilfield was found in Saskatchewan and when its commercial development proved likely to be long and costly, Catawba negotiated the sale of these interests to General American for $4,300,000 for reinvestment in some other venture which promised stockholders a quicker return; Buckley traditionally never was satisfied with a slow payout and already had his eye on a more important play in British Columbia. Then the Smiley light oil field was found, and was thought to have huge reserves. At that point diversification ran into its own sea of troubles, which for a while seemed as formidable as those of Pantepec in Venezuela, though for a different reason.

Before that blow fell, Pancoastal had spun off its first two new companies. Apropos the process of spinning-off, stockholders who stayed with Buckley along the line, as one new company after another was spun off, and kept their stock through moments of misadventure, prospered exceedingly. Others who bought high just before some major setback lost heavily if they sold without waiting for the rescue operation.

The first spun-off company was Coastal Caribbean for the Florida leases, which Standard of California undertook to explore and develop on a long-term program against a half-interest. This company was a gift-wrapped package to Pancoastal's stockholders.

Next, Pancoastal set the Canadian venture on its own feet by assigning all its Canadian holdings, plus the Ecuadorean interest, to a company, Canada Southern Oils. The market was feeling so blithe about Canadian oil in general that Catawba was able to arrange a $10,000,000 convertible debenture financing for it. Then trouble loomed.

This was during the "false growth" (580 per cent) boom which is a familiar feature of the early period in a new area where public interest has far outrun actual development and factual proof. That phase of wild speculation began when the Leduc gusher blew in in 1947. It was followed by the equally familiar decline in oil stocks;

in the next five or six years most of the new independents failed or were swallowed up through lack of funds, mismanagement or ill-placed lands.

At that moment of general depreciation in Canadian oil shares, Buckley took a hard knock from a separate quarter. It was decided to split Canada Southern Oils into trifoliate companies, each standing on its own firm feet: Canada Southern Petroleum for the British Columbia properties, Canso Oil Producers for the Smiley light oil field in Saskatchewan, and Canso Natural Gas for the Saskatchewan and Alberta gas areas. Then the alarming discovery was made that one of the companies had no firm feet; the Smiley reserves had been grossly exaggerated by the engineers of Imerval Oil Co., the operator; in good faith to be sure, but in a published report.

Buckley was reminded once again on that rueful day never again to rely on estimates of reserves before they were fully proven. A dramatic fall in Canada Southern stock followed and at Catawba headquarters rehabilitation was set as the watchword for the next several years. The path of diversification for a while looked as rough as that of eggs-in-one-basket (in Venezuela, Pantepec was still battling the C.F.P. lawsuit and the back-taxes problem).

Nevertheless, at the end of the debacle W.F.B., wounded, criticized and with many enemies, was still in Canada, bloody but unbowed, still sure that his philosophy and method would be vindicated. Not only that but, as if nothing had happened, he was serenely seeking fresh oilfields and permits new. The Canadian and Venezuelan situations were overcast enough to have kept most men under cover. He was out in the Pacific and the Middle East, on his old quest bent.

He was negotiating in the Philippines (a venture later taken over by Pantepec and Pancoastal). For once he found all the desiderata present: an area of new interest, a friendly people and government, political stability, equitable oil and tax laws, reasonable concession practice. When the concessions eventually were issued, after negotiations guided by Catawba, W.F.B. held another large spread of carefully chosen acreage, and in time one more new company was spun off, San Jose Petroleums.

Then Catawba appeared in Israel. In this case W.F.B. deviated from the principle of seeking politically-stable areas. The political uncertainty in those parts kept the major companies out of Israel; possibly his poor opinion of their nerve prompted W.F.B. to go in. Leases were acquired and two more companies were added to the Buckley group. Pantepec received stock in these companies in return for doing their drilling at cost and passed on the stock (then worth about $1,500,000) to its stockholders. The Buckley luck held; within the year oil was found nearby, though not on the Buckley permits and the two companies' stock for a time appreciated 300 per cent. To date, no oil has been found on the properties.

If the name Buckley is not written on any oil leases in Africa, the venture in Israel is the reason; Catawba made a bid for concessions in Libya but this was refused when the Libyan authorities learned of its activities in Israel. Somewhere along the line of these years concessions were obtained or were under negotiation in Australia, Italy, Greece and Guatemala, and a producing field in Wyoming was picked up.

The difficult situations in Canada and Venezuela remained, and in time the basic Buckley philosophy promised to vindicate itself again there. In Canada, W.F.B.'s counsel, or policy, in the depreciation days was to hold on to the properties, period. By 1956 general confidence in Canadian oil and gas was recovering and the acreage came into the middle of the competitive picture; Catawba, which had earlier negotiated a farm-out of part of the British Columbia acreage to Pacific Petroleum, then concluded what it believed to be potentially the biggest deal in Buckley history.

This was the agreement whereby Phillips Petroleum took over the exploration and development of the remaining Canada Southern properties on a profit-sharing basis. The company's shares began to recover from their nadir of 1954 and rose steadily, though due to collapse again in 1957 with the general depression. The management group holds this to reflect the general opinion of an agreement whereunder Canada Southern, without further expenditure, is guaranteed a minimum of 50 percent of profits from properties where large gas reserves, this time, have been definitely established.

At that very moment of vindication Buckley learned of the arbitrator's finding that Pantepac in Venezuela must repay the C.F.P. its $3,000,000 option money, and made the unbridled comment above recorded. Almost at once, however, came news of a big discovery in Venezuela, directly offsetting one on Pancoastal's properties there, and Pancoastal shares also began to rise. Then Pantepec's name, too, began to appear in the "most active stocks" list; in the whispering world of oil word seemed to have gotten around that Buckley was up to something that boded good for the original company.

In 1956, when he looked back on the ten years that began with the Pantepec-Pancoastal split and the first ventures into new lands, Buckley saw ten oil and gas producing fields where there had been two, and eight listed companies, holding several million acres in six countries, in place of that original one. He also saw his life's experience and philosophy embodied in the staff he assembled in Catawba headquarters in New York. During the past eight years he had remitted more and more responsibility to it, in a process of gradual transition, and thus ensured a smooth continuity whenever he let go.

Catawba is both advisory group and service corporation, but was first and foremost, under W.F.B., the planner of strategy. Its strength continues to be in the associations built on Buckley's experience, the multi-linguality of its principal officers and its intelligence staff. It aims to anticipate, rather than to keep abreast of worldwide petroleum developments through its agents and associates in many countries.

It represents only companies in which its officers and stockholders hold strong stock positions (at this writing, these are the various companies founded or acquired by Buckley himself). Its primary function is to give the companies guidance at the high policy levels in matters financial, corporate and exploratory; and to provide them with the necessary liaison with American groups and agencies in effecting such policies.

It believes that its location in New York, its contacts with the financial world and the wealth of experience deriving from W.F.B.'s now completed odyssey put it in a strong position to discover likely new ventures which it can either pursue independently or make available to the associated companies. As an example of this it cites the current Philippine venture; it was devised and launched by Catawba but the stock is primarily held by the original Pantepec and its first offshoot, Pancoastal.

Each of the companies is a separate corporate entity with its own operating staff and a largely independent stock ownership, but all of them are guided by this group of men in vital decisions on policy, the conduct of major negotiations, and the undertaking of commitments. Catawba believes that this makes available to all the companies experience and contacts which none could separately amass.

It is Catawba's task and responsibility to be at all times knowledgeable of the special problems and capacities of each of its client companies; and it often happens that this intimate knowledge redounds to the mutual benefit of these clients, as one company's needs may be another's opportunity. W.F.B. used to cite the arrangement by which Pantepec was able to earn a stock interest in the two Israel companies, through performing their drilling at cost, as an example of the mutually-beneficial contrivances which a central intelligence can devise. (In that case, again, the regular international drilling contractors were reluctant to enter the field because of the Arab-Israel conflict.)

W.F.B. from the days in Mexico was used to being shot at (literally, at that period) and so firmly believed he knew what was best for the companies that he was never intimidated by the crossfire of stockholder-complaint, which the existence of this single management group sometimes drew.

In each of the companies stockholders occasionally arise who, peering through the ramifications, cry that the other companies are being favored at the expense of the one which carries their money. It seems part of human nature, W.F.B. saw, to forget past capital appreciation and to pine for present dividends. Since the time of the Pantepec reorganization, however, it has been his position that he has an implicit mandate to reinvest earnings realized by the companies in new situations for the benefit of stockholders, who receive a direct participation in these ventures through the recurrent spin-offs and stock-distributions.

The men associated with Catawba are dedicated to the Buckley philosophy and method, believing that the visible benefits have fully justified the unorthodox approach they have entailed. They admit to having made mistakes and the big one in Canada is obvious, but they think this one in time will more than pay its cost in a lesson learned and applied. The other setbacks have been normal business ones such as pursuing diversification into too many small but costly ventures, or sidestepping into collateral activities (such as asphalt supply, in Ecuador) which lay outside the natural Buckley expertise.

In future Catawba proposes to advise adherence to the classic Buckley pattern which has stood the test: the discovery of areas of new interest and the acquisition there, early and on good terms, of large spreads of acreage against the time of keen competition.

The group in the control tower comprises two elders who accompanied W.F.B. in his odyssey for more than a quarter-century and four juniors who trained with W.F.B. during the last decade.

W.F.B.'s closest associate was George S. Montgomery, Jr. Only a complete individualist, probably, could have worked in such in-timate association with that other notable individualist, William F. Buckley, for over thirty years. This may have been the secret of their mutual and fruitful understanding. Being twins in this basic tenet of their *Weltanschauung* they were able to differ widely on any question without damage to their relationship, and they com-plemented and supplemented each other perfectly.

Montgomery, who was a naval aviator in World War I, has been a partner in the New York law firm of Coudert Brothers for many years and is a director of the Schlumberger Corporation. He is an expert in international law and down the years no major decision has ever been taken without his full participation.

The same goes for the third senior triumvir, Joseph H. Himes, who was associated with W.F.B. as a large stockholder in all his ventures since 1929. He is the other elder statesman of the group, whose consultation and concurrence in major matters is manda-tory. The name of Buckley, the founder, inevitably attaches to today's large group of companies, but its growth is the joint work of these three men, governed by the original Buckley idea, and their names are inseparable from the story.

Himes, a onetime cinder pitman in a Pittsburgh steel mill who rose to executive rank and served a term as an Ohio Congressman, has an exceptional grasp of business and finance, in and outside of the United States, and far-reaching connections in financial and political circles through his partnership, presidency or directorship in many big corporations (the New York brokerage firm of Mer-rill Lynch, Pierce, Fenner and Beane; the Himes Company; Mid-Century Limited of America; Acacia Mutual Life Insurance of

Washington; Canadair of Montreal; Electric Boat Company of New York, etc.).

After these comes the second echelon, the young men from the wars returning who came in and came on during the decade that saw the parent Pantepec put out its many branches. Dean Reasoner, a senior partner in the Washington law firm of Reasoner and Davis, joined the management group as general counsel at its birth ten years ago and developed a specialized talent for translating legal practice into practical oil transactions. He was a principal negotiator in all the big deals made by Catawba for its associated companies, including the big Phillips agreement. Reasoner, an Iowan from Oscaloosa, was a World War II naval officer.

John W. Buckley, W.F.B.'s eldest son, after army service in North Africa and France began to absorb the parental philosophy in the land department of the first diversification company, Coastal Caribbean in Florida. Then he spent two years in Venezuela, where he worked primarily in liaison with Creole, C.F.P., and Atlantic, and gained an early insight into the minds and methods of the big operators.

As president of Catawba he has had much opportunity to apply the experience gained in Florida and Venezuela during major negotiations. With the elders of the group and Dean Reasoner he put through all the most important transactions of 1950-1956, including the $10,000,000 financing of Canada Southern Oils through Gairdner and Company in 1956 and the Phillips agreement of 1957.

There are no rigid apportionments of responsibility in the Catawba hierarchy, which is built on consultation between the group's members with proper regard for experience and seniority, but John Buckley's particular purview, within those limits, comprises the two Venezuelan companies (he speaks Spanish almost as fluently as his father and even better French), Manabi in Ecuador, and the three Canadian companies.

Benjamin W. Heath, in charge of Catawba's public relations, came out of the Air Force to join the group, starting in 1946 as manager of Coastal Caribbean. He has been an officer or director of many of the companies, but has given the bulk of his energies to the Florida and Israel situations.

James L. Buckley, the youngest member of the group, saw much combat service in the Pacific as a naval officer and then practised law for three years with the New Haven firm of Wiggin and Dana, after graduation from Yale Law School in 1949. He joined Catawba in 1953 and today has a voice in all the strategic decisions. He specializes in the legal aspects of the acquisition of foreign concessions and was responsible for securing the Philippine concessions on good terms. His lengthening experience of concession negotiation has also taken him to Libya, Israel, Guatemala and Italy. He has devoted himself particularly to the Philippine venture and, with Ben Heath, to the Israel companies.

W.F.B. let go active personal guidance of his companies at a rate that corresponded almost exactly with the years he had left to live and when the last day came, he had only just before fully effected the transfer of responsibility. The last years he divided his time between his old Northern home in Connecticut and his old Southern one in South Carolina, looking back on nearly fifty years of romantic privateering in the seas of oil. He raised a family of companies nearly as numerous as his own family of children (ten) and in the new generation both families grew rapidly, through spin-offs and grandchildren.

As far as man can provide for the future, he did by creating an organization to carry on in his spirit the venturing which he began and he allowed it to take over, under his watchful eye, so that there should be no jolts or jars when he relaxed control of it. It has not a cast-iron constitution or rigid frame, for that would be the denial of his original concept. He built up a group of men who accept his basic philosophy and the practical method of applying it which he evolved in an odyssey that took him through the gales of two wars and two revolutions.

He never compromised on the principle with which he set out fifty years ago, independence of thought and act, and had small patience with much that went on in the increasingly penned and herded world about him. He stood against that tide when he first met it and always thereafter, believing it contrary to human needs —in the oil business as in all human affairs.

He meant to make money, and succeeded, and looked on money as a fructifying agent, not as an end. To him it was the raw material of new ventures, proving an original philosophy.

He came a long way from San Diego, Texas. If oil one day

should give way, among the requirements of man, to something else that comes out of the ground, the big operators when they arrive on the scene will find the name of Buckley or of one of the companies he organized on the claim-stakes already planted, and Catawba will be pegging claims somewhere else, outside the range of that moment's interest. That will happen if his philosophy is continued.

II. *Post-Mexico:*
The Business History

By GEORGE S. MONTGOMERY, JR.

" '*How many shares will you command at the next meeting,*' *W.F.B. asked the man who liked to think of himself as the Terror of Wall Street, which in point of fact he had frequently tyrannized.* '*An absolute majority,*' *he answered—hoping to bring Buckley to his knees.* '*That,*' *W.F.B. answered,* '*is exactly what you will need*'*—which was W.F.B.'s quiet way of saying,* '*You, sir, can go to hell.*' "

O N A SUNDAY AFTERNOON in April, 1927, I entered an office build-ing on Park Avenue at 46th Street, signed my name on the admission-sheet and was taken to the sixth floor by the attending elevator operator. As I ascended, I did not realize that this after-noon meeting was to channel my life, not merely in the professional field of law but in practically every area of life, to an extent com-parable to that of the Great Divide.

This was the occasion of my first meeting with William Frank Buckley. I was in my fourth year of the practice of law in New York City following my graduation from law school.

W.F.B. at that time was engaged in the second step of a carefully planned project involving the building of an oil empire.

The first step had been completed in Venezuela, where he had gone after his expulsion from Mexico in 1921. An account of the first Venezuelan phase of W.F.B.'s activities illustrates his broad understanding of human nature and the Latin American temperament.

The results of W.F.B.'s activities in Venezuela are vividly seen by looking at a map of the country on which are delineated the oil and gas concessions he obtained. When he arrived in Venezuela, the oil industry was in its infancy. Eastern Venezuela was virtually un-explored—a jungle.

I have often heard W.F.B. generalize that the majority of the people in the oil business have no curiosity about unexplored areas. For this type of man, he said, there is no oil anywhere until some-one brings it to the surface. His rejection of this proposition moved him to go into unexplored territory, using all available geological and geophysical information for locating drilling sites.

On arriving in Venezuela, W.F.B. traveled extensively through eastern Venezuela where, at the time, the presence of oil was merely a geological speculation. Not a well had been drilled. With the advice of his geologists (Henry Hinds, in particular) he selected, on a checker-board basis, a large number of widely sepa-rated concessions. The idea was to own property near wherever oil was discovered in eastern Venezuela.

Contrary to the practice of visiting foreigners, W.F.B. did not immediately on his arrival, seek out an interview with the omnip-otent President Gomez. He went, instead, about his business traveling about the country appraising the merits of the land. So unusual was his conduct that the President, out of curiosity to meet the renowned independent who had had so flamboyant a career in Mexico, sent W.F.B. an "invitation," "requesting" a visit from him. (Dictator Gomez' invitations were not often refused.) The first encounter between these two strong men occurred in 1924. A healthy relationship took hold, based on mutual respect that lasted until the President's death. It proved a considerable asset when W.F.B. put together his remarkable selection of concessions and throughout the many troublesome years when they stood endangered.

Having collected these extraordinarily well-located concessions, spread over the map of Venezuela, W.F.B. was ready to take the second step in his plan. He had taken on substantial financial obliga-tions to the Venezuelan Government in carrying charges and ex-ploration requirements on the concessions. He had now to raise the money to meet these obligations—to finance Pantepec Oil Company of Venezuela.[1]

In the early 1920's, New York was already the unquestioned financial center of America and was rapidly becoming the world financial center. But W.F.B. could not bear to live there any more than he had to. Already he had three children (with seven more on the way). He acquired a house in Sharon, Connecticut, which was to become the unforgettable "Great Elm," named after the largest elm tree in Connecticut, which rose majestically on the grounds, south of the main house. On the lovely main street of this beautiful New England town, Great Elm, consisting of about thirty acres, was transformed under W.F.B.'s direction not merely into a showplace, but into a home for a large American family with almost all the advantages of indoor and outdoor family life.

Initiating his contacts with the investment world, W.F.B. acquired associates who, as was typical of him, remained his life-long friends and partners. One of the earliest was Fergus Reid of Norfolk, Virginia. Mr. Reid was a very substantial, strong-minded individual with a sound financial background, of highest integrity and intellectual enthusiasm. I know of no occasion when, following a period of analysis and discussion, these two friends and associates ever differed on basic policies. Though Reid had no roots in Wall Street, his reputation as a power in the investment world, his numerous directorships in important corporations, made him an effective instrument in the search for capital. The association lasted until Mr. Reid's death when his son, Fergus Reid, Jr., succeeded to the position held by his father for so many years. W.F.B.'s fourth son was named after Fergus Reid.

Another friend and associate of the highest stature was Joseph H. Himes of Washington, D. C. From the time W.F.B. and Himes met in the middle twenties to the time of W.F.B.'s death in 1958, Mr. Himes was the tower of strength in all of the projects which Buckley undertook. A man of substantial wealth and influence, with numerous activities in the financial and political world, the contribution which Mr. Himes made to the success of Buckley's plans cannot be overestimated. Again, I know of no instance

---

[1] W.F.B. chose the name "Pantepec" for his operating companies in Venezuela after a little river in Mexico of the same name, in whose hospitable banks he once took shelter against revolutionists who were after him.

where these two great friends ever differed ultimately on any major problem.

Another associate who continued a close relationship with W.F.B. for many years was E. A. Pierce, then of the investment firm of Potter & Company. This firm was the first Wall Street house to engage in financing Mr. Buckley's projects. In 1926 an issue of common stock was distributed with good reception and many of the purchasers have retained their investment ever since, including all of the resulting stock distributions over a period of thirty years.

Mr. Pierce later became head of the firm of E. A. Pierce & Company. This firm, during the years following the stock crash of 1929, absorbed house after house with the result that it became the most important unit in the brokerage business in the country. The present name of this brokerage firm is Merrill Lynch, Pierce, Fenner & Smith.

Simultaneous with the financing of his projects, W.F.B. carried on negotiations with large oil companies with a view toward exploration and development on a partnership basis of the extensive concessions in Venezuela. On September 11, 1926, he entered into an agreement with Union Oil Company of California. This contract covered nearly one million acres of oil concessions. It required the Union Oil Company to expend a total of three and a half million dollars in exploration work on the concessions.

On March 2, 1927, a second contract was entered into with California Petroleum Company which covered approximately 757,000 acres of concessions in Venezuela on virtually the same terms as the Union Oil Company.

The odds against any wildcat well drill discovering oil is estimated at over fifty-to-one. W.F.B. did not affect the ratio: none of the wells drilled by either Company under their contracts turned up oil or gas.

This inauspicious start did not discourage him. During 1928 and 1929 he acted on the assumption of failure by Union and California, shoring up the financial structure of Pantepec by a loan from a bank in Paris in the sum of $1,000,000. At a time when the investment world was stock-conscious to the extent of speculative excess, this arrangement was an extraordinary achievement: it saved the stockholders from the extreme dilution of additional shares to which an ordinary manager would undoubtedly have resorted.

Additionally, W.F.B. arranged with the Union Oil Company to divert a part of the total amount due to be expended in wildcat drilling in Venezuela, to the purchase of properties in the United States. During the lean years that were to follow the stock market crash, Pantepec would have died, had it not been for those two acts of foresight by its founder.

During the early thirties, Pantepec found itself with an accumulated debt and tax obligation of over $2,000,000. Its stock was selling on the market at the nominal figure of 6¢ per share. The Wall Street world regarded W.F.B. as washed up.

During this period of agony, an incident indelibly painted for me the stalwartness of W.F.B. in the face of overwhelming odds and seemingly certain destruction. In the small office staff which W.F.B. maintained, there worked a boy of about twenty, who served in a variety of capacities, as messenger, telephone operator, receptionist and general handyman. One morning while I was seated with W.F.B., the boy, Robert, came into the office and diffidently informed W.F.B. of his mother's illness and his need of a raise. Knowing the desperate financial straits of W.F.B.'s affairs, I silently commiserated with Robert on the futility of his request. To my utter amazement, W.F.B. not only offered Robert's mother help with genuine sympathy and concern, which was predictable in him, but complied instantly with Robert's request, putting into immediate effect a raise higher even than what Robert had asked for.

How many burdens of this sort W.F.B. voluntarily took on without visible evidence of concern, I do not know. I do know that without his advice and assistance during the speculative days which found me as feverishly enmeshed as any other little speculator, I would have been completely submerged myself. And that goes for a great many other people.

By his courage and determination, before the thirties had gone by, W.F.B. had (a) completely funded and discharged an accumulated indebtedness, and (b) arranged a contract with a subsidiary of Standard Oil Company of New Jersey, which after extensive operations on the Venezuelan properties, ultimately resulted in the first discoveries of oil for the Pantepec organization.

The year 1935 actually marked the dividing point in W.F.B.'s business career. In this year he negotiated the all-important contract with Standard Oil of Venezuela. In order to make this contract operative, Pantepec had to discharge all of the accrued obligations affecting the concessions in Venezuela. While these accumulations were relatively modest in size, nevertheless, the job of raising funds to meet them was not simple. It was out of the question to obtain any sort of credit, and the stock of the Company was still selling at less than one dollar per share. However, W.F.B. succeeded in interesting a small group of investors by offering them attractive options over a period of time, in conjunction with the sale of a small block of stock. In this manner he avoided, in his usual skillful way, any substantial dilution of the stockholders' equity.

The operations under the so-called Standard contract were blessed with success from the beginning. The first well drilled under this contract gave a showing of gas in one of the East Venezuela concessions. This initial encouraging sign galvanized the speculating public, which took a renewed interest in Pantepec. With this interest came an additional threat of the welfare of the stockholders.

Pantepec was still in a precarious position due to its shortage of operating funds. One or more of the Wall Street operators, learning of this condition and sensing an opportunity for a lucrative stock market move, approached W.F.B. with proposals which, had he accepted them, would have virtually doubled the outstanding capital stock—with a trifling return to existing stockholders. W.F.B. rejected the proposals, whereupon the dealers shot back with a threat to take over control from him. They tried, and failed. I remember another crisis, when an arrogant Wall Street group assured W.F.B. that he would find himself out of power at the very next stockholders' meeting. "How many shares will you command at the next meeting?" W.F.B. asked the man who liked to think of himself as the Terror of Wall Street, which, in point of fact, he had frequently tryrannized. "An absolute majority" he said—hoping to bring Buckley to his knees by so conclusive a prediction. "That," W.F.B. answered, "is exactly what you will need."—which was W.F.B.'s quiet way of saying. "You, sir, can go to hell."

The loyalty of W.F.B.'s friends was evidenced in the battle that ensued. The stockholders' meeting came and went—and Buckley remained at the helm. The Wall Street operators abandoned their imperialistic blitzkriegs against Pantepec, which continued to prosper under the Buckley management.

In 1939 the first commercial oil well was struck on Pantepec property.

The next ten years represented a steady process of development in two important fields in Venezuela. These fields were developed jointly with the subsidiary of Standard Oil Company of New Jersey under the 1935 agreement. Pantepec was able to finance its operations initially through bank loans with the Chase National Bank and The Empire Trust Company. The Company became self-sustaining and began payments of cash dividends in the middle forties.

In 1944, W.F.B. succeeded in placing a large area of concessions not covered by the agreement of 1935 under an operating arrangement with the Atlantic Refining Company. The agreement provided for drilling operations by Atlantic in consideration of a fifty per cent undivided interest in the concessions.

In 1946, W.F.B. projected Pantepec into its first venture outside Venezuela. The venture involved oil and gas leases in the State of Florida of over four million acres, consisting principally of offshore concessions and concessions on lakes and rivers. A pattern on a map of Florida reveals how precisely W.F.B. stuck by his preference for a systematic diffusion of acreage. The Pantepec holdings extended throughout the State in such a way as almost to guarantee to Pantepec stockholders an interest in any important discovery in the State.

By 1946 W.F.B. had also arranged a sales and option agreement with Compagnie Française des Petroles under which the latter Company agreed to supply several million dollars' worth of capital for drilling on Pantepec properties, and to purchase Pantepec's production, obtaining an option to acquire one-half interest in Pantepec properties for a large cash consideration. This was an excellent arrangement for Pantepec based on conditions as they were understood in 1946. However, owing to a miscalculation as to the oil resources in one of the fields, the drilling program provided for in the contract could not be carried out. Compagnie Francaise sued and won an outrageously large judgment against Pantepec.

In 1948, as a result of a number of developments and diverse

points of view of large stockholders, W.F.B. decided to divide
Pantepec into two different companies. The producing properties,
operated under the New Jersey agreement, were held by Pantepec;
all other properties, including those held under the Atlantic agreement and the Florida properties, were placed under the new
Company, called Pancoastal Oil Company. Every stockholder of
Pantepec was given two shares of Pancoastal.

Shortly after the spinoff, The Atlantic Refining Company en-
countered some important discoveries on jointly-owned properties
with the result that interest in Pancoastal developed to the point
of rivalling Pantepec itself on the New York Curb Exchange.

In 1949 W.F.B. made a second important investment outside of
Venezuela. By trading out its own stock, Pancoastal acquired important exploratory areas in the Dominion of Canada. The oil
prospects of the country were almost entirely unexplored at the
time. The acreage acquired by W.F.B., mainly in Saskatchewan
and Alberta, very shortly gave promise of oil and gas reserves. In
1951 another splitup took place. This time Pancoastal held the
Venezuela and Florida properties, and the Canadian properties, together with an investment in Ecuador properties which had been
acquired in the meantime, were transferred to a Canadian company, Canada Southern Oils, Ltd. The stockholders of Pancoastal
became the holders of all the stock of Pancoastal and Canada
Southern.

In 1951 W.F.B., through a Canadian investment banking firm of
Toronto, succeeded in floating, in Canada, a ten million dollar issue of convertible debentures. At the very time that the negotiations began, the first oil well in Saskatchewan was brought in on
the Canada Southern properties.

The flotation of the convertible debentures in Canada was a
pioneer project in the investment world. It was the largest issue
of this kind of securities ever disposed of entirely in Canada. The
debentures were speedily distributed. The funds raised were used
to great advantage in extending the land play in Canada. Promising
properties were acquired by the usual Buckley formula of covering
a vast area with substantial blocks, so placed as to assure a high
probability of success.

In 1954, after a careful survey of existing conditions in the oil
and gas industry in Canada, it was decided to divide the Canadian

properties into three individual operating units. The pattern was based primarily upon the theory of having one company specializing in the search for and production of gas; one to engage actively in the production of oil properties and one to remain primarily exploratory in its activities. The stocks of the three companies were distributed to stockholders just at the time that a severe recession struck the Canadian industry and the reaction on market values put the Canadian enterprises in a most unfavorable position for several years. In addition to the doldrums in which the companies labored, the problem of discharging the debentures, the maturity of which grew steadily closer, threatened the survival of the companies. Fortunately, about sixty per cent of the issue had been converted before the slump struck. The balance, however, caused great concern. Finally, in 1957, a plan was conceived and carried out which resulted in the conversion of all the outstanding debentures into shares of the three companies. This conversion was completed just before another wave of pessimism swept over the Western Canadian petroleum industry. It put all three companies in a position to survive the storm and to emerge with adequate resources to take advantage of the inevitable turn for the better in which W.F.B. always believed.

W.F.B.'s clear-sighted thinking in times of stagnation or distress was akin to the confidence which made him the ideal pioneer searching for new fields for exploration. I recall his confidence in the basic soundness of the oil industry following the Second World War. With no visible exception, the major companies anticipated a catastrophic decline in world demand for petroleum products and an equally catastrophic increase in available supply. Unconvinced, W.F.B. took in his stride the termination by a major company of its contract for the purchase of Pantepec's Venezuelan production, by this time substantial, and negotiated a contract with other purchasers on far better terms.

His friends, on occasion, observing how frequently events followed his predictions, regarded him as gifted with an uncanny foresight. Actually, the phenomenon was explainable by his comprehensive and untiring study of all relevant factors and his constant rejection of the emotional factor of unwarranted hopes and fears.

The impression W.F.B. made on others is a study in human nature. The initial impact varied with the nature of the individual, but after any extended contact I found an amazing similarity in the final appraisal. Certain obtuse, self-centered individuals would see at the outset nothing unusual in the quiet, soft-spoken, unassuming gentleman, the most considerate of listeners, who from innate politeness endured so much of others' volubility and ego. However, always in the area of business, and with few exceptions in social contacts, the qualities of mind and character and the background of wide and varied experience, brought the newcomer to join the ranks of those who recognized here a man of singular stature, a man of penetrating mind, of wide cultural experience, who aroused respect and admiration and, in most people, affection.

W.F.B. was not without enemies. His career in Mexico alone brought him powerful enemies who never relented in their malicious efforts to destroy him. To the cynical policy of business-by-corruption which obtained in Mexico at the time, W.F.B. remained firmly and constantly opposed. In his own personal dealings, he adhered at all times to the principle that a true representative of the Mexican nation must in no way be diverted from service to his trust. Moreover, as one of the Americans of force and influence, W.F.B. did not hesitate to exert his efforts to the maintenance of honorable relations by other Americans with the Mexican authorities. W.F.B. predicted that the harvest of a practice of general bribery by Americans would be disaster for all Americans. With the expropriation of oil in 1938, history proved him correct.

I do not have to speculate as to the constancy of Mr. Buckley's adherence to principle, since the public record establishes this clearly. The Congressional investigation which took place in the early 1920's, in which he took such an effective and constructive part, rolls back the curtain from those troubled years when he was active in Mexican affairs. The picture is of a strong, determined man unostentatiously working to convince his fellow-Americans that fair play with the Mexicans in power was the only means of achieving permanent advantages. Obviously, such a position was calculated to make enemies, not only among Americans tempted to follow the venal path, but among their Mexican counterparts, ready to sacrifice national for personal interests. W.F.B.'s enemies never tired of spreading rumors which carried stories of conduct diametrically opposed to his actual actions, both political and private. One of the most malicious of the slanderers was motivated by a personal hatred arising from a strange incident so illustrative of human nature in its defensive mood that I am impelled to relate it.

The incident occurred one day in a small Mexican town, where a few Americans and their wives were having dinner. A skirmish between rival revolutionary forces was under way in the vicinity and suddenly gunfire broke out in the town square. Stray bullets spattered the front of the hotel. One of the American ladies asked W.F.B., in a terror-stricken voice, where her husband was. At her insistence, he began a search for the man—and ultimately found him cowering under a bed in one of the rooms on the second floor.

It so happened that this American gentleman was an important representative of a large American company. It was one of the most unfortunate occurrences for W.F.B. that he should have been a witness to this state of blue-funk. The man assumed that W.F.B. would spread the story far and wide—a mistake on his part—and acted to discredit W.F.B., to cast doubt on his veracity. This later proved to be one of the most vicious sources of malicious slander.

Due to the general resentment at W.F.B.'s interference with the policy of purchasing public officials in Mexico and to the superficially disgraceful act of expulsion, he was to encounter through his life reverberations of these rumors which were overcome only by direct contact with Buckley himself. I recall many occasions when strangers, who had been influenced by the insidious reports, met W.F.B. and discovered how grievously they had been misled.

A strong man of integrity—constantly protecting the interests of his stockholders against raids by high pressure operators, he was bound to make new enemies. And the combination of the Mexican calumnies with the bitterness of the thwarted Wall Street manipulators assured him of a constant barrage of secret attack.

The crisis of the 1930's, when the fate of Pantepec was so seriously threatened by the ambitions of unscrupulous operators, made a lasting impression on W.F.B. The fruit of his experiences led him in the late 1940's to set up his companies with voting trusts, to obstruct irresponsible outsiders with designs on them. To the Wall Street of that day, trained to mouth platitudes concerning industrial democracy, the voting trust was an evil anachronism, belonging to the age of the robber barons. W.F.B.'s first venture with the voting trust brought vitriolic attacks from certain elements of the press as well as the financial world. He stuck to his guns, however, and practically every one of the present group of the Buckley companies is operated under the voting trust arrangement.

It is interesting to observe that the destructive raids by irresponsible groups on the management of traditionally sound American companies, which became prevalent in the 1950's, went far to restore public respect in voting trusts. Criticism of this method of management had emanated principally from those sources which were frustrated in their efforts to gain control of attractive industries through the manipulation of an effective portion of the voting stock. The wreckage which followed upon such irresponsible depredations served as a significant lesson for investors caught in the coils of unscrupulous speculators.

During his lifetime, W.F.B. built up an oil empire which virtually encompassed the globe. The following companies were created by him and the shares of each company were being actively traded on the American Stock Exchange in New York and in other Exchanges in the United States and Canada at the time of his death:

> Pantepec Oil Company, C. A.
> Pancoastal Petroleum Company
> Coastal Carribbean Oils, Inc.
> Canada Southern Petroleum, Ltd.
> Canso Oil Producers, Ltd.
> Canso Natural Gas, Ltd.
> Pan-Israel Oil Company, Inc., and
> Israel-Mediterranean Petroleum, Inc.

Following certain developments making mergers advisable, Canso Natural Gas, Ltd. and Canso Oil Producers, Ltd. were united into United Canso Oil & Gas, Ltd. The two Israel Companies have been merged into Magellan Petroleum Corporation.

The Buckley Companies, at the time of Mr. Buckley's death, had important holdings in Venezuela, Florida, Canada (including the North West Territories), Guatemala, Ecuador, The Philippines and Australia.

The period from 1953 to Mr. Buckley's death in 1958 found him in ill health but still active right up to the last hours, in the supervision of his companies. This was an age of transition during which his two oldest sons, John and James, achieved a stature, in the light of responsibilities which were devolving upon them in greater and greater degree, adequate for the performance of these arduous duties. These sons, whose abilities and energies complement each other admirably, are more and more recognized today as carrying on the philosophy of William Buckley in the oil industry with remarkable capacities required for the sort of pioneering of which their father was such a great exemplar.

III. *Above All a Teacher*

By C. Dean Reasoner

"What he taught first—through his own actions—was gentility and courtesy."

To meet this man on the path of life and walk a way with him was an exciting experience. The path thereafter was never without challenge. W.F.B. was a man respected by friend and foe, the ordinary and the mighty. Self-confidence born of self-reliance accounted, in part, for this. He was called a pioneer, a lawyer and a businessman, as well as a patron of the arts. He was all of these, but his first, and to me, his true profession was that of a teacher. He taught by example. What he taught first—through his own actions—was gentility and courtesy; next, respect for one's own conclusions and the drive to carry them through; and then, the utility and enjoyment of property.

He had the natural pedagogical gift of stimulating the student in the true sense. He was not given to pedagogical relationships with those he taught. What he left one with, rather, was a latent interest in profound avenues of thought. This was the unique result of his teaching. The end product was one's own. But on hard analysis, one could trace its origin to the teacher. Not infrequently the student, in fresh possession of the product, thoughtlessly found himself attempting to teach the teacher. This must have furnished him deep enjoyment, although he seldom betrayed this outwardly.

This legacy survives. It can be appreciated and used, but it is not a tangible that can like property be readily transferred. The legacy is a living thing that could only be learned from the man himself. It could never have been fashioned of words alone.

I think the importance of example was the crux of W. F. Buckley's firm views on human, national and international relations. Just as a nation becomes more stalwart from the stalwart example set by its leaders; just as other nations are encouraged to establish a worthy government through the example of a nation where it has been successfully established; so this man felt that his country's international role depended on its conduct at home; that constant, zealous vigilance was required to attain and preserve good government here, and that this was the essential prerequisite to a benevolent international role.

Few Americans have gone "foreign" and returned to spend the greater portion of their creative years in this country. W.F.B. was not the "ugly American" away from home. In Mexico and later, in Venezuela, he learned to speak better Spanish than most Spaniards, to serve better Latin food than most Latin households and became more closely acquainted with their politics and politicians, their courts and customs than most native-born. When he reestablished himself in the United States he saw his country not only through the provincial eyes of a native son but through the eyes of a foreigner as well. This unique bifocal view confirmed his belief that Americans should first set an example at home.

I think his solution to this national inadequacy, although he never spoke of it to my knowledge, was the proper kind of education. To learn the language, the history and the customs of others —these were prerequisites to understanding how to handle ourselves in relations with others, never forgetting to keep our own house clean and our own windows polished, that others might observe and became inspired by our way of life. Teaching and example, really the same, were his banner and as proudly and effectively as ever it was borne, he bore it.

IV. *Love Affair with Oil*

By JOHN W. BUCKLEY

> *"The stockholder stormed out of the room saying,*
> *'This is the God-damnedest oil company I've ever run*
> *into!'*
> *"He was telling the simple, unvarnished truth."*

B Y ALMOST ALL of the commonly accepted norms, Father should have been a cataclysmic business failure. Where the rule book says that one should be cautious, he was a reckless plunger. Where the mores of business conduct (and a goodly percentage of Father's stockholders) thought that the corporate assets should be carefully conserved, nurtured, and, God help us, distributed, he would commit all of the assets in sight, and a lot not in sight, to some wild, harebrained scheme that had a way of making millions for the stockholders, and Father more distrusted and unpopular than ever before—a situation which he hugely enjoyed.

His business concepts might be exemplified by the following incident: When he was in the hospital in Charlotte in 1947, I went to visit him prior to going to Venezuela to start working for Pantepec. We were talking about the place in Camden, and he mentioned that he wished he had bought and built there many years before he had actually done so. When I suggested that the many hundreds of thousands of dollars that were required to create the minimum *pied a terre* suitable for his requirements had been conspicuously absent in the early thirties, he was visibly shocked. "Good Heavens," he said, "if an idea is good, if you see or think of something you really want, you should grab it and *then* think of the money."

Neither I, nor, so far as I know, anyone else who worked for Father with the exception of Mr. Himes and Mr. Montgomery (one didn't work *with* him!) has ever been able to figure out whether Father worked purely from intuition, or from a consummate intelligence, or from a combination of both. He was generously endowed with both, but these two qualities need not necessarily work in harmony. When one of his enterprises was successful, and established, and was even earning money, he would visibly lose interest in it—except to the extent that it would churn out money for new and more exotic adventures that would enrage the stockholders and saddle them with additional, unexpected capital gains.

Father was an expansionist and couldn't stand still. There was *always* a tremendous amount of oil to be found in an area where Father's company or companies just happened not to be, and the pattern, never the same in details but surprisingly consistent in general outline, went along these lines:

First, the area in question had to be looked down on by the majors. It generally had to be in a country, province or state where the business climate was unpromising if not actively hostile. To be truly irresistible, the terrain should be inaccessible, and the markets or pipelines nil. If he didn't find it himself, it had to have been brought to his attention by a fast-talking individual who was a demonstrable failure or an even more demonstrable mountebank. Then, and only then would Father decide that (a) the majors were too stupid, and too timid to seize upon this priceless opportunity; (b) the area was underlain by oceans of oil; (c) the stockholders of Pantepec (or Pancoastal, or Canada Southern, etc.) could not in good conscience be deprived of this priceless opportunity; (d) that the directors and officers who were against the play were timid, if well meaning, conformists of sadly limited imagination; and (e) that W.F.B. was the man to get it for them.

Then, and only then, the show began: conferences far into the night, conferences at breakfast, lunch and dinner, conferences on the week-ends when the trout were rising, the sun was shining and the birds were flying. Acres of maps were tacked on the walls, strewn on the floors and airmailed special delivery all over the world. The secretaries were kept overtime and more were hired. The lawyers ground out contract after contract, the principals were

wined, dined, week-ended, threatened, cajoled, charmed and outwitted. The directors were worried sick, the stockholders were
about to make money, and Father was enjoying himself hugely.

Sometimes a geologist was consulted.

But the show had only *just* started. The stockholders were furious. Their priceless assets were being squandered all over the
world. They *knew* there was no oil in Florida, or Saskatchewan, or
whatever. Poor people, well meaning mostly, they must be shown
the error of their ways. Some were converted, some rebelled. Proxy
fights ensued, Father would win 95 to 1, or better. The latest proxy
fight resulted, once again, in a resounding victory for Father, but
was a little too close for comfort: 1,300,000 shares for us, 900,000
agin. Unlike some of the others, however, it was a popular win.
The enemy was a notorious Wall Street bully, and fought dirty.
And, incidentally, from this fight came one of the nicest compli-
ments *I* have ever received. One of the enemy, a young man who
approaches all problems with an open mouth, told somebody recently: "John Buckley's getting to be as crooked as his old man
was."

The new acquisition required money; none was available. Bankers X, Y and Z were courted. They were lovely, charming men,
but a little timid. Days and weeks of intense negotiations followed.
A public offering was made and the bankers were lovely, charming
men. Or, the bankers would say that the project was not financ-
able. They then became damn fools. When a situation was completely unfinancable, Father would cheerfully put up his own,
Mother's, his children's and grandchildren's money. Time after
time, Father saved his and the stockholders' investment from collapse with Buckley family money. This little practise of his used to
drive the auditors crazy. The recent Annual Report of one of
Father's younger companies had two pages of text, and thirty-two
pages of fine print footnotes!

Wells would be drilled, and they would be dry. The stock
would drop and the stockholders' letters would be increasingly
abusive. Then a discovery would be made and the stock would go
up. The company looked as if it might become self-supporting.
Father was getting bored.

Had we ever heard of Patagonia?

Director A went back to his psychiatrist, and Director B was

beginning to drink too much. Major stockholder C paid an un-
expectedly heavy capital gains tax that day and beat up his wife
that night.

Father's business life was not comic opera. Far from it. It was
deadly earnest, it was risky, it was a fight all the way, and he loved
every minute of it. The situation was generally critical, but never
serious. Father was a *force* in business. He was distrusted and disliked by large and important segments of the oil industry, the
financial community and the investing public. I would not say that
Father had contempt for the bulk of his enemies; he was basically
too kindly for that, and he was not arrogant. I think, fundamentally,
he felt *sorry* for people who were timid, or unimaginative, or dis-
agreed with him, or controlled millions but wouldn't invest in his
latest idea, or hated him, or were dull or stupid, or didn't enjoy
life. But he also did have some great enemies and enmities: these he
fought uncompromisingly, but always cleanly. Once in a rare while
he found people *beneath* contempt. As far as his awareness was
concerned, these people simply disappeared. The head of a large
European oil company was a notable exception to this last. He gave
one of the companies a savage, and nearly fatal, mangling in the
courts. This one Father neither forgave nor forgot, (a) because the
loss was totally unjust, but primarily (b) because the enemy was
arrogant, devoid of a sense of humor and not a gentleman.

In business, Father naturally gravitated to the people at the top,
and they to him. He was too deep, and imposing and charming to
waste his time and talents on the dull, the uncouth and the unsuccessful—unless the unsuccessful were neither dull nor uncouth.
Many years ago Father took me to see the cockfights in Caracas.
Shortly after we had arrived, there was a great commotion in the
crowd. The dictator, General Gomez, had arrived with his staff,
his hangers-on and his bodyguards. He was no sooner seated than
he saw Father and dispatched an aide to invite him to join the
presidential box. The conversation started as follows:

> General Gomez: "Mr. Buckley, you have been in Caracas for
> over a month and you haven't come to see me. Why is that?"
> Father: "General, I didn't call on you because I knew how
> busy you were, and, as a matter of fact, I've been pretty busy
> myself."
> General Gomez: "Mr. Buckley, it would be well if you were to

remember this: I am never too busy to see you, and you are never too busy to see me."

He was too retiring and modest to project his image or permit it to be projected. (He refused even to permit his name to be listed in *Who's Who.*) It was a great mistake.

Father's principal operative prejudices—call them right or wrong, were that (1) bankers are fools (all, that is, except the ones he knew and liked); (2) the major companies are cowardly and unprincipled; (3) he knew best; (4) the large land play was the ideal medium for oil people with modest, or scarcer, resources; (5) the next well was going to be the biggest discovery yet; and (6) judges of horse shows drank cocktails before lunch and were therefore corrupted.

Father was incapable of thinking in small terms, though in some particulars he was a perfectionist (he once had an architect redesign a staircase fourteen times). He painted with a broad brush—but he might argue for a week over a word in Article XXV, subparagraph 4.1 of Exhibit E of the Tentative Agreement. He was completely independent and unorthodox, and so frequently—but *not* always—right, that he inadvertently made his critics to appear foolish—which was no way of winning a popularity contest that he wasn't running in anyway.

In business, Father had not one but two Achilles heels: He was a monumentally poor judge of character, and he would instinctively believe what he wanted to hear rather than what might prove unpleasant or contrary to his cherished premises.

As to the first, Father was one of the rare natural aristocrats who genuinely liked people provided they lived up to his exacting standards. His business associates and adversaries had to have a minimum of two of the following characteristics: ability, wit, imagination, optimism, generosity, a sense of humor, a glib tongue and gentility. If they did have any two or more of these characteristics, they could also have, and conceal from him indefinitely, crookedness, avarice, disloyalty and a strong addiction for the fruit of the grape. Father was once connected with an unscrupulous vulgarian because he had imagination and a glib tongue. Being a boor, he was never a member of Father's inner circle, and it took Father several years to realize that the glib tongue and the imagination had been used exclusively for the purposes of deceiving Father and fleecing the stockholders. This man is, incidentally, still at large.

Others who were not dishonest, but who grew prideful and would attempt to interpose a truncated imagination on Father's visions, would be eased out. Many of them remained among Father's dearest friends.

On the other weakness, Father refused to give credence to any advice that ran contrary to his preconceptions or hopes. Suffice it merely to say that many an uneconomic or dry well was drilled because Father was told by a geologist or engineer what he knew he wanted to hear rather than the truth.

This weakness was a weakness of degree. It was just one overly-developed facet of the general characteristic of optimism which made Father a founder, a builder, a success.

Father's business life was an enormous success; but in terms of financial reward, it never measured up to his incredible natural endowments. This was due, in part, to sheer bad luck, to over-tenaciousness (he would devote as much time and energy to a hopeless cause as he would to a meritorious one), and to the fact that he really had to devote the bulk of his time and energies to the matter of sheer personal and corporate economic survival. He always operated on the heroic scale; but on the personal or corporate basis, he was never able to get sufficiently far ahead of the game to utilize to full fruition his vast talents. It was a sad irony that Father should have died before any of his ventures had reached their full fruition.

I have referred to Father's poor judgment of character; but that, I feel, is only part of the story. The reverse side of the coin is the fact that, such was Father's own character that he made, and never lost, some monumental friendships with people who had one great common denominator: integrity and, for lack of a better word, sweetness of mind. First and foremost among these were: Cecilio Velasco, George S. Montgomery, Jr., Joseph H. Himes, Garcia Naranjo, the Misses Mildred and Ethel Hembdt, the late Fergus Reid, Sr., and the ever irrepressible Chicha Freeman de Dougherty.

Finally, Father enjoyed business, just as he enjoyed everything else he did. There is the story that just after Father's expulsion from Mexico, he was living at his Mother's house in Austin, as was his brother Edmund. Uncle Edmund, who was showing no visible signs of extreme poverty, was devoting his energies to hunting and golfing. Father, meanwhile, freshly exiled, with no company, no holdings and, for that matter, very few worries, was working twleve to eighteen hours a day and had two full time secretaries working as hard as he. After a while, apparently, Mother Buckley couldn't stand it any longer, and she asked Uncle Edmund why it was that he, Edmund, seemed to do nothing but enjoy himself while poor Willie was working himself to death. Uncle Edmund's answer was the essence of simplicity: "You see, Mother, Willie likes to work and I don't."

Father carried on a love affair with oil all his adult life; it was the perfect medium for his talents. And yet, he persistently refused to take himself too seriously as an oil man. One of his favorite stories relates to an early stockholders' meeting of Pantepec in New York. At the meeting there was a persistently troublesome stockholder who finally asked the directors what were their qualifications to guide the destinies of an oil company. Three of the five confessed to being investment bankers, and the fourth to being a lawyer. "Do you mean to say, then," said the stockholder, "that only Mr. Buckley is an oil man?" "Heavens, no," Father answered him. "I know *nothing* about oil. I'm a lawyer, too." The stockholder then stormed out of the room saying, "This is the God-damnedest oil company I've ever run into!"

He was telling the simple, unvarnished truth.

V. *How W.F.B. Took Tallahassee*

By Benjamin W. Heath

". . . And without opening his eyes, the Governor said, 'Give it to the yardboy.' "

Although there are many incidents I recall from the several years spent with W.F.B., one in particular remains in my mind as something he seemed to find much pleasure in recounting as the years went by.

The scene of this episode was Tallahassee, Florida in 1947. W.F.B. had just acquired from one of the old-time promoters three State oil and gas leases covering more than 4.5 million acres of the so-called tideland areas of Florida's west coast, for which he had paid $1 million—in cash. While the number of acres involved and the price paid were both impressive, the status of the leases left much to be desired. He inherited from the former owner an 11,500 foot drilling commitment for a well that was supposed to commence within a matter of days. W.F.B.'s philosophy was: If you see something you want, get it, then worry about how you are going to keep it.

The time for worry had arrived. It was somewhat complicated by the fact that W.F.B. had spent all of the available cash to acquire the leases and had nothing left to drill a well. The appeal to the State for relief from this onerous commitment was to be made in person at the Capitol Building in Tallahassee. The day before the big event W.F.B. and his retinue, including his wife, a few children who happened to be too young for, or were suspended from, school at the time, four or five attorneys, two secretaries, a chauf-

194

fer, a butler and this humble neophyte, arrived and took over the Presidential suite of the town's leading hostelry.

The local attorneys put in their appearance shortly thereafter to assure W.F.B. that the approaching battle would be a tough one indeed; next to impossible, to say the least. I have learned over the years that this is standard practice, designed to support the outrageous legal bills to be submitted as soon as the battle—which they really know will be a lead pipe cinch to win—is out of the way. It was decided that we would ask for a 60 day reprieve.

Our case was carried before the Governor and his staff by a prominent Florida attorney, who, we had been assured, had excellent political connections. He began with a stirring tale of W.F.B. and his oil empire, emphasizing that the people of Florida really did not realize how fortunate they were that he had chosen the Sunshine State as his next oil search area. Within a short while all assembled turned with awe toward this handsome oil baron from New York—all except the Governor, that is. At the time of this meeting, the destiny of our southernmost state was in the hands of a rangy, six-foot-four Floridian who appeared to sleep through the entire presentation; I don't recall that he opened his eyes for even a minute. We didn't know it then, but learned later that he was quite an actor in his own right, and was really putting on a show. What was currently unfolding left little doubt in our minds, however, that this fellow was a tough cookie and was little impressed by what he must have considered Yankee invasion of one of the last bastions of the Stars and Bars. In any event, we were soon convinced that he was a firm believer in the old adage that action speaks louder than words. *His* first words of the two-hour session were to ask what the oil giant from New York was prepared to do to insure the drilling of the well within 60 days, provided the State granted an extension?

Upon hearing this, W.F.B. whispered in the ear of our No. 1 man that he would escrow $250,000 in a bank of the State's choice. Obviously impressed with the figure (he later charged one-tenth of it for his work) and by the calm manner in which his client with the pince-nez had passed it along to him, our boy chose to make it the climax of a half hour courtroom appeal that would have done justice to Clarence Darrow. The Governor, apparently, was considerably less impressed. Still seemingly in deep slumber, and without opening his eyes, the great man said, "Give it to the yardboy."

W.F.B. did not take kindly to this treatment (or perhaps he was hurt that someone had mistaken him for a damned Yankee), but he forthwith marched out of the hearing room. He did take the precaution, however, to tell one of these lieutenants to tell the Governor that he, W.F.B., was on his way back to New York and to h--- with their leases. He, of course, had no intention of going to New York, where it was cold and snowing (it was 75° in Florida), but his ruse worked, as I'm now sure he knew it would. Within an hour the No. 1 boy arrived at W.F.B.'s suite in a breathless state (presumably to stop the packing which was then supposed to be underway) and announce that a clean victory was ours.

In later years, and after learning that much of the by-play between the Governor and our attorney had been carefully planned at a poker game the previous night—principally for the benefit of a press that imagined the Governor was giving away all of Florida's wealth—this became one of W.F.B.'s favorite anecdotes.

PART FOUR

Connecticut

Aloise S. Heath

W. F. B.

Van Zandt Wheeler

I. *Supper at Great Elm*

By Aloise Buckley Heath

*"Papa is the handsomest man in the world, and aside
from the King of England, the richest: he owns personally ONE HUNDRED DOLLARS."*

WHEN FATHER DIED last fall, at the age of 77, fewer than a dozen
of the hundreds of letters and telegrams his family received
were from people who thought of him, or who had ever thought
of his as anything but "Mr. Buckley." For, in the last fifty years of
his life, he almost never reached the intimacy, much less the mean-
ingless familiarity which is implied between two people who address one another by their given names. He felt a warm affection for
many of his friends and associates, a genuine liking and admiration
for many more, a fiercely enveloping and protective and, at times,
possessive love for his family; but he was never completely at home,
completely at ease with anyone but his wife, his brothers and sisters, his children, and any very young child. His own sons and
daughters, as they entered adolescence, were taught to call him
"Father." This, however, is about the days when his children were
still children; when they were closest to him and he was closest to
them.

The years when Father was still Papa seem, through the haze of
twenty and thirty years, to consist only and forever of family supper in the shadowed summer twilight of the big dining-room at
Great Elm. Dinner must have been early on those evenings, for in
memory, the sun glints strongly through the heavy elms beyond

the western windows, and a curtain is always being drawn, or a blind lowered in order to present a child with a clearer and more comfortable view of his unfinished tuna fish on toast. There are no guests on these occasions, which is the reason Aloise and John and Priscilla and Jimmy and Mademoiselle are having dinner in the upper dining-room with Mama and Papa. Jane, Billy and Patricia, too young to be so honored, are at their own table in the lower dining-room, happily not eating their vegetables, because Mexican Nana, *their* supervisor, has her meals in the kitchen. Reid, Maureen, and Carol are placidly unborn.

Great Elm, 1925 . . .

One of the delicious distinctions of dinner in the upper dining-room is that you have to speak English because it is not polite to speak French in front of Papa, whose other language is only Spanish, poor thing. Sometimes, though, Mademoiselle, who is absent-minded, relapses into middle dining-room *mores* and says: "Parlez français, s'il-vous-plait," instead of: "Parlez anglais, s'il-vous-plait," which is very amusing indeed. But sometimes Jane or Billy or Patricia calls: "Papá! Papá!"—They, who speak only Spanish and a little French, aren't even *trying* to learn English!—and the big chil-

. . . 1958

dren try to wring from a reluctant Mademoiselle the admission that
if it is "pas poli" for them to speak French in the presence of Papa.
it is equally "pas poli" for Papa to speak Spanish in *her* presence.
Mama is neutral: she speaks inaccurate French and Spanish with
great fluency and nonchalance and she has told us that what Papa
says about how she must practise her mistakes, making so many of
them, is not true; they just come out naturally when she opens her
mouth.

Mama sits at the pantry, or "bell-end" of the table—("Just your
Mother's polite way of putting it. She's afraid if she admits it's the
head of the table, you children will realize she's the head of the
family," and "Oh, *Papa!*" the children giggle, thrilled by the out-
rageousness of his invention). Aloise sits next to Mama, because
Aloise is both plain and argumentative and Papa, often articulately,
deplores these characteristics in any female of any age. Jimmy is in
the chair on Mama's other side because Jimmy (a) makes smacking
noises when he chews, (b) never gets the backs of his hands clean,
(c) chatters incessantly in a physically unbearable penny-whistle

screech, and Papa, often articulately, deplores these characteristics in any person of any age. (Another reason Jimmy sits beside Mama is that (d) Jimmy and Mama are each other's favorite.) John and Priscilla sit in secure serenity on either side of Papa because they are by nature, clean and pretty, sweet-tempered and mellow, and can therefore only be teased about things they don't mind. Mademoiselle's place is between Priscilla and Jimmy because they are very young, still, and in more need than the others of the little, murmured: "Pas avec les mains," and "Finissez vos legumes, s'il-vous-plait," and "Ne parlez *pas* avec la bouche *pleine*, Zhee-*mee!* (Jimmy)" with which she punctuates all meals in the upper-dining-room.

Mademoiselle—*any year.*

At the foot of the table sits Papa, eating, talking, laughing, teasing, dominating the table with the gusto and vigor, the gaiety and the concentration on the moment at hand which, until his last illness, entered the house and left it only with him. (Only when he turns to Mademoiselle does his manner change to the grave and slightly puzzled courtesy with which he treats all plain women: "Father's 'What *can* God have been thinking of?' expression," his daughters called it, many years later.)

Great Elm, 1934: *(standing)* Jim, Aloise, Patricia, W. F. B.;
(sitting) Bill, A. S. B., Maureen, Priscilla, Jane, Reid, John

Papa is the biggest man in the world and the smartest. He can lasso children by the leg while they're running. He is the strongest man in the world but also the kindest, which keeps him from beating up other children's Papas. He has the bluest eyes and the pinkest cheeks in the world and he is 99 years old (Mama is 16). He is the handsomest man in the world, and aside from the King of England, the richest: he owns personally ONE HUNDRED DOLLARS. He has never told a lie in his entire life except for jokes and kneels by his bed every morning to say his prayers. God will, naturally, send him straight to Heaven when he dies, except for perhaps an hour or so in Purgatory so as not to show favoritism. He is the most modest man in the world, because he says none of these things are true; that Mama made them up to show what good taste she had when she proposed to him. He is the funniest man in the world.

Papa is George Washington and Douglas Fairbanks, Will Rogers and Robin Hood, King Arthur and Stonewall Jackson. Mama thinks so too, (and thought so, to the day of his death), although as her children, growing up, began to come to her with stories of how absolutely *impossible* Father was getting to be, she used to confuse them into silence by retorting that: (a) they could count themselves lucky if they ever again, in the course of their lives, laid *eyes* on a man of their father's calibre, and (b) they were all beginning to exaggerate just like their father.

At supper in the summertime, Papa talks to the children about the olden days when he was young, and those are the things he tells them:

—His father's name was John and John was so strong that when he was only 17 years old he used to go to Country fairs without telling his parents, and win ten dollars by beating the wrestler. It was no wonder, therefore, that when he grew up he became a TEXAS SHERIFF. Unfortunately, he never shot anyone, but then, on the other hand, no one ever shot him—a circumstance from which the children are supposed to derive more comfort than they, in fact, do. He once let Papa ride all the way to Kansas City with him in a cattle car, even though Papa's mother thought he was too little.

—His mother's name was Mary Ann, not Mother B., as the children had always supposed. She was very beautiful and very good but very strict, and though Papa was born on July 12th, she celebrated his birthday on July 11th because July 12th is Orangeman's Day. (Father's 77th and last birthday was celebrated, as always, on July 11th.) When she saw Grandfather talking and laughing with a man who didn't like him, and whom he didn't like, she would say later: "John, how *can* you!" She would say: "I can forgive by an act of *my* will, but can only forget by an act of God's will." And Papa telling this, rocks back his chair, mouth opened wide in one of his great bursts of laughter. "You kno-o-w?" he says, "I don't remember God's ever willing my mother to forget a single thing she willed herself to forgive!" (Yet when Aloise once asked, all big-eyed and fraudulent innocence, if Mother B. would have shot people if *she* had been the Texas Sheriff, Father lost his good humor at once and answered shortly: "That will do, Aloise. My mother was a saint, and don't any of you ever forget it." Thus early do the children learn, as their own children and husbands and wives have since learned, that Buckleys tolerate disparagement of Buckleys only from Buckleys—and only from Buckleys within the same degree of consanguinity, at that.

—There was Uncle John, who was the oldest, and who died when he was sixteen (and in such a way as to at least mitigate the callous and unromantic pacifism of the children's grandfather, for he died of pneumonia after he was waylaid and stabbed in the lung by a boy who believed he had been the victim of an unfair decision in a baseball match John had refereed); and there was Tía (Aunt) Priscilla, and Papa, who was Willie then, and Uncle Claude and Tía Eleanor and Uncle Edmund, who was the baby. (It seems strange to the children, when they are very small, that the next-to-youngest should have the whitest hair, but by the time they are ten or so, it has become evident that Tía Eleanor's hair was a good forty years older than Tía Eleanor.) John and Priscilla and Claude and Eleanor and Edmund were all paragons of intelligence, wit, honor, diligence, piety, courage, CHARACTER (Papa's capitals), and any other virtue you could think of. They were all far superior to Papa, he says, and if Mama had not already explained that all the Buckleys were additionally gifted with the quality of modesty, the children might have pitied their poor, inferior Papa.

—Uncle Claude, who had a terrible temper when he was small, but when he got old, when he was 19, he lost the handball doubles championship of the University of Texas because he insisted on having Papa as his partner, so the children forgive him the fact that he once hit Papa on the nose with a brick and broke it, which is why his nose is so big and curved. ("Big and crooked," says Papa. "Aristocratic," says Mama.) "Your Father must be getting very vain in his old age if he's taken to inventing wild tales to explain the Buckley nose," says Tía Priscilla, whose nose is small and straight. "Your Aunt would rather face my terrible nose than your Uncle Claude's terrible temper," says Papa. Uncle Claude smiles and shakes his head and winks at the children, which is what Uncle Claude mostly does. The issue is, to this day, unresolved.

Great Elm, 1929: *Patricia, A. S. B., Bill, Jane, W. F. B.*

—When Papa was a little boy, he used to creep out of the house at four o'clock in the morning and run down to the town jail to share the prisoners' breakfast of doughnuts and *café con leche*. The jailer allowed him this privilege because his father was the sheriff; the coffee, perhaps because it was served with milk, fortunately did not stunt his growth, though it will stunt the children's growth if they drink it before they are sixteen. (Once, when John asked Papa something about those early breakfasts, he said, *"café con leche* with milk in it." Papa laughed at him—very rudely, the children thought; after all John's language was *French*— and, calling down to the lower-dining-room, explained the joke to the little children, whose unduly prolonged and insufferably Spanish-y giggles were ignored by their seniors, who sat in silence coldly hating Papa. As was truly meet and just, John beat up Jane, Billy and Patricia right after supper, but Papa, who was supposed to be strolling in the garden, unfairly walked into the nursery during the height of the fracas and sent John to bed with harsh language—which is why John got the .22 he'd been promised only when he was 12, four years early. (Twenty-five years later, one of the young men in the Company remarked to a group of the younger Buckleys that his personal retirement-old age insurance plan was to "make Mr. Buckley fire me. . . . First, of course, I have to figure out how to make him mad enough to fire me with a really *big* pension." Mr. Buckley's children agreed that the plan had every chance of success.)

—Papa's school had only one room and only one teacher. The teacher was a man and he had a red beard, but he was a very good teacher, nevertheless. When someone had dirty finger-nails, he would say: "Are you in mourning?" When someone said *"pres*-piration," he would say: "If you can't say *per*spiration, say 'sweat'." When someone talked about the "kids," he would say: "In my school there are no young goats." And he would say: "In my school, however little you learn, you will learn to express correctly," so every morning they had a grammar drill on sentences like: "Each of the stories told by the three men were amusing," or "While ill in the hospital, my house burned down." He would say: "In my school you will use words *accurately*" when he heard a big boy swear, and he would make the boy write three sentences on the board using the word "damn" or "God" or "hell" accurately. He would say " 'Gosh' and 'heck' and 'darn' are cowards' swearwords." Papa learned what he was taught, and he remembered and told the children. (Many years

Grundelwald, Christmas, 1932: *Priscilla, Jane, John, Jim, Aloise, Bill, Patricia*

later, one of his daughters heard her father say quietly into a telephone: "Mr. X, as far as I'm concerned, you can go right straight to hell," and, smiling to herself, thought of the red-bearded teacher in the little Texas town. It was obvious that Papa was expressing himself *correctly* and using his words *accurately*.)

—When Papa was still young, poor grandfather died one night, after a stroke, surrounded by his family. When he died, he didn't have enough money in the bank for Papa and the family to finish school, so for a while Papa became a school teacher himself.

Great Elm, 1929: *"Bo," Bill, Father, Patricia*

He had a little school on the Mexican border, where he taught all eight grades, in Spanish mostly, because practically all the children were Mexican. The school was a day and a night away from home, by train or horseback, so from fall to Christmas and Christmas to Easter and Easter to summer, Papa boarded at a nearby ranch. Once, in January, when there was a long cold spell, he pulled back his covers at bedtime and found a rattlesnake coiled between his sheets. Unfortunately, Papa did not know about putting the pan of warm milk on the floor, like Kipling, so he called the rancher's wife (after all, it wasn't *his* house, or *his* bed or *his* rattlesnake, the children would explain to each other later), and she swept the snake onto the floor with one end of her broom and killed it with the other. "And did she say: 'Tsk, tsk, them pesky critters'?" one of the children, who were all in the age of conformity, would ask. "Of course," Papa would answer gravely. "Then why are you winking at Mama?"

—It took over three years (half a lifetime, if you were Jimmy's age) for Papa to get to be 20 years old and by that time, as might be expected, he had accumulated vast hoards of money not even counting the money that Tía Priscilla gave him from what she earned translating Spanish and English in an Office; so at last Papa could go to the University. (The children know *what* University: *the* University, that's what University) but even at that University, even though Papa was a schoolteacher, even though he was 20 years old, they made him take examinations to get in. When he passed those, they made him take Freshman final exams *in Spanish!* Then they made him take the Sophomore finals and then the Junior ("Weren't you *tired*, Papa?" asks the sympathetic Priscilla) and finally the examination that Seniors had to take before they graduated with a degree in Spanish. After all that, the University told Papa that he could be in the Freshman class, but had to take English and History with the Sophomore class and be an Instructor in Spanish, which turned out all right, because every month the University paid him 28 dollars and 50 cents for instructing. ("Lucky *duck!*," the children murmur, wide-eyed and proud).

—These are the things Papa told the children about his bright college years:

They were among the happiest years of his life.

His first year was lonely, because he lived in a freshman dormitory, where the other boys were 17 and 18, and Papa was 20 and an Instructor.

After his freshman year, he lived in an off-campus house with students from all four classes, and he was happy.

Great Elm, 1929: *John, Priscilla, Aloise*

Great Elm, 1929: *Jane, John, Priscilla, Jim, Aloise*

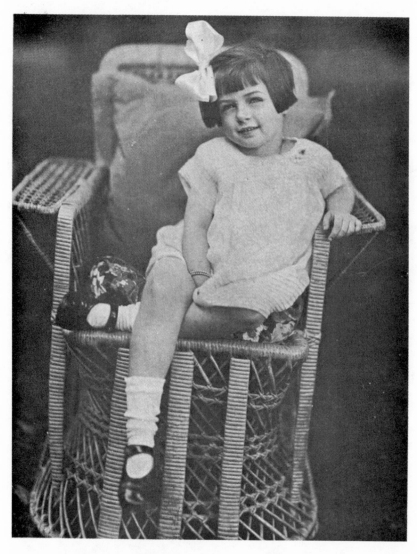

Great Elm, 1925: *Priscilla*

He never saw a football or a baseball game away from the University, because he never had enough money to buy a train ticket, but he often saw home games.

He ate at a restaurant in Austin where you could buy a meal of pea soup, steak, fried potatoes, bread and butter, apple pie and coffee for 25¢. ("Yum *yum*," Jimmy murmurs, late on the cue only because he is busy trying to find out how much asparagus hollandaise can be safely hidden beneath a lamb chop bone.)

He and Uncle Claude once convinced a freshman whose final report card was studded with A's, that he had flunked out of college because E stood for "Excellent," D for "Doing Well," C for "Can Do Better," B for "Bad" and A for "Awful." "The thing *is*," the children point out to one another in the insomniac hour between summer bedtime and summer sleep, "Papa and Uncle Claude could say it, all right, but the thing *is*, how could they think that freshman really believed it?" The thing *was*, the children were to learn, that Papa, at least, most certainly did think the freshman believed it, for he never entertained the slightest doubt of the success of his practical jokes, which tended to be elaborate and transparent. "She pretended she'd known all along, but you should have seen her blush," he would say about one of his "victims," who had indeed known all along; or "He tried to laugh the whole thing off, but I could see by the look in his eyes. . . ." "Don't tell *me* you didn't think that house was haunted! You were all as white as sheets," he would delightedly inform the children who protested that they had instantly recognized the paternal

Great Elm, *1929*

"wo-oo-oo-oo's" emanating from the cellar of the empty house next door. Then there was the yearly irritation of Christmas. *All* the children were firm believers in Santa Claus, Papa maintained, in the teeth of impassioned statements to the contrary; in spite of Jimmy's pointing out, Christmas after Christmas, that although Santa Claus experienced no difficulty in conversing in English with half the household, in Spanish with the other half, he always answered Mademoiselle's: "Joyeux Noel, Sawhnta Close" with a courteously formal: "Thank you, Mademoiselle. Merry Christmas to you too." (In their young adulthood, the children decided that just as the dignity and reserve which Father kept between himself and all the world except for very young children demanded occasional release in the form of practical jokes, so that same dignity and reserve demanded that these jokes be uniformly successful. In middle-aged adulthood, the children have not changed their minds.)

One year at the University, when Papa was worried about not having enough money, he heard of a hundred dollar prize that an insurance company would give to whoever wrote the best composition about some kind of insurance, so he read about that kind of insurance and wrote the composition and won the prize. The next year he was worried again about not having enough money. But because he had won once, he wasn't allowed to try again, so one of his friends agreed to sign his name to Papa's essay for ten dollars, so he won the prize again, though this year it was about a different kind of insurance. The next year, though, he didn't write the composition, because he didn't think he could bear to learn any more about insurance.

In the summer vacations, Papa and Uncle Claude and Uncle Edmund—or was Uncle Edmund too young? Was it Dr. Garnett? —went to Mexico and earned money and had adventures. One summer they travelled from village to village showing movies, which they were not very good at doing. However, the audience didn't mind much when the reels were in the wrong order, or when they got parts of some movies mixed up with parts of others, but they did mind very much when Papa couldn't seem to keep from showing the film upside down, ("*C'est assez!*" Mademoiselle whispers sharply, as the children catch each other's eyes across the table, for it is well and disrespectfully known that, for Papa, locks do not respond to keys, nor corks to corkscrews, nor cars to starters) so after a while the boys decided that Papa could only take turns between being the usher and the ticket taker, but never the movie man. Papa said that was fair. Another time they sold soap that they made every night. It was wonderful soap; the boys used to ask for something very dirty to wash, and after they had washed it, it was all clean and bright again and the people in the villages were very pleased. By the middle of the summer they had sold so much soap that they didn't have anything left to make it with and they had loads of money so they decided they might as well go home. The way home was through some of the same villages they had sold soap to, and at the very first one, all of the women came running out of their houses, screaming and scolding and calling the boys *"ladrones"*—("Robbers," Jimmy translates squeakily, for Jimmy has only very recently been promoted from Nana and the nursery, and sometimes forgets that he is pretending not to know Spanish)—and the women held up the clothes they had washed. The clothes were still clean and bright but ("How can Papa and Mama and Mademoiselle *laugh?*" Aloise and John, who know the tragic last act, wonder) they were full of big ragged holes. So Papa and Uncle Claude and Uncle Edmund—or was it Dr. Garnett?—paid them back the money they had spent for the soap and gave them money for new clothes and "we got home with 16 cents between the three of us," Papa finishes, simply roaring with laughter. "But they didn't *have* to buy the soap," argues Priscilla in the ensuing pause. (Priscilla is always tiresomely living up to the reputation she established at the age of three, when she answered Aloise's unflattering comments on a group of Japanese by sweetly lisping: "Maybe *they* think *we* has funny faces, *too!*" —or that's what Mama says she said.) "No-o-o," Papa agrees, thoughtful and instantly intent, "nobody made them buy the soap. They bought the soap because they trusted the three American boys who told them it was good soap." Papa glances round the table once, then begins to eat his lemon pie. The children look triumphantly, but not unsympathetically at Priscilla. After all, you can't always guess right.

And then . . . and then . . . But the stories of when Papa lived in Mexico, the days when he was a lawyer and when he was an oil man and when he was in revolutions and when he met Mama must wait, for the candles have flickered down and the sun has set. It is almost time for baths and prayers and bed.

Soon—too soon, it seems today—Papa has turned into Father, and the big children are sons and daughters whose eyes no longer widen as they listen. It is only the smaller children who still have Papa, and to them the stories are told.

Great Elm, 1929: *A. Ṡ. B. and "Jocko"*

II. *Memorandum to:*

Aloise
John
Priscilla
Jimmy
Jane
Billie
Patricia
Reid
Maureen
Carol

"Protruding teeth and romances; poor diction and sophomore marks at college; quarreling, careers and the choice of a fraternity, were all subjects to which he gave time and thought; about which letters and memoranda—often from a hotel in Caracas, a sleeping car in Spain, an apartment in Paris or a rented room in London, arrived in due course in college letter box or on Great Elm's breakfast table."

THERE WAS NOTHING complicated about Father's theory of child-rearing: he brought up his sons and daughters with the quite simple objective that they become absolutely perfect. To this end his children were, at one time or another, given professional instruction in: apologetics, art, ballroom dancing, banjo, bird-watching, building boats in bottles, calligraphy, canoeing, carpentry, cooking, driving trotting horses, French, folk-dancing, golf, guitar (Hawaiian and Spanish), harmony, herb-gardening, horsemanship, history of architecture, ice-skating, mandolin, marimba, music appreciation, organ, painting, piano, playing popular music, rumba,

Great Elm, 1939: *(foreground) Maureen, Reid;
(sitting) Patricia, Aloise, Priscilla, Bill, Carol, A. S. B., Jane;
(standing) Jim, W. F. B., John*

sailing, skiing, singing, Spanish, speech, stenography, swimming, tap-dancing, tennis, typing and wood-carving.

And from a random culling of the old filing cabinets (until lately stored in the unused part of the chicken coop at Great Elm) it appears that there was very little in the human personality, or in the personalities of Aloise etc., Buckley, which he considered unworthy of his attention.

Protruding teeth and romances; poor diction and sophomore marks at college; quarreling, careers and the choice of a fraternity, were all subjects to which he gave time and thought; about which letters and memoranda—often from a hotel in Caracas, a sleeping car in Spain, an apartment in Paris or a rented room in London, arrived in due course in college letter box or on Great Elm breakfast table.

The more ephemeral fields of perfectibility he took over himself and (since, from their adolescence on, he and his children were on terms of affectionate inarticulateness) conducted by means of letters and memoranda, usually signed "Father." Every memorandum was, as a matter of principle, directed to all "the children," so as to conceal from those for whose benefit it was intended the fact that it was they upon whom Father's *ojo* was *puesto*. In March, 1956, for instance, 16-year-old Carol received at boarding-school a letter informing her that:

> Your Mother and I feel very strongly that your children should have at least two injections of the new polio vaccine by June 1 at the latest. This is a matter of such importance that I am sure you realize that any procrastination on your part may result in the death or a life of total paralysis for one or several of your children.
>
> I am informed that these injections are relatively painless and can be given to children as young as two months of age.

Carol, realizing that Father would have considered it indelicate to the point of rudeness to address these instructions *only* to those of his grandchildren's parents whom he knew to be procrastinators, was only momentarily startled. In the interests of common courtesy, the memo was, as usual, headed "To the Buckley Children" and followed by "cc: Aloise, John, Priscilla, Jimmy, Jane, Billy, Patricia, Reid, Maureen, Carol."

Often, however, he addressed his children as a unit, as members of a family which he hoped and planned should become and remain

Carol: *Shortly before being advised by W. F. B. to "give all your children polio vaccine."*

a family or a clan in a very concrete sense. Thus, in 1949, he wrote his children:

> I have just read *Prairie Avenue*, by Arthur Meeker, an impressive novel about wealthy families in Chicago during the golden period of 1885 to 1918. These people were pure materialists, without morals or religion, although uniformly contributing members of churches. Notwithstanding their conviction that they were establishing families that would last forever, these had disintegrated entirely by 1918. The following are the appropriate forewords to the three books and epilogue of the novel:
>
> Book I — "The sunny street that holds the gifted few . . ."
> *Old Chicago Saying*
>
> Book II — "This is the rejoicing city that dwelt carelessly, and said in her heart, I am, and there is none beside me."
> *(Zephaniah 2:15)*
>
> Book III — "Their inward thought is, that their houses shall continue forever, and their dwelling places to all generations . . . Nevertheless . . . man that is in honour, and understandeth not, is like the beasts that perish."
> *(Psalm 48)*

The Patio, Great Elm: "'Their inward thought is that their houses shall continue forever.'"

Epilogue: "For he remembered that they were but flesh; a wind that passeth away, and cometh not again."

(Psalm 79)
Affectionately,
Father

This seemed unduly critical in view of the fact that Father had just circulated another

MEMORANDUM TO THE CHILDREN:

As you probably know, Americans are famous for being the poorest conversationalists in the world. Education and cultivation of the mind do not seem to improve us. We can't stay on a subject and we are constitutionally incapable of listening. As a people we are always thinking of something we are going to tell the "bore" as soon as he stops talking. A political conversation is never a "give and take," but leads to a monologue — usually by the least interesting and least informed person present.

I am enclosing an article from December's *Reader's Digest,* which you should all read again and again. It is the best thing I have.ever seen written on this subject.

Father

and none of the children was quite sure to which it was *really* addressed. Needless to say, the end generation made it a point to be intelligently mute, or mutely intelligent for a good two weeks.

On one occasion, Father, who considered smoking a sin just this side of adultery, or dirty talk, was irritated to the point of addressing only the guilty. In one of the very few memoranda addressed not to "The Children" but to individuals called Aloise, John, Jane, Billy, Patricia, Reid, he offers the passing comment that:

Knowing your catholic interests in literature, I am quoting from a life of Columbus which recently appeared. Rodrigo, one of Columbus' associates, landed in San Salvador, and made the following quaint statement:
"They pressed lighted tobacco upon us,
and Luis de Torres and I, being
Andalusians and nothing daunted,
inhaled the smoke and straightway
were seized into a spasm of coughing
and into a dizziness that
lightened our heads and mellowed
our humors and then to vomiting.
Surely this weed was a drug and
all the natives used it and

perchance that accounted for their
debility, for, indeed they were a
fragile people; seemingly not ill
and yet never robust."

Father

This preoccupation with the collective character of his children did not, however, deter Father from coming down to earth, if earth needed to be come down to. "My dear John," he wrote, just before John's 14th birthday:

> On Sunday you told me that you would see Mr. Tuttle Monday and would write me that day the name of a book on saddle horses. You did not do this Monday, Tuesday or Wednesday.
>
> My getting a letter from you about this matter is not of great importance, but it is very important that you do what you promised to do. I have noticed invariably that those of my friends who keep their slightest promise are successful and those who don't keep their small promises are not successful.
>
> This is a very slovenly habit to get into and one which promises to be a lifelong habit with you and Aloise if you don't correct it right away. After this, when I ask you to do anything I wish you would think it over seriously and if you decide it is too much trouble tell me then that you won't do it. I quite understand that your training in doing things has been very deficient, but you and Aloise are now old enough to do some thinking for yourself and develop your own character.

Affectionately,
Father

cc to Miss Aloise Buckley

Again, to Jim, aged 16:

Mr. James Buckley,
Millbrook School,
Millbrook, New York

My dear Jimmy:
    I am returning to you my check for $10.00, and am sending you additional check for $24.00. The $34.00 is a return of money you paid me to reimburse me for the purchase of the binoculars, which I am giving you as a present. Your Mother and I remarked Sunday afternoon that we were very pleased at the seriousness with which you take your debts. She said you had paid her everything you owed her.
    With lots of love,

Affectionately,
Father

Honest Jim, 1940: *"Your mother and I remarked Sunday afternoon that we were very pleased at the seriousness with which you take your debts."*

On another occasion, Father wrote the headmistress of the Ethel Walker School:

> "I have intended for some time to write or speak to you about Maureen's speech. She does not speak distinctly and has a tendency, in beginning a sentence, to utter any number of words almost simultaneously. Anything that the school may do to improve this condition would be greatly appreciated by us. I have always had a feeling that there was some physical obstruction that caused this, but doctors say there is not. She is one of two or three children in our family who have no wisdom teeth — perhaps this has something to do with it. I hope you will pardon my adding to your many burdens."

(He did not circulate, beyond the eldest five of family, his description of the night when, in Mother's absence, Father and 8-year-old Maureen were roommates:

> After Maureen and I had played two games of Parchesi and I had read her one story and she had read me one story, I mentioned the fact that it was almost two hours past her bedtime. Your sister asked me pointedly where her Mother and I habitually undressed for bed. I replied that your Mother usually undressed in the bathroom while I read the evening paper, and when your Mother had come to bed, I took my turn in the bathroom. I added that, in view of her superior sex, Maureen would be given priority in the bathroom.
>
> Your maidenly sister gave vent to an enormous sigh and said: "Well, I'm glad to know our *main* problem is solved!"
>
> I hope you all appreciate the ladylike delicacy of your sister's instincts.

Father's own delicacy was manifested far less directly than his young daughter's. During Reid's sophomore year at Yale, in a "Memorandum to William F. Buckley, Jr." Father writes:

> Jane tells me that Reid has quite extensive sideburns. When he started growing them I mentioned them to him very casually and he said that that was required of the Glee Club—which sounds rather extraordinary. If you could gently suggest to him that he remove them, it would be a great relief to the family. I would rather he would not belong to the Glee Club.
>
>   Father

John, 1928: *"You did not do this Monday . . .*

1935: *". . . Tuesday . . .*

1938: *". . . or Wednesday."*

Not long after this, however, Father, repenting his rebuke, sent out to the Phoenix Bank in Hartford, a

Memorandum for Mr. Fenniman:

It seems to be the consensus of opinion that Reid should be getting an allowance of $100.00 a month beginning in June, and that out of this he should be able to accumulate enough money to buy clothes and books and so on at the beginning of college; and that thereafter his room and board bills should be paid, and that in addition he should get $100.00 a month.

One or two of the children were so presumptuous as to suggest that Reid be given a lecture on the value of money and on the difficulty of acquiring it, which I will not pass on to Reid.

W. F. Buckley

WFB: cpr
CC: Miss Mildred Hembdt
    Mr. Fergus Reid Buckley

For Father's atonements were as roundabout as his remonstrances. Reid's small pomposities, when he was growing up, were a source of continuing joy and exasperation to Father, and at times his correspondence with or concerning Reid almost doubled the volume of mail at the Sharon Post Office. In 1939, for instance, when Reid was nine years old, Father wrote from New York:

My dear Reid:
    I have just submitted your music to a music house here and have sold it for $1.00. I will give you the dollar when I get out to Sharon.
    They fully agreed with you and with me that your music was a masterpiece.

Affectionately,
Father

When Reid was 15, he received a routine letter from a firm of certified public accountants, asking him to confirm his balance at the bank. Reid answered:

Dear Sirs:
    In reply to your inquiries concerning my account at the Sharon National Bank, I have at the present date the above mentioned ———. I drew a check for the amount of———in late January: It

was made out to Miss Celia Reilly. The recent bank statement sent to me by your firm confused the issue as you see by crediting my account for———. I delayed answer till the matter was cleared up. I received word from C. R. that she had as yet not cashed my check a few days hence.

I would appreciate it if you informed me what your business is with me: purely a question of curiosity concerning why any person deems it necessary to become acquainted with my personal account.

Yours truly,
F. Reid Buckley

Impressed with the manly dignity of his reply, Reid sent a copy to Father, adding that "I do not intend in the future to tell anything about my pecuniary affairs to any company that feels it would like a bird's eye view of me financially." The episode filled Father with such fearful joy that he circulated one hundred copies of the correspondence to his relatives and friends.

In 1953, when the family newspaper, the *Grelmschatka*, finally got around to covering Reid's wedding, three years and two sons after it occurred, Father wrote the following biography:

Maureen, 1938: *"Well, I'm glad to know our main problem is solved."*

Reid, 1934: *"Reid became almost speechless, a rare condition for him."*

To the Editor of GRELMSCHATKA:

In connection with Reid's wedding, you have asked me to give you a short account of his youthful career.

Reid started life by being born in the American Hospital in Paris on Bastille Day, July 14, 1930, having in mind undoubtedly the prospect of entering French politics and becoming President, since the locale of his birth precluded his occupying a similar post in the United States. We had lived in Paris since 1929. In the fall of 1932 your Mother took you all to England where we rented a house in Edward's Square. Billie and Patricia attended school for a year at Cavendish Square Convent, Parkman Place, located very near our home, and Reid and Maureen were of course at home.

Reid by 1933 spoke Spanish fluently, but no English. Being very fond of talking as a young man, and finding himself with no audience, he proceeded to master the English language within a few weeks. It seemed to be no problem at all.

Shortly after our arrival in London Reid told me that he wanted to see Buckingham Palace, thinking no doubt that he would walk right in and have a chat with the King. I took him to see the Palace from the outside; Reid was greatly impressed at its size and its isolation. As we passed by the two guards in their magnificent uniforms standing in the small cupolas on either side of the entrance, Reid became almost speechless, a rare condition for him. Reid told me that he had thought there was only one King and was surprised to find two, thinking of course that each of the guards was a king.

Reid used to come into his Mother's and my bedroom while in England dressed sometimes as a Bishop (he skipped the Priest stage) and sometimes as a Major General and occasionally as a King. He would march past our beds and look into the mirror at the corner to see how much he had impressed us, never suspecting that at the same time we could see him through the mirror.

I stayed in France on some business most of the time but came over to England very often. On one occasion when I appeared unannounced and to the surprise of Reid and Nana who were sitting on the stairway, Reid exclaimed to Nana, "El Señor!" Nana was much embarrassed and asked Reid what he meant by El Señor, to which he replied, "Oh, that Señor that comes once in a while and eats and sleeps here. They also call him 'mi papá."

While eating his meals in the children's dining room Reid entertained the servants and others and continued this practice after he got to Sharon. One time, after Dr. and Mrs. Chaffee had had lunch with us, we asked Reid to perform, which he was always willing to do; he was about to start when he noticed that Mrs. Chaffee was talking. This bothered him tremendously, and after waiting a few seconds, he exclaimed "Jesús, Mariá, José! Cómo habla esta señora," to the great amusement of Dr. Chaffee when we translated this for him and also of Mrs. Chaffee.

We returned to London in 1938, where we had an apartment on Portland Place. The President of France and his wife made a ceremonial visit that year to the King and Queen of England, who met their distinguished guests at the station, and proceeded from there in a regal procession to Buckingham Palace.

Thousands of English people, as is their custom, lined the route to view the ceremony, coming early and bringing lunches. Miss D'Arcy took Reid and Maureen to see this spectacle, and Reid, as Miss D'Arcy told us later in the day, lost no time in getting acquainted with the spectators in his section. He modestly asked them if they would like to hear him sing, and when they of course said "Yes," he again modestly asked them whether they wanted him to sing in English or Spanish or French, with the result, as he may have planned, that he was urged to sing in all these languages. He complied with great dramatic fervor. After his repertoire was exhausted, and possibly the spectators, he volunteered to dance and did some very intricate steps to the delight of these very nice and hospitable people.

He then gave them his views on a number of matters that seemed to be puzzling the world. Among other things, he told them he did not think very highly of English cooking; he also thought the English were not very proficient in music, especially classical music. However, he was tremendously impressed with the English military display in the procession and when asked if America had an Army, he said, "Oh, yes, a very fine Army." They asked how large an Army and he said that it was very large, that his guess would be that there were over 100 soldiers in our Army.

Reid on "Vagabond," Rhinebeck, 1938: *"Reid reported that he had gone right up to the car and looked at Mr. Roosevelt but that the latter, evidently, did not recognize him, because he did not speak. After this slight, he put on his Willkie button again . . ."*

In 1940, when Reid was about ten years of age, we were at the Rhinebeck Horse Show where Reid was displaying a large Willkie button. President Roosevelt came in to see the show and sat in his car with a Swedish Princess, surrounded by secret service men. We were in the grandstand and Reid decided to go over and call on the President. He first took the precaution of removing his Willkie button. When he returned in about an hour it was apparent that he was very disappointed that the secret service men had not questioned him as they did others, and he reported that he had gone right up to the car and looked at Mr. Roosevelt but that the latter evidently did not recognize him because he did not speak. After this slight, he put on his Willkie button again and resumed his loyalty to this mountebank. (Not meaning by this that President Roosevelt was not one also).

Reid (and I hope the rest of the children will pardon this statement) is the real intellectual of the family. He reads nothing but good literature. There are few young men of his age that have as extensive a vocabulary. He was at one stage in his youth so given to quotations that the rest of the children dared not mention at the table any play by Shakespeare, or the poetry of Keats or Shelley or Milton without Reid standing up and delivering himself of quotations from these authors that sometimes occupied most of the mealtime. Reid graduated at the head of his class at Millbrook School and distinguished himself at Yale. As a sophomore he was head of the debating team, with juniors and seniors under him, and he won many important debates including the one with Oxford. He was highly thought of by the professors and especially in the English Department. He also wrote a lot of poetry, and good poetry. He was a member of Fence Club, The Elizabethan Club, Torch Honor Society and Skull & Bones, and Vice-Chairman of The Yale Daily News.

He had the good judgment to marry the very beautiful and gracious Elizabeth (Betsy) Howell.

— Father

Rhinebeck Horse Show, 1937: Bill, Patricia: *"If you expect to entertain them, you will find it necessary to furnish them with 1) a horse, 2) a yacht, or 3) a private airplane."*

It is worthy of note that here Father's flow of entertaining anecdotes about his son ended at Reid's tenth year, though entertaining incidents had continued for some years longer. The absurdities of adolescence were far less amusing to him than those of children, and what amusement they did provoke in him was apt to be tinged with exasperation. Carol's easily outraged dignity, at the age of 13, gave rise to the practical joke which can be read between the lines of the following "Memorandum to the Children."

Ex Catawba

Editor of Grelmschatka:—

It is with great humiliation that I find it necessary to report an incident in our otherwise pleasant tour this summer of Spain and Portugal. When we got to the beautiful hotel at Bussaco, Portugal, I stopped to register while your Mother and the two girls took the elevator. Unfortunately, and in the presence of two bell boys, Maureen had a recurrence of the hiccups, a malady from which she suffered on occasion during our trip to the great embarrassment of Carol. When the three ladies arrived in their room, Carol's face was red and she expressed the thought that it might be well to leave before night or at least have our meals served in our rooms, as she feared that news of this occurrence would spread over the hotel like wildfire. To our amazement, immediately after dinner we received the following communication (in Portuguese, of course) from the manager, which I am sure you will all understand and which I am glad not to have to translate into English as it might fall into alien hands.

"El Senhor Gerente presenta sus cumplimentos al distinguido Senhor Buckley y a su distinguida familia y espela que gozaran de heste humilde hotel.

"Al mesmo tempo—y perdone Uste nostro atrevimento—se sente obliggato a le participar que en heste establecimento esta estrictamente prohibido— pe le Capitulo 34, Articulo 10, Regla 203A—o hicope. Me despos de consutla con nostros socios, estamos intermente dispostos a le servir sus comidas en su habitazio.

"Ahora, perdone Uste pelo me atrevo a la confianza, inspirado en los francos semblantes de Vd. y de su distinguida Senhora, de sugerir un remedio eficaz para esta desagradable enfermadad— y es, nala menos, se abstener de comer tan vorazmente, reforzado per cuantiosas dosis de carbonato de soso.

"Me, si Uste se ofende con hesta bien intencionada insinuacion (que espelo no sea el caso), Vd. podra largarse de este hotel, e irse con Dios, junta con su Senhora (siempre distinguida) y su afligida hija y su hermanita quien, siento insinuarle, esta dema-

siada disposta a la coqueteria, calidad menos desagradable, per
supuosto, pero si mas reprensible que ei hicopo—verificando su
despedida, per suposto, despos de pagar su cuenta (incluyendo
esta noche por ser ahola despos de la cinco).

q. s. m. b.
Father

**Aboard the United States, 1954: W. F. B., A. S. B., Carol,
Maureen:** *". . . perdone Uste pelo me atrevo a la confianza,
inspirado en los francos semblantes de Ud. y de su distinguida
Senhora, de sugerir un remedio eficaz para esta desagradable
enfermedad—y es, nala menos, se abstener de comer tan
vorazmente . . ."*

Sometimes Father got into what can only be described as a
rut, on a given subject. One of the longest was the "car" rut—
probably because cars and Father always disliked each other in-
tensely—and the car rut consisted of at least twelve memoranda
dealing with their effect on character, on physique, on intelligence;
their stupidity, brutality, malice and wilful disobedience, etc. Only

a few of these can be found, but the series seems to have started with the following letter to "My dear Jane:"

> We were having a general conversation last night and Priscilla said that you had recently found out that you were charged with your car. I suppose I didn't take the precaution to tell Mr. Fenniman that this was a graduation present from your mother and me. Would you drop me a note about this and confirm this sad news and tell me just what the price of the car was. I will send a check within the next week or two to the bank to reimburse your account. After this, when you get hard-up, you should always write me about it; I may not be able to help you but I can give you a lot of sympathy.
>
> > Lots of love,
> > Affectionately,
> > Father

Jane, 1946: ". . . *when you get hard-up, you should always write me about it; I may not be able to help you but I can give you a lot of sympathy.*"

Perhaps it was the memory of Jane's firm rejection of (a) a
hunter (a horse that hunts), (b) a pearl necklace, (c) an ermine
jacket in lieu of the car Father promised her in a moment of aber-
ration, that reopened the smouldering feud. At any rate, the
memos of the following two years were devoted almost exclusively
to cars.

For instance:

I think there is entirely too much driving of cars by our children. It is not unusual for two or three cars to come into New
York in a day. In the first place, the best and most sensible way of
getting to New York is by train; that is how over 90% of the
people from Sharon move from one place to the other. The cars
are extremely expensive and their operation is expensive, and they
are dangerous as well. I am sure that there is a very large mileage
registered on the car of every member of the family.

Outside of John and Priscilla, none of you has earned enough
money to buy a car and I think that you should be very careful
in your use of one.

Some of you have gotten into the practice of arriving swankily
in a car and turning it over to Mr. Cronin to park, asking him to
put up the dollar for parking charges. Anyone who hasn't a spare
dollar, or having one fails to carry it in his pocket, should not be
driving a car into New York.

I have thought of this matter a number of times, and I am sure
your Mother has.

W. F. Buckley

Another memo, from Camden this time:

Now that most of you have your own cars, and the so-called
(by the children) "family cars" which suffered greatly during
the War for many and varied reasons have been replaced with
new ones, I hope you will all try not to age them too much
during the coming Holidays.

First of all, if those of you who are nicotine addicts should be
overcome by your craving while you are driving, please use the
ashtrays. While I agree with Mayor McCorkle that everything
possible should be done to keep Camden clean, I also would like
to keep the inside of the cars clean, so please do not throw papers
and trash on the floor. Regarding the City of Camden, I feel that
you are all old enough to make your own decisions.

Second, Ben Heath tells me the station-wagon should never be
left out over-night. So if you use it in the evening, be sure it is

put in the garage, no matter how exhausted you may think you feel when you come home. Moreover, be careful when you do put it away, because station-wagons have become too wide to enter normal garages.

Third, if you are unfortunate enough to scratch or dent a fender, report it to the main office. We carry expensive insurance policies to cover all damage over $50.00; any damage under that figure will be paid for by the responsible party.

I hope that none of you younger children will take the preceding sentence as a suggestion that you have only major accidents.

Affectionately,
Father

Aloise and "Red Mike," 1939: *"I have been much concerned of late with the apparent inability of any of you, at any time, to go anywhere on foot, although I am sure your Mother would have informed me if any of you had been born without the walking capacity of a normal human being."*

The following communication, circulated the summer after the war, was a mere recapitulation of several others.

Memorandum to the Buckley Children:
I have been much concerned of late with the apparent inability of any of you, at any time to go anywhere on foot, although I am sure your Mother would have informed me if any of you had

been born without the walking capacity of a normal human being.

A few of the older children, notably Priscilla, occasionally walk a few hundred yards behind a golf ball, but all the others "exercise" exclusively by sitting on a horse or a sailboat.

Concurrently, I have noticed that the roads around Sharon are crowded with Buckley cars at all hours of the day and night, and it has been years since any of you has been able to get as far as the Town Clock, much less the Post Office without a car, or if under 16, a car and a chauffeur.

All the cars are left out every night in all kinds of weather, undoubtedly because of the dangerous fatigue involved in walking from the garage to the house.

I think that each of you should consider a course of therapy designed to prevent atrophy of the leg muscles if only for aesthetic reasons, or you might even go to the extreme of attempting to regain the art of walking, by easy stages of course. The cars might then be reserved for errands covering distances of over 50 yards or so.

Affectionately,
Father

And a resigned protest to Bill's future father-in-law.

Memorandum to Austin C. Taylor:

I have tried for many years to interest my children in conventional sports, but I have not been very successful. Billie is easily the worst in this regard, having no interest in tennis, golf, or other activities which satisfy the great majority of the nation. If you expect to entertain him, you will find it necessary to furnish him with 1) a horse, 2) a yacht, or 3) a private airplane.

Aloise joins me in affectionate regards to you and Babe.

Will

The Buckley children were at all times kept *au courant* with the life and times of their brother Bill, sometimes unkindly referred to as "The Young Mahster," by means of memoranda of which the following, dated May 25, 1941, is typical.

Memorandum to Aloise et al.

You will all, no doubt, be glad to know that Billy has again achieved his high B average, and is subsequently back on the Millbrook School Honor Roll. The reason for this academic improvement is the fact that he has terminated all connections with the Silo and the Mill (and vice-versa), has completely ostracized the piano, and has let Pantepec and the foreign situation go to the dogs.

It may come as a surprise, therefore, to some of them, that one of Father's "ruts" was critical of Bill, and lasted from the time Bill learned to write, at the age of six, till he learned to type, at the age of eighteen.

February 16, 1940

My Dear Billy:

I think more strongly than ever that you should take hold of your handwriting situation and work on the new system along the lines that I had discussed with Miss Reilly. You will never be able to take your present handwriting and do anything with it, in my opinion. It is not very intelligent to go through life with a handwriting that people cannot understand. Aloise has done that and has almost incapacitated herself for writing. I am sure that you will get down to work with Miss Reilly and correct this situation.

Affectionately,
Father

Again:

October 10, 1940

Mr. Edward Pulling,
Millbrook School,
Millbrook, New York
Dear Mr. Pulling:

My wife sent me a letter from Billy today which reminds me of his very illegible handwriting. He uses the backhand, very awkwardly, and it seems to me it will cause him a lot of inconvenience and annoyance in the future as well as retarding his speed in writing. I realize that such things as handwriting should have been taken care of long before a boy gets to Millbrook, but nevertheless I wonder if there is anything you could have done for Billy in this connection.

And a year later:

My dear Billy:

Your Mother and I were delighted to receive your mid-term reports and to learn through Miss Reilly that you were back on the "A and B" list again. You should be very proud of your work, in which you have shown great character and determination.

The only stumbling block seems to be your handwriting, which continues to be illegible. I do think that you should buckle down now and correct this. I am sure you will be able to do so with a little application.

With lots of love,
Affectionately,
Father

(Bill's handwriting is still illegible, but he types very well indeed.)

Any other criticism Father made of Bill positively reeks of insincerity. When the young Mahster was 15, for instance, Father wrote:

> My dear Billy:
> In thinking over my letter to you it may have appeared very critical and I hope you did not take it that way. Your Mother and I like very much your attitude of having strong convictions and of not being too bashful to express them. What I meant was that you would have to learn to be more moderate in the expression of your views and try to express them in a way that would give as little offense as possible to your friends.

Vancouver, 1950. W. F. B., Bill: *"In matters of love and engagement, my children are a most unscrupulous lot."*

His real feeling about Bill's moderation in the expression of his views can be gleaned from the speech which Father wrote but was too shy to deliver on the eve of Bill's wedding.

I feel that the honor of the Buckley family, or what is left of it after the activities of my children during the last year, requires that I now, somewhat belatedly I confess, divulge to the Taylor family that they have been the victims of fraud.

In matters of love and marriage, my children are a most unscrupulous lot. They were determined to get Ann and Pat as sisters-in-law and, as usual, let nothing stand in their way. I must tell you that my children's tactics vary with the character of their victims: with Ann, who is extremely wily herself, they resorted to prayer; with Pat, however, whom they consider very strongminded, they despaired of prayer and resorted to artificial wile.

For the last five or six years our daughter Patricia had announced each spring that Pat was going to visit us in Sharon and each Fall that she was coming to Camden. After Pat failed to materialize for several seasons, I asked Patricia about this mysterious girl and the answer was, "Pat looks like a queen, she acts like a queen and is just the wife for Billy." Poor Pat's fate was inevitable after this. When Pat did not come to visit the Buckleys, Patricia decided to visit the Taylors. She then shrewdly suggested to an oil company that Billy and Patricia's fiance, Brent Bozell, could do excellent work for the company in Alberta and Saskatchewan. In due course she casually suggested that the Taylors invite Billy for a short visit. I will explain later why the other Buckley children joined in the plot.

Brent's name moves me to digress from my story for just a second to illustrate the lethal qualities of these children when they are on the hunt. Billy and Brent became inseparable friends the day they arrived at Yale. Billy told Patricia how wonderful Brent was, and notwithstanding that she had not yet met him, Patricia immediately fell in love. Parenthetically, Brent had shown some radical tendencies in his career in Yale, which Billy deplored but which he said had greatly moderated since their acquaintance. After spending one evening with Patricia, Brent asked Billy how he would like to have a radical for a brother-in-law, whereupon Billy telephoned Patricia that she was engaged. Nothing that Brent said could change this fact—he was engaged and that was that.

But to return to our subject. The alarming thing about Patricia's plan is that it immediately developed into a conspiracy among the rest of the children, in which Patricia and Billy had no part. Billy has always been regarded by the rest of the family, except Patricia, as being slightly deficient in a sense of humor, and unbearably arrogant and dictatorial. The latter quality, I gather from chance remarks, they attribute in part to the former defect. Now, his brothers and sisters have devised all kinds of plans to tame Billy without any success whatever, and when Patricia and Billy told them how strongminded and determined Pat was, they had the inspiration that here was the instrument to use for their purpose. In mitigation of the determination of the other children, but that you may understand fully the gravity of the role that is being assigned to innocent Pat, I must give some illustrations of the character and imperiousness of the Taylor's future son-in-law.

When he was six years old, he wrote the King of England demanding that England pay her war debt.

When Billy was eight and a half, a guest remarked in the presence of her daughters, ages 25 and 28, that she had no religion and that her daughters had not been baptized. Within three hours Billy reported to his Mother that while the two daughters were taking a nap he and Patricia had baptized them. Their souls were thus saved regardless of their will or their mother's

When Billy was ten, he attended Beaumont College, near Ascot, and within two days of his arrival he called at the office of the President, a distinguished scholar, and told him that there were a number of things about Beaumont that he did not like. Father Sharkey, who recounted this incident to us later, said that the shock rendered him too paralyzed to speak and that before he recovered Billy had explained the deficiencies of this venerable college.

One week-end Jane, about two years older than Billy, brought to Sharon a little girl about her own age. This girl was not a bit shy and when we sat down to dinner began expounding on world affairs. Billy arrived late and after listening to not more than two sentences said, "Look here, (what's her name?) Cecily, you are entirely too young to have such positive convictions, and besides I am going to tell you something that will surprise you—you are mistaken in every statement you have made." He then turned to me in an aside, which everybody could hear, and said, "I took a dislike to her as I came in the door."

When in 1938, the older children founded a local newspaper in Sharon devoted to the advocacy of isolationism, which brought on the family animadversion of the entire community, Billy was given the special job of delivering the paper to the post office because he was too young and innocent to realize that he might be mobbed on the way. Considering himself a member of the staff he solemnly announced at dinner that evening that the Editorial Board must make no decisions in policy without consulting him.

It was decided to send Patricia to the Ethel Walker School when she was about thirteen years of age in spite of the misgivings of

Billy. Based on his experience with the weaker sex he felt that the
girls at the school were not sufficiently refined for Patricia, although his sister Jane had been attending the school for a couple
of years without any protest from him. As we left her at school
we could see a look of consternation on Billy's face. He had, in
his preoccupation with global affairs and some correspondence
with congressmen overlooked a very important item. He felt that
the girls' dresses at Ethel Walker were a little too short, so he
located Patricia at a distance from the car of about 30 feet, and
then had her reach up with the right hand and then the left hand
until he found the proper length for her dresses. Then he pinned
her dress in the right places and gave instructions for alterations.

At Millbrook School he appeared uninvited at a faculty meeting
to report that a member of the faculty had deprived him of the
right to express his political views in class and proceeded to ex-
pound to the stunned faculty on the virtues of isolationism, the
dignity of the Catholic Church and the political ignorance of
the school staff.

Having no witnesses here to corroborate all of these statements
(my wife, while entirely too gentle to attempt fraud, is nevertheless too loyal to condone this exposure of her children) I
appeal to Dr. Shumiatcher here present for a confirmation of the
following:

A summer ago when Billy spent the summer at Regina (he was
gradually being moved nearer to Pat by Patricia) he and Brent
were leaving Dr. Shumiatcher's office as a professor from Yale
was entering. According to Dr. Shumiatcher, the professor asked
if that could possibly have been Bill Buckley of Yale. When advised that that was the same person, the professor said, again
according to Dr. Shumiatcher, "That boy took a course under
me last year on politics and I give you my word he talked twice
as much as I did during the entire year!"

Fortunately, there is another objective witness here, Mr. Mac-
Donald of San Antonio. Billy was transferred to the San Antonio
Military Base when demobilization started, and after being there
forty-eight hours wrote a letter to the Commanding General
telling him that he had found a great waste of manpower and
his staff was inadequate, and expressed surprise that such things
could be. He submitted a plan of his own redesigning the entire
system. This letter and plan had to go through Mr. MacDonald,
who intervened and saved Billy from an immediate court martial.

There are many other instances but I have given you enough
to satisfy my own conscience and enough to warn Mr. and Mrs.
Taylor that there is a purpose behind this assiduous courtship by
the entire family and that Billy's brothers and sisters expect to
use Pat to accomplish what they have failed to do and that is to

beat Billy into submission, even if it requires his being beaten into insensibility. If Pat survives in her course between Scylla, the family, and Charybdis, her husband, it will be a tribute to the stamina that she has inherited from her Father and Mother.

I feel that this report, while very belated, will serve to be a vindication of my wife and myself. I can now, however, foresee from the frowns on my children's faces the storm that is gathering and which will descend on my head if I do not isolate myself until after the wedding tomorrow afternoon at 1:30.

Father

W. F. B., A. S. B.: *"I can see from the frowns on my children's faces the storm that is gathering and which will descend on my head if I do not isolate myself until after the wedding tomorrow afternoon at 1:30."*

But the old filing cabinets are also crammed with testimony to the fact that Father's children were far more to him than a source of mingled amusement, exasperation, pleasure and disapproval. He loved them with a watchful and an anxious protectiveness which, moreover, was not in the slightest *laissez-faire*. Not that his children didn't make their own mistakes, but only

after the long exchange of formal memoranda (in the Buckley
family, the equivalent of a tooth-and-nail battle) which invariably
ended one memo short of the ungentlemanly ultimatum which
might have led to the discourteous refusal. Thus ended, for instance, the correspondence with the college senior who planned
to go into editorial work; a correspondence which began:

> Dear Maureen:
>   Your Mother and I have thought for a long time that you are
> intellectually and temperamentally suited for a law career, which
> you would find you would enjoy very much.
>   I am sure that Jimmy would have no trouble getting you into
> the Yale Law School and as a matter of fact I don't think he
> would allow you to go anywhere else.
>   You should write to the Dean of the Law School as soon as . . .

Another exchange, this time with the middle-aged mother of
seven children:

> Dear Aloise:
>   Your Mother and I both think that it would be far more sensible
> for you and your family to live in Sharon than in Hartford. The
> Bingham house is now on the market and I am sure it can be
> bought very reasonably.
>   Mr. Cole can take you through the house either this Saturday
> or next. Be sure to let him know which is . . .

Father's plans for the lives and careers of his sons were couched
in far more deliberate and thoughtful terms, than he used to his
daughters (men have *reasoning* power), but they did not the less
present decisions on his part, not suggestions. In 1953, the year
Bill's *God and Man at Yale* came out, Father wrote him:

> I had planned to have a long talk with you in the East about
> your future. . . .
>   In the first place, I will state that if you are in this country
> during the next electoral campaign, I think it would be invaluable
> experience for you to . . . participate in X's campaign. I liked this
> man's letters very much, as did your Mother. Maureen got so
> enthusiastic I think she would like to volunteer, with the reserva-
> tion only that you must adopt all of her views, or none. I have
> the feeling that you will inevitably be drawn into politics, or
> alternatively catapult yourself into this field. What this country
> needs is a politician who has an education, and I don't know of

one. There hasn't been an educated man in the Senate or House of Representatives since Sumner of Texas quit in disgust three or four years ago. Joe Bailey and Spooner were great constitutional lawyers with a broad knowledge of history; Borah was a thinker and had a thorough knowledge of American constitutional law; and John Sharp Williams, of Mississippi, was a thoroughly educated man. I don't know of any other educated Congressman or Senator in the last 25 years.

If you are going into politics, or if without going into politics you want to continue to discuss public questions, you should spend a couple of years in study. . . . If this is to be your course, I would think that you could very profitably spend from 8 to 10 months a year for two years at Oxford or Cambridge, and study under one or two of the outstanding scholars there. . . . You could, of course, do the same thing at a French or German university, but you could not afford in addition to go through the struggle of either perfecting your French or of mastering German. Besides, the English have an innate mastery of politics and government which is not reflected in their stupid incursion into Socialism.

The other alternative, and this could be deferred until you get back from your trip to Europe, or even until after your return from two years of study there (unless the business should go bankrupt because of your absence for so long a period) is the matter of going into business with John and Jimmy and their associates. . . . In my opinion, you would make a great executive, and it would not take you long to get into the spirit of what we are doing and trying to do, and I believe this is a field that would fascinate you. You would get primarily the pleasure coming from adventure (and gambling), and in addition the multiple interests of dealing with governments and bankers and oil companies. . . .

I do hope that you will discuss this matter with Mr. and Mrs. Taylor, while you are there, and possibly permit Pat and Christopher to sit in the room while you are doing so. (A little phenobarbital would help to keep them quiet!)

Lots of love. . . .
Father

If Father noted in later years that Maureen still gobbled her words, that Bill's handwriting was totally unreadable and Aloise seemed never to emerge from a cocoon of cigarette smoke; that, in fact, the barrage of memoranda he had shot at his children had remained to a large extent unheeded, this was no reason to desist. And so, from his hotel in Bad Gastein two weeks before his death came an admonitory note to a 36-year old daughter.

My dear Priscilla,
    Since you and Carol plan to spend several weeks in Mexico, I
think you should know that young ladies of good families do not
go unescorted in Mexico City. This is a custom I think you girls
should respect. . . .

                                        Affectionately,
                                        Father

                                                        A.B.H.

Winter, Great Elm: *"For he remembered that they were but flesh; a wind that passeth away, and cometh not again."*

III. *The Squire:*
A Reminiscence

By VAN ZANDT WHEELER

"Whenever he was trapped in conversation with boring people, the expression on his face was that of an early Christian martyr...."

MY FIRST MEETING WITH Will Buckley came about in a curious way. We had both been residents of Sharon for several years, yet our paths had never crossed, a circumstance we often spoke of with regret later on. W.F.B. was a Conservative in politics and, on the occasion in question, he had written a letter-to-the editor of *The Lakeville Journal*, a lively weekly published in the nearby town of that name, taking issue with the views of some other letter-writer. What the controversy was about has long since slipped my mind, but it must have involved some phase of the then raging Conservative-Liberal "cold war." Being very much in the Conservative camp myself, I wrote W.F.B., commending his position. He was so surprised to find an ally in this exceptionally well-fed, well-clothed and well-housed area, where the smart sophisticates and intellectual elite present a Liberal front as solid as a Greek phalanx, that he wrote, inviting me to lunch.

Thus began the most close-knit, rewarding friendship of my life, if such can be measured in terms of respect, admiration and the deep and abiding affection I was to feel for this extraordinary, many-sided man. And many-sided he surely was, as the record of his career amply attests. However, as this career is adequately sketched in other chapters of this book I shall confine myself to the phase of which I have first-hand knowledge; our friendship.

Almost from the start, we were on first name terms with the Buckleys, so it is only as Aloise and Will that I seem able to think of them.[1] We dined frequently at each other's homes, and Will and I lunched together on almost a weekly basis, particularly in the period following his breakdown in health, when he was confined to his bed or room. As he gained strength, and was able to get around, these lunches were served in the library or living room. Invariably, on rejoining my wife, Claire Louise, she wanted to know what the menu had been; and just as invariably, I could not tell her, my entire attention having been engrossed in the matters W.F.B. and I had been discussing. There was a single exception to this; the coffee. Will was very definitely a crank on this beverage and would have nothing short of the superlative, served piping hot and as strong as Samson. What enjoyable hours those were for me; and they must have been equally so for W.F.B., since he kept up the ritual of further invitations.

I never met a man whose personality so impressed me. He was human to the core, kind beyond measure and generous to a fault, but not one to invite the back-slappers of this world, since he was as dignified as he was agreeable. He had a grand sense of humor, and a well stocked mind. As a close and understanding friend, I never had occasion to sample the iron force of his character, though out-croppings of its ore were everywhere in evidence. In a word, W.F.B., I think, possessed all the qualities I had admired all my life, yet never before found packaged in one man.

The Buckley saga, as I have come to think of it, would never have taken the form it did, but for what I called luck, and what Will, himself, really believed to be an act of divine intervention in his behalf. He was well into his mid-thirties when he met, wooed, won and married Aloise. Both of them have told me that it was a case of love at first sight. She was fourteen years his junior, beautiful of person, finely endowed of mind, like himself a Catholic, and the very essence of old New Orleans charm. Aloise was Will's full partner in everything. In my thought, they were indivisible. It was as though they shared one heart and one mind. More than once, when we drove to Sharon in the late

[1] It was only in the last ten or fifteen years of his life—and then with the closest friends that W.F.B. adapted the familiar first name style of address. His friends of twenty or thirty years or more, he addressed by their last names. [Ed.]

afternoon, we'd meet them out for a stroll, arm in arm. Such love must be good for a woman, since ten children and forty years later, Aloise is still beautiful, still as shapely as when she was a bride, and she would add, if she were here, much better dressed. Oddly enough, I knew her quite a while before I realized that beneath the velvet facade of her Southern charm, there dwelt a spirit and mind as resiliant as tempered steel, plus an efficiency and competence equal to Will's own. I told this to Will once, when he and I were lunching together.

"Yes," he replied, "I will say this for Aloise, she's about as perfect as God ever intended a mortal to be."

The struggles of his early days forced W.F.B. to become an adult while still hardly more than a boy, and developed and toughened his mental and moral muscles to a degree of strength capable of coping with the problems and tasks he was later to confront.

Will and I were of a generation, both of us having first seen the light of day in the eighteen-eighties. I think this accounted in a large measure for the political ideas and ideals we shared. Up to, and even a little beyond, the turn of the century, pretty close to 100 per cent of our citizenry were outright jingoes, patriots to the core. At the outbreak of the Spanish-American War, John L. Sullivan announced at a rally: "Gimme a hundred New York cops with their night-sticks, and I'll go down to Cuba and throw every damn Spaniard off the island." A publicity stunt? Possibly. But the point is that Sullivan himself, as well as thousands of his admirers, probably believed he could do it. In those days, the surest way for a boy or a man to get a punch on the nose was to sound off with any criticism of America. Present day Liberalism was yet to be born.

Will always claimed to have a bad memory. I had occasion to test him out on this several times, and, in consequence, arrived at the conclusion that in trivial matters, he did; in those of con-sequence, or real interest, his memory was good. To illustrate, in the days before his illness, he always carried a notebook and a pencil around with him. He was eternally doing nice things for his friends. If at dinner at Great Elm, for example, my wife hap-pened to praise a certain wine, he'd say: "I'll send you a few bottles of it"—and he'd make a note of it. Or it might involve a book. But the article, whatever it might be, always came through on schedule. My view is that he simply didn't want to clutter up his mind with things he considered trivial, hence he confided them to notes. In his business affairs as well as in matters of consequence, his memory was excellent. I was often amazed at the amount of miscellaneous knowledge he had stored up.

W.F.B. was, by all odds, the most modest man with respect to his own accomplishments, I ever knew. But his admiration for his children knew no bounds. Several years back, in one of my letters to him, I recall commenting on the brilliance of mind they all displayed. In his letter of reply, referring to this, he wrote, "I just don't know where they get it from." It never seemed to occur to him that, over and above their natural aptitudes, the rearing and education he had given them, plus his own wise supervision of their developing minds, had anything to do with the admirable end results.

As I previously noted, W.F.B. was forever doing nice or generous things for others, such as at Carol's coming-out party. What I call "Buckley Luck" as to weather, surely held good on that occasion, just as it had for the several big parties we had previously attended at Great Elm. A magnificent night, a huge tent on the lawn, and an immense dance floor set up therein. A name-orchestra that played, and played and played. No stops at all. Nor did the crowd thin out or the dancers stop. At about a quarter to three, Will, who had been watching the festivities from a strategically located chair, got up, and on the arm of his man (he was semi-paralyzed at this time) proceeded to the elevator, Carol tagging alongside, her slippers in her hand.

"It will all be over in a few minutes now," said Carol.

Will smiled down at her. "You all seem to be having such a good time, Carol, that I've arranged with the orchestra for another hour. You've got until four."

"Oh, thank you, Father, thank you so much!"

That was all Carol said; but I shall never forget the note of gratitude, nor yet Will's smile as he stepped into the elevator. To give pleasure to those he loved was Will's own greatest joy.

Much that I have set down about W.F.B. may seem to be on the sugary side. If so, that is only because the camera happened to snap him from a particular angle. In the arena of affairs, where he had spent well over half a century, he was no man to take lightly. "The oil business, at the time I entered it," he once said to me, "was a jungle. The only law was devour or be devoured. Even now," he added with a smile, "eternal vigilance is the rule unless you plan to lose your shirt."

"Isn't that the rule of business as a whole?" I asked.

"To a certain extent it is, no doubt," he conceded, "but hunting oil is a gamble. And many of the operators are as slippery as the oil they handle."

We were lunching across a card table in his room that day, and he got to reminiscing about things that had happened in the long ago. I forget the details, but there was a villain in the story. Merely telling the yarn, revived an old feud and the emotion that went with it.

"That man was a scallywag—the worst I ever ran up against," he said in a harsh voice. "He dealt from the bottom of the deck. He was an all around, unmitigated S. O. B."

That was the first and only time I ever heard W.F.B. swear, though I had never doubted that he had an adequate vocabulary of invectives, stored away for use in the event of a suitable emergency.

In the spring, about six years ago, I contracted pneumonia, a rather severe case. I refused to be hospitalized, so a bed was made up for me on a couch in the living room, close to the fireplace which was kept aglow day and night with oak logs. W.F.B. came up to see me almost daily for a week or more. In my mind's eye, every time I go into that room, I seem to see Will sitting there in the fire glow, a glass of Bourbon in hand and a platter of sandwiches alongside on a tray. It was not until some time later that I found out *why* he had been so attentive in the matter of his calls. Apparently I had looked so badly that he had expected me to die, so he later told my wife.

To me, the enigma was the manner in which W.F.B. managed to keep going. He had, in health, been an extraordinarily active man; then came the crippling strokes that paralyzed his left side, and forced him for several months to remain abed and physically inactive, but not mentally by any means. Soon, whether by grace of God, or his remarkably developed will power, he was on his feet again, and with the aid of a cane and a supporting arm, getting around pretty much as usual. He travelled, here and abroad, as before; he gave and attended parties, as before; he kept a vigilant eye on his business affairs, as before; he took his daily drive with Aloise, as before.

I was never at Kamschatka, the Buckley's winter home in South Carolina, but I know their life down there was, in many ways, more strenuous than it was in Sharon. The place was top-heavy with house guests; their own sons and daughters drifting in at frequent intervals, usually bringing along cascades of grandchildren, always to W.F.B.'s delight, though he confessed he couldn't at all keep track of their names. Some of his letters from Camden as I read them bring out his warmth of character and his wit.

This paragraph from a letter dated December 13, 1956:

> What you say about Reid's book means a great deal to us as we know you wouldn't say it if you didn't mean it, and you are more-than-well qualified to give an opinion of it. It encourages me very much and I do hope Reid will get it published. He is down here now and is working very hard on its final revision. He goes every morning to seven o'clock Mass, comes home and has a cup of coffee, then closes himself in his room, shuts off the telephone and works until two o'clock. The rest of the day he spends with his children and his dogs, the latter, I suspect, getting most of his attention.

After I had mentioned that Aloise's chirography was more difficult to decipher than the hieroglyphics in the tomb of King Tut-ankh-amen, this reply:

> I sent your letter over to Aloise, as I always do; but I have in mind particularly in this letter how you pay your respects to her handwriting, in which I entirely agree with you.

On the newly established school he had set up at Great Elm, and the brick-bats that were being thrown at it by the press at large: "I know that in the end I will have no one there but my own grandchildren, which is exactly what the school is for."

Once I asked Will what he thought of Catholic-Protestant marriages, seeing that two of his own children had crossed the line in this respect. He did not answer for a moment, obviously reflecting on his reply, as he always did when any question out of the ordinary was put to him.

"Generally speaking," he said at last, "I suppose it is best for people to marry in the faith in which they are brought up. But sometimes it works out another way and no harm is done. Besides, I can't forget that, but for such an intervention, I would have been a Protestant, myself."

"You?" I exclaimed in genuine astonishment.

Will nodded, and I could see an amused twinkle in his eyes. "Yes," he went on, "my Buckley grandfather was an Irishman, but a Protestant. However, he fell in love with a pretty girl, who was a Catholic. They wed. My father's generation was brought up, as is customary in such cases, in the latter faith, which, in turn, accounts for me following in their spiritual footsteps."

The Buckley sons and daughters had all gone through college at a time when unbridled liberalism was the order of the day and they had emerged, as Will put it, uncontaminated by all the social and political quackery to which they had been subjected. In discussing this one day, Will reminded me that, in his own youth, he had had to work his way through college and help support a family besides, which had left him no time or inclination to reform the world. Besides, he said, the intelligent and ambitious young men of that period were eager to follow in the footsteps of Rockefeller, Schwab, Carnegie and others of their kidney. These men had all achieved great success and wealth under their own power, starting from scratch. They were to be emulated. Their careers furnished incentive and hope.

"The opposite seems to be the ideal of this day, unfortunately," W.F.B. concluded. "Now they want to lop off the mountain tops and fill the valleys with them till all is level."

At lunch one day, W.F.B. did all the talking, and his subject was his oldest son, John. John had just closed an oil contract. The biggest oil deal in the last twenty-five years, Will said. It was with the Phillips Company and John had handled the negotiations from first to last. That was what Will was most proud of.

"This will teach certain people in Wall Street that the Buckleys have still to be reckoned with," he chuckled, "and in a big way, at that."

He then proceeded to do a bit of philosophizing about the oil business. The big operating companies such as Standard, Shell and the rest, he told me, are eternally on the hunt for the stuff, have their own experts combing the earth to find it. The aim of the smaller operators in the oil field Will informed me, is to locate oil and then sell or lease it to the operating company that eventually puts it into the filling stations where we buy our gas. But the battle over terms and price is often of epic proportions.

"If I do say so myself," concluded Will, "I was rather apt when things reached this point. First, I knew the real value of what I was selling; and second, and I think, most important, I had patience. After stating my terms I could wait, and was never in a hurry. Patience really came easily to me, since it was part of my nature. In John's case, it is the other way around, for he is impatient by nature. But he was patience to the Nth degree in his negotiations with Phillips."

As a writer, speaker and debater, his son, Bill, was the essence of all W.F.B. himself had stood and fought for politically. Will never missed being in the audience when Bill spoke if it were at all possible for him to be there. Neither Will nor Aloise was proud, on such occasions, merely because their son happened momentarily to be in the spotlight; their pride in him was because of the brilliant way he battled for the cause and values in which they both believed . . . forthright American standards as opposed to Communism, and the type of Liberalism which so often unconsciously promotes its aims.

Out of one of Bill's debates there developed this exchange. It was in the course of one of my coffee-sessions with his Father. I forget who Bill's opponent was, other than that he rated as one of Liberalism's top hatchetmen. Will had taken in the show, however, and gave me an account of it. At the end, I stated that I had always considered this man a monumental egoist.

Will nodded, then, after a reflective pause, he remarked, in his slow manner something to this effect: "Do you know, I'm beginning to think that egotism functions as a sort of mental anaesthetic which deadens the pain its possessor would otherwise feel, were he conscious of his own stupidity."

Most of the talks I had with W.F.B. over the years, were on the serious side. He was the only man I have known in recent years with whom such conversations were possible. He was, besides, the wisest man I have ever known. Wisdom, I believe, is one of the rarest mental qualities found in the *genus homo,* and is not to be acquired in classrooms or attained from books; rather it is innate, something you are born with, like personality, for example. It is the faculty to think through problems and come up with the right answer, as I conceive it. Unhurried reflection was W.F.B.'s habit of mind. He first made sure his premises were correct and sound, then the conclusions reached followed the same pattern. He never went off half-cocked on any subject I ever discussed with him, which, to me, made him the most delightful of companions.

Every time I drive past Great Elm, I think of Will and the unforgettable, stimulating sessions I had with him. Conversation has become a lost art these days. He was, I admit it, easily capable of being bored. Once, at a party, I recall seeing him captured by two middle-aged ladies of the type I call "professional collegians." They literally sprayed him with intellectual twaddle. The expression on his face was that of an early Christian martyr.

Earlier in this piece, I mentioned and paid tribute to Will's wisdom. Nowhere had he displayed that quality more than in the education of his children. He loved them devotedly, yet without weakness. They had to do their work and no maybe about it; nor was there any Pop and Mom style of address. Father and Mother was the order of the day. For the rest, the family life was animated, wholesome and deeply affectionate. But once the children had completed their educations, and variously set up for themselves, Will automatically and absolutely removed his hand from their affairs. If any of them chose to discuss problems of any sort with him, as they had all done in childhood, he was always at their service.

Will was the founder and architect of the Buckley family as it exists today. He was, at the same time, the founder, in my thought, of a great and noble tradition. He is imperishably enshrined in the hearts, not only of his own kin, but of so many others who, like myself, feel the richer for having known him as a friend.

This book, I think, will best serve the true purpose for which it was designed, when today shall have become a long-ago yesterday, when generations of his descendants yet-to-be-born, should be made proudly aware of the stock from which they are sprung, and thus seek to be worthy of their heritage.

PART FIVE

October, 1958

I. *The Last Days*

"At the end, he was not called upon to suffer more."

FATHER AND MOTHER spent the late summer of 1958 at Bad Gastein in Austria, as they had two of the preceding three sum-
mers. Bad Gastein was one of the few places in which Father found
refuge, in his lifelong flight from hay fever. Reid and Betsy and
their children joined them there and spent several weeks with them.
They met again in Paris. From there, Reid and Betsy returned to
Spain where they were living; and Mother and Father took the
train to Le Havre, and boarded the *S.S. United States*.

Father had been in high spirits. He was feeling well, and had enjoyed and profited from the daily baths at Bad Gastein. He spent
hours every day playing with Hunt and Job; he read voraciously
letters from his children, and kept abreast of developments in the
office. And Mother, as always, was at his side. But by the time he
reached Paris he was eagerly looking forward to the return trip,
and reunion with his children. The night before he left Paris, he was
suddenly nauseated. That was the beginning, the doctors later de-
duced, of his fatal brain hemorrhage.

But the disturbance was not prolonged, and they left on schedule
for Le Havre; again, Father was feeling well, and had a hearty dinner on boarding the liner Thursday evening.

On Monday afternoon, the day before the ship was due in New
York, the office at 103 East 37th Street received a cable from
Mother addressed to John. The cable was read to Bill, because
John was in Canada hunting, and Jimmy was in the Philippines.
Father had become ill, Mother cabled, giving no details, and we
should request Dr. Touart to meet the boat when it docked the
next morning. Bill telephoned the *S.S. United States*. He reached
Mother who told him that during the preceding day and a half

Father had slowly been losing consciousness. The ship's doctor, and an internist who was among the passengers and had been consulted, diagnosed the trouble as probably due to a stroke. By Monday afternoon, Father was only intermittently conscious.

At eight that night, Mother called again and spoke with Maureen. Father had been moved to the ship's infirmary, she reported, at the suggestion of the doctor. Arrangements had been made for Mother to spend the night with him in the adjacent bed. Fearing the worst, Mother had called in a priest, who administered the last rites. Father remained unconscious except for an occasional intelligible remark addressed to Mother.[1]

We lost touch with the boat after nine. The ship-to-shore Transatlantic telephone service is suspended at that hour, until eight the next morning. The entire night was consumed by devoted friends of the family, notably Bill Shields and Austin Taylor, in attempting to arrange for Bill to go out to The Narrows the next morning on the Coast Guard cutter that takes out customs officials, reporters, and persons whose presence is indispensable to the serenity of very important passengers. The bureaucratic logjam was finally broken early the next morning, thanks to Ralph de Toledano, and permission was secured a bare ten minutes before the cutter set out at ten in the morning. Mother meanwhile had been reached by telephone. There was no change in Father's condition. Bill reached the S.S. *United States* at eleven. Father was unconscious; Mother had not slept.

The boat docked at one and Father was taken immediately to the Lenox Hill Hospital by ambulance.

Dr. Touart took immediate charge. A spinal tap confirmed his suspicion that there was, or had been, bleeding within the skull. They would wait to see whether the blood vessel would mend itself, and whether the brain had been damaged. By Wednesday, Father had not recovered consciousness, and an exploratory brain operation was indicated, to repair the blood vessel and examine the damage that had been done. The hemorrhage was located by X-

---

[1] Four years earlier, gravely ill after his first stroke, Father lay seemingly unconscious on his hospital bed at Charlotte, N. C. Mother opened his bible and began to read aloud from the psalms in the Old Testament. Father's voice rang out for the first time in four days: "Boy, could those Jews write!" And, having paid tribute to good prose, which he always admired, he relapsed immediately into his coma.

ray, and the operation performed on Thursday, by Dr. Juan Negrín.

Except for Reid who was in Spain, and Jimmy who was in Manila, the entire family had come to New York (John was reached in Canada and returned immediately), including Father's youngest sister, Aunt Eleanor. We hoped the operation would reveal the point of pressure against the brain which was causing the unconsciousness, and that, relief having been effected, Father would revive, and recover. Meanwhile, he was not in pain, or so the doctors assured us; and there is no reason to believe that he was ever aware of what went on during that week. After Monday, the last day aboard the *S.S. United States,* he did not have a moment of consciousness; or a moment's apprehension. There had been plenty, in the last four years, against which to exercise his enormous reserves of courage: a paralyzed left side, the treatment—and the inevitable condescension—that is meted out to all cripples; yet he was never heard by any living soul, including the woman in whom he confided everything, and reposed all his trust, to utter a single word of complaint—against the pain, the boredom, the humiliations, the immobility. But at the end, he was not called upon to suffer more.

Twenty-four hours after the operation, he had not revived; and his blood pressure was alarmingly low. But on Saturday, it began to rise, and danger of post-surgical shock appeared to have been surmounted. Priscilla and Jane drove to Sharon to pick up a fresh set of clothes. Mother had dinner on Saturday night, after leaving the hospital, with Aloise, Patricia, Gerry, Maureen and Carol. She talked after dinner with the nurse in attendance, who reported that Father was sleeping peacefully.

At ten minutes to three the next morning, on Sunday, October 5, the telephone rang. Mother picked up the phone. The nurse told her to hurry to the hospital, that Father had taken a turn for the worse. Within fifteen minutes she and Aloise and Patricia and Carol arrived at Lenox Hill. Father was dead.

That afternoon the family met at the Church of Our Saviour at 38th Street and Park Avenue where a priest read the rosary. The word had got out quickly, and many of his friends and associates, from his office and elsewhere, appeared at the church, and joined the family in prayer.

Mother decided to bury Father in Camden, having inferred from

a casual remark he once made that this was Father's preference.
Monday evening, the family, including Aunt Eleanor, boarded a
private car at Pennsylvania Station. We reached Camden at 11:30
the morning of October 7th, a bright and beautiful day. Father was
taken to the funeral home, which was a sea of flowers. At 4:00 P.M.
the pallbearers,[1] Austin Sheheen, Carleton Burdick, Cyril Harrison,
Thomas A. Ancrum, David R. Williams, John Whitaker, Henry
Carrison, Sr., Ross Buckley, and Edmund Buckley, Jr., brought the
casket into the crowded church, and Father Jeffords performed a
funeral service that lasted about ten minutes. The procession to the
cemetery included about a hundred cars. We took a circuitous
route, to avoid a parade which the mayor of Camden had postponed
a half hour, to make it possible for us to cut through the town to
the cemetery. Six months before, the mayor had called on Father
with a delegation, to present him with a silver bowl, a token of
Camden's gratitude for Father's generosities over the years. As we
drove by, the policemen saluted the hearse.

Father's tombstone, which is on the northern side of the Quaker
Cemetery, and is shaded by a magnolia tree, bears the inscription
"W.F.B., 1881-1958."

—W.F.B., Jr.

---

[1] Honorary pallbearers: Cecilio Velasco, Van Zandt Wheeler, Joseph H. Himes,
Warren W. Smith, George S. Montgomery, Jr., J. MacMillan Harding, Dr. M. D.
Touart, John deLoach, and John Villepigue.

40th Wedding Anniversary, December 29, 1957 (*Missing: Aloise, Jane*)

II. *From Posthumous Comment,*
Letters:

Editorial from *The State*, Columbia, South Carolina, Oct. 7, 1958

William F. Buckley, whose untimely passing is greatly deplored by the people of this, his adopted, state, once told the writer of these inadequate lines that the only regret he had about establishing a home in Camden was that he had not done so sooner.

He came to love South Carolina and though he had strong ties elsewhere decided some years ago that when his time came to go he would like to be buried in her soil. In keeping with this wish, he will be laid to rest in Camden this afternoon.

Mr. Buckley's extraordinary career as an oil pioneer and as an advocate were covered in our front page story of yesterday chronicling his death in New York. In that same article there was reference to his benefactions, notably in Camden, where he had made himself part and parcel of the community life. He was not just a tourist seeking only the sunshine. He was deeply concerned with the welfare of our section. Sympathetic with, and understanding of, our problems, he was helpful in our efforts to solve them. An outspoken conservative, he had no time for those who would undermine our constitutional form of government, and was exceedingly active in movements to preserve our way of life as declared by the Founding Fathers. He was a man of positive views, and from young manhood his life was marked by courageous stands. He was ready to fight for what he thought was right.

A man of pleasing personality, a gracious host, a churchman given to wide charity without ostentation, Will Buckley had friends in many places, but none more devoted to him than those he made during his 20 years of residence in this state.

May God rest his worthy soul.

". . . a man who did not go through life unnoticed, who left deep footprints, through a life of honorable work and justice." (O.V., *Mexico City*)

"One could gauge his personality by the power and the pull it exercised. You have lost much—but you have given much, in your father's personality, and what it has meant to you is forever yours." (G.N., *South Bend, Ind.*)

"I shall always remember him as a twinkling-eyed, doughty warrior, a man of charm and courtesy—and courage." (I.C.K., *New York City*)

"How happy I am that I allowed nothing to interfere with my getting to the Gare Saint-Lazare that afternoon. I had the last vivid impression of a great patrician. . . ." (A.O'G., *Paris*)

"I honestly feel that he was the greatest man I shall ever be privileged to know, not just because he was such an honest, ethical and successful businessman but primarily I was impressed by his great love and concern for his family, his religion and friends." (T.P., *Atherton, Calif.*)

"How he must have epitomized everything a father and a friend should be." (Gen. A.C.W., *Boyds, Md.*)

"Some years ago, when I was a trumpet player with Clarence Brazell's orchestra, I had the rewarding experience of performing for you, your family, and guests on several occasions. Because of the gracious consideration and friendliness shown to me personally —and to all the musicians—on these occasions, they remain among the best memories of my musical career. . . . I wish to add this undoubtedly unremembered but sincere voice to the thousands of others who are expressing their sympathy." (D.A., *New York City*)

"Let me tell you something you cannot have known. With-

out knowing you very well, and never having met your father at all, I have nevertheless more than once thought of the relationship which existed between you as the ideal possible in this always perilous human conjunction. The world about me is full of example, on a scale running from Purgatory to Paradise, of father-manship, and I am interested in all of them."
(M.S.P., *New York City*)

"He had been invaluable to me over the years as an example of all that I now strive to be. . . ."
(W.K., *New Haven, Conn.*)

"Rarely if ever does an adopted son enjoy the genuine respect and affection [he] had from our people."
(C.R., Mayor, *Camden, S.C.*)

"Something strong and positive in the lives of all of us has passed with his going out. I know that he was a guiding spirit to so many for so long, that as the months and years go by, his memory will not diminish, but rather the sense of loss which you will feel will grow. . . [We will miss] his vast reservoir of human sympathy."
(M.S., *Regina, Sask.*)

"His courage and his indomitable spirit will always be remembered by those who were privileged to cross his path. His unfailing devotion to that which he thought was right—his brilliant mind and his common sense and his life with his family combined to make him a truly great man."
(W.W., *Bedford Hills, N.Y.*)

"We fraternity brothers loved him for his generosity, his fine work in establishing Delta Tau Delta and in being the best editor ever of the *Cactus*."
(E.T.B., *Houston, Texas.*)

"In him I saw not only originality of character, great vision and inspiring courage but, above all, a vivid, colorful and great *human* being whose spirit was instinct with generosity to all those around him."
(I.B., *New York City*)

"I would like you to know how much all of us who associated with him in his enterprises in Saskatchewan appreciated his

fine character and great vision. He was one of the pioneers in developing our oil industry in Saskatchewan and we all feel that we owe him a great debt."
(T.A.D., *Premier, Saskatchewan*)

"He was so gay and gallant. . ."
(J.B., *Barboursville, Va.*)

"But no one can record the courage, the nobility and the kindly friendship of the Will Buckley that I have known and loved for 57 changing years. It's a book of many chapters, recording so many devotions to the various members of his family, his church, his college fraternity, the University of Texas and the cause of Education. As his friend, I have preserved in my files and memory a record of his pioneering courage and wisdom."
(W.S.P., *Abilene, Tex.*)

"I feel I have lost something which never could be replaced but it is survived by a heritage from my friendship with [him] which I hope never to lose. This heritage of an approach to life with confidence, pride and courage which he so magnificently practiced and inspired in others is one of my proudest possessions."
(C.D.R., *Washington D.C.*)

"It is one of the greatest privileges of my life to have known [him]. He was truly one of God's noblemen."
(L.Y., *Camden, S.C.*)

". . . Always thoughtful, interesting and interested, entertaining and cheerful."
(D.E., *Taormina, Sicily*)

"How can you replace a gracious, gallant, brave, wise and vigorous man. There is no substitute."
(W.L., *Manchester, N.H.*)

```
┌─────────────────────────────────────┐
│  WILLIAM  FRANK  BUCKLEY             │
│           1881-1958                  │
└─────────────────────────────────────┘
```

[From National Review, Oct. 25, 1958]

The vital statistics are that he grew up in Texas, and as the oldest
surviving son undertook, upon the premature death of his father,
to look after the health and welfare of his mother, and the education of his two brothers and two sisters. He did this, and educated
himself at the University of Texas by teaching Spanish, which
he had mastered while living as a boy on the frontier. He went
to Mexico to practice law, and saw the revolution against the
benevolent and autocratic Porfirio Diaz, and what followed in
its wake: and learned, and never forgot, his distrust of the revolutionary ideology.

There are not many alive who knew him then, but those who did
remember keenly the intelligence, the wit, the largeheartedness
and—always—the high principle, which brought him a singular
eminence in the community. That eminence the American government repeatedly acknowledged, as when three successive Secretaries of State called on him for guidance; as when the Wilson
Administration offered him the civil governorship of Vera Cruz
(he refused indignantly); as when the Mexican government appointed him counsel at the ABC Conference in Niagara; as when
he was called by the Senate Foreign Relations Committee as the
premier American expert on the tangled affairs of Mexico. And
in 1921, the end of the line: exile from Mexico. At that, he was
lucky. For he had indeed materially aided a counterrevolutionary
movement. The fact that the counterrevolutionists were decent
men, and those in power barbarians, does not alter the political
reality, which is that it is a very dangerous business indeed to
back an unsuccessful insurrection: and he knew it, and barely
escaped with his skin.

He had married, and had three children, and would have seven more, all ten of whom survived him. He launched a business in Venezuela, and his fortunes fluctuated. But as children we were never aware of his tribulations. We knew only that the world revolved about him, and that whether what we needed was a bicycle, or an excuse to stay away from school for a day, or the answer to an anguished personal problem, he was there to fill the need: and when he thought the need exorbitant, or improper, he would, by a word, bring us gently to earth. He worshipped three earthly things: learning, beauty, and his family. He satisfied his lust for the first by reading widely, and by imposing on his lawless brood an unusual pedagogical regimen. The second impulse he gratified by a meticulous attention to every shrub, every stick of furniture that composed his two incomparable homes. The third he served by a constant, inexplicit tenderness to his wife and children of which the many who witnessed it have not, they say, often seen the like.

In his anxiety for the well-being of his country his three passions fused. Here in America was the beauty, the abundance, that he revered; here in the political order was the fruit of centuries of learning; here his wife, and his ten children, and his 31 grandchildren, would live, as long as he lived, and years after. So he encouraged us to stand by our country and our principles. To his encouragement, moral and material, this magazine owes its birth and early life. It was only two weeks ago, crippled and convalescent in Austria, that he registered, in turn, joy, and indignation, and amusement, and sadness, as his wife read aloud to him from the latest issue of this chronicle of America's glories and misadventures.

My father died last week at 77, and we take leave of him in the pages of the journal which had become his principal enthusiasm. We pray God his spirited soul to keep.

W. F. B. JR.: For the family